CONTENTS

The
Presidents
of the
UNITED STATES
1789–1962

A SELECTED
LIST OF REFERENCES

Compiled by

Donald H. Mugridge
Specialist in American History

GENERAL REFERENCE AND BIBLIOGRAPHY DIVISION
REFERENCE DEPARTMENT

U.S. LIBRARY OF CONGRESS

Washington : 1963

L.C. Card 63–61781

For sale by the Superintendent of Documents, U.S. Government Printing Office
Washington, D.C., 20402 – Price $1.00

Back in the days of Calvin Coolidge, this Library's Division of Bibliography prepared a 7-page, 75-entry, typed list of "Biographies of Presidents of the United States" (June 1926). It proved of such continuing usefulness that in December 1930 a page of supplementary references was added, and a year later an augmented list, grown to 11 pages and 120 entries, was typed up. A third expansion was prepared by Mrs. Grace Hadley Fuller and mimeographed (200 copies instead of 6) in June 1937; it offered 507 entries on 49 pages. Before long it went out of "print," and a further updating was several times begun, but each time accident intervened and prevented its completion.

When the work was entrusted to the present compiler, a change of plan was considered to be in order. Instead of a practically complete listing of separately published biographies and collective biographies, the present compilation offers a selection from such works of those which retain biographical value in the light of present-day historical scholarship, or have a literary interest transcending their information, or are of special interest in view of their authors or associations or of their priority among a certain kind of publications. In the place of a considerable number of campaign biographies, hack compilations and time-eroded lives, the present list includes several classes of material absent in the older plan. In the first place, the concept of biographical material has been widened, and there are many entries which throw light upon a President's life and administration, although they are not formally biographies. Each group of biographical entries is preceded by a substantially complete, although by no means minutely detailed, listing of the President's own writings. Each such group closes with biographies or autobiographies, when such exist, of the First Lady (or Ladies) and the Vice President (or Presidents) pertaining to each administration--but, of course, only of Vice Presidents who did not subsequently become President.

As the present list will attest, literature on the office of the Presidency, as distinct from chapters or sections of general works on the government and politics of the United States, was still quite scanty in 1926 and little more abundant even in 1937. During the last quarter-century it has proliferated at an accelerating rate, and so we have begun this compilation with a list of the more significant titles. The same acceleration is true for generalized treatments of Presidential elections, to which our second section is devoted; the 3 or 4 titles of 1926 have increased to 37 in 1962. The third, entitled "Collective Biography," has the same augmentation as our individual biographical sections; it includes collective Presidential writings, of which the indispensable Messages and Papers of the Presidents is the first exemplar. The fourth section, "The White House," is a miscellany which includes the historic building, the domestic and social life which has gone on in it for most of 163 years (with breaks in 1814-17 and 1948-52), and the reminiscences of aides, social secretaries, guards, chefs, seamstresses, etc.--a type of backstairs literature which has lately become so abundant that a determined attempt has recently been made to choke it off altogether, with what success only the future can show. This section was easily put together by selection from Mrs. Ann Duncan Brown's The White House, a Bibliographical List (Library of Congress, 1953) and the present compiler's supplement of 1961, to which lists the user is referred for further materials of the same kind. Even the Vice Presidency has now acquired a small literature of its own, to which our fifth and last preliminary section is devoted.

The object throughout has been to include in a list of moderate size the more important, interesting, and useful materials, so as to be serviceable to both the general reader and the serious student of history and government--although by no means to the specialist in particular administrations or in the minuter aspects of political science, who will find this selection an inadequate guide to further research. However, by indicating all substantial bibliographies in the individual works entered, means have been provided whereby the student can very rapidly expand his knowledge of the literature and come at unpublished sources for which we have no room here. We have given a full share of attention to books which are primarily pictorial or in which pictures are a major ingredient, requiring only that the pictures be responsibly assembled and identified.

The entries are for the most part for separate publications, from multivolumed sets to pamphlets. However, an important part of current research and interpretation makes at any rate its first appearance in the form of articles or essays in learned periodicals or symposia. Of these we have given rather a sampling than a complete selection and can only plead that time and space for a closer approach to the latter were both lacking. In the section on Abraham Lincoln, indeed, we have had to omit articles altogether but have indicated a bibliography (in no. 783) in which an expert selection may be found.

The present list departs from its predecessors and from the majority of this Library's bibliographies in that in every section and subsection the titles are arranged in the chronological order of their publication rather than by the alphabet. This, it is believed, will enable the user to perceive how the literature of the Presidency has developed in complexity, subtlety and depth, and how advantaged the reader of today is in comparison with his predecessor of only a few decades back. All the advantages of alphabetical order are preserved by the Author, Editor, and Title Entry Index which concludes the publication. The chronological order has, however, entailed some artificialities and compromises. For the most part, titles are entered according to the date of their first editions, and reissues, with unchanged text or only minor corrections or alterations, are indicated in a note. But when a title has been substantially revised or enlarged in a subsequent edition or editions, our entry is for the edition in which the book assumed its final form, with the earlier edition or editions indicated in the note. Giving, as it were, a condensed publishing history in a single entry has proved more time-consuming than was anticipated, and it is to be feared that some of our entries are incomplete and others inconsistent in these respects. In a related matter we have departed from strict chronology; a classic in the field is regularly entered according to its original publication, but when a modern edition or abridgment has become standard, the latter immediately follows the original as a second numbered entry; thus Thomas Jefferson's Notes on the State of Virginia is entered under the date of the first public edition, 1787 (no. 395), but William Peden's annotated edition of 1955 immediately follows as no. 396; and Allan Nevins' standard abridgments of the diaries of Presidents J. Q. Adams and Polk immediately follow the original publications of 1874 and 1910, respectively (nos. 539-40, 658-59). When any section or subsection contains more than one publication of the same year, the alphabet determines the order of the contemporaries.

In the subsections listing the writings of the several Presidents, the user will note that the order follows that of the Library's card catalogs: sets of collected writings (together with collected writings of a particular kind, such as diaries or letters) come first, volumes of selected writings follow, and individual works, including correspondence with a particular individual or on a particular subject, conclude the subsection. Within each of these three groups, however, the order is according to the date of publication. In the Biography subsections will be found several kinds of publications which it was at first intended to list separately under their own headings. Works on particular elections, such as those of 1860 and 1864 in the section on President Lincoln, appear according to their date of publication. Works on First Ladies, on White House hostesses, and on Vice Presidents come at the end of the section, in a chronological order of their own. The attempt to segregate these materials resulted in too many headings with but a single entry or pair of entries under them for comeliness. Avoiding this evil has created a lesser evil for recent elections and the large and specialized literature which has been springing up concerning them; there are, for instance, 10 analyses of the elections of 1952 and 1956 among the 33 biographical entries for President Eisenhower. To compensate for the loss of visibility of these materials, on page 147 will be found three special indexes; one to the entries for each election since 1824, one for the First Ladies or their surrogates, and one for the Vice Presidents.

It was originally intended to keep annotation, apart from the indication of alternative editions, down to a minimum. But the individual writings of the earlier Presidents so frequently called for some clarifying context that the minimum was soon exceeded, and momentum carried annotation into the other sections. The result, it is to be feared, is a bibliography partially and somewhat inconsistently annotated. Completeness and consistency were quite beyond our resources, and it is hoped that the notes, as they stand, will prove useful to some. Beside elucidation the notes have sometimes a further function: that of indicating another publication or publications related to but normally of slighter importance than the entry proper.

Some overall reflections on the literature of the American Presidency, as here listed, are in order. Several hints have already been given concerning the recent date of the general literature which falls within the first two sections, The Presidency and the Presidential Elections. In 1960, which was, to be sure an election year, there appeared 15 titles on the Presidency, nearly all publications of some importance. Assuming that our selection is adequate, and counting in the first edition (1937) of no. 72, it was not until 1939, the 150th anniversary of the Presidency, that there were accumulated 15 titles concerned with it. Again, 1960 saw the publication of 6 titles concerned with Presidential elections in general; only 7 such titles had been accumulated before 1940. Why, one is moved to ask, is the detailed, the mature literature on the American Presidency a product of the last quarter-century? The answer is probably a dual one: it is only so recently that political science or the study of government has reached a level of development at which it can analyze the actual operations and effects of the Presidency, as against its theoretical basis and its formal "powers"; and it is only in this latter day that the sources revealing the inner workings of particular administrations have become available in sufficient quantity and thoroughly enough studied to permit of significant generalizations. Now that this double breakthrough has been achieved, it seems likely to go on with unslacking mementum; but here we can only look backward and point out a few landmarks in the development. It will be considerably more convenient to reverse the arrangement of the present list and to consider the development of the literature on the individual Presidents, especially the publication of the sources, before we return to the general works on the office.

The Presidency has two aspects, an outer or public one, and an inner or personal one. In the first aspect, it is self-recording and abundantly recorded: inaugural addresses, annual messages, special and veto messages, proclamations, and executive orders are all promptly published and, sooner or later, collected into serviceable sets. It is interesting to note that this collecting, first carried out under public auspices (no. 113) and then reverting to private enterprise (nos. 114, 1251, and 1287), finally became a continuing public charge during President Eisenhower's administration (no. 151). In the second aspect, which is quite as essential to a penetrating understanding of any administration and so of the office and its potentialities, the Presidency is anything but self-recording. We can only know why the President does what he does or refrains from doing what he does not do, and what influences or pressures are exerted upon him--in short, the whole story of which the public record is only the visible fraction of the iceberg--if the President himself or someone close to him tells us. The President is a busy man and, until quite recent times, has always been undersupplied with secretarial assistance; if immediate duties are caught up with, there is always the next national election looming up. All the more honor, therefore, to those Presidents who have doggedly kept up their diaries during their administrations--to Washington, who started out well if he finished with little but the weather; to Jefferson, who unfortunately did not begin to record cabinet meetings until 1806; to Hayes, of the extent of whose recording his editor has left us in doubt; to J. Q. Adams, whose complete diary we are now promised; and especially to President Polk, who had not kept a diary until he entered the White House, but thereafter left us the most perfect record of any administration, and in the process doubtless hastened his early demise.

As against the five diarists, twelve Presidents have left more or less in the way of autobiography. John Adams did not get beyond the Revolution, nor Jefferson beyond his return to the United States from France in 1790. Van Buren's is considerably

longer and more diffuse, but it was left incomplete before it reached the Presidency.
Fillmore's is only a brief sketch of his youth. Lincoln prepared only some brief
sketches for the press, which have nevertheless been made into a book (no. 710).
Grant's Personal Memoirs (nos. 882, 883) deserve their fame, but death broke in as he
struggled to reach Appomattox. Theodore Roosevelt's Autobiography of 1913 (no. 1034)
includes his retrospect of his administration and is an outstanding achievement.
Coolidge's of 1929 (no. 1230) is bare of political or administrative detail. The full-
dress Memoirs of Hoover and Truman (nos. 1259, 1377) represent a new departure in Presidential writing and must always remain primary sources of the first importance; their
changed conception of the obligations of an ex-President form a part of that breakthrough from which our discussion took its departure. Eisenhower's book (no. 1399) is
a masterly narrative of his exercise of the supreme command in the European Theater,
1942-45. We should mention, but cannot review, Presidents' letters as a source poten-
tially as valuable as either diaries or autobiographies; those of Washington, Jefferson,
Cleveland, Wilson, and especially Theodore Roosevelt (no. 1005) deserve particular
notice.

A President's private secretary seldom receives much notice as a person during the
administration, but he may become an important source of information after its close.
(This remark does not apply to the recently emerged Press Secretary who, as the contact
man with the White House and Washington correspondents, gets a full share of the lime-
light, as the cases of Steve Early, Jim Hagerty, and Pierre Salinger attest. However,
the only Press Secretary who has contributed a memoir is Hoover's Theodore G. Joslin
[no. 1269]). In 1890, the same year that Lincoln's two principal secretaries, John G.
Nicolay and John Hay, brought out their massive and objective life and times (no. 730),
their sometime colleague William O. Stoddard published a volume of secretarial reminiscence (no. 731). Two years later, Pierce's secretary, Sidney Webster reprinted two
long newspaper articles in which he had come to the defense of his principal (no. 637).
In 1913 the papers of W. G. Moore, Johnson's secretary, were drawn upon to amplify the
records of his administration (no. 867). After Wilson's retirement but before his
death, his secretary, Joseph P. Tumulty, published an uncommonly revealing memoir (no.
1154). Both Tumulty and Nicolay have themselves become the subjects of books (nos.
1182, 804). In 1939 an edition of Hay's diary during the Civil War (no. 767) added
many vivid touches not allowed to transpire in Abraham Lincoln; a History. Grace
Tully's sympathetic sketch of her boss (no. 1326) contributes to the composite portrait
of Franklin Roosevelt.

The importance of the Cabinet varies from administration to administration, but it
is never a nullity, and much can be learned from the records of its members. The first
and largest part of Jefferson's Anas records his views of the widening breach within
Washington's cabinet; it is interesting that it was put into print as early as 1829,
in volume 4 of T. J. Randolph's selection from his papers (no. 380). J. Q. Adams'
diary for the 8 years he served as Monroe's Secretary of State fills 3 volumes of C. F.
Adams' edition of 1874-77 (no. 539) as compared with the volume and a quarter covering
the 4 years of Adams' Presidency. Thomas Ewing's brief diary was occasioned by the
approaching crisis in the Tyler Cabinet as its Whig members found themselves increasing-

ly dissentient from the first "accidental" President. For the administrations of Lincoln and Johnson, there is the great diary of the Secretary of the Navy, Gideon Welles, which we can only regret that he did not begin to keep earlier than he did (no. 742), supplemented (for Lincoln only) by the less penetrating ones of Edward Bates and Salmon P. Chase (nos. 761, 818). Some light is thrown upon the last 14 months of Cleveland's second administration by the recently published diary of the Postmaster General, William L. Wilson (no. 973). For the New Deal, there is the extraordinary Secret Diary of Harold L. Ickes (no. 1337), which takes a dim view of most of the colleagues of the Secretary of the Interior. The Forrestal Diaries (no. 1385) have come to us so early because of their author's premature and tragic end.

Cabinet memoirs prove to be a quite recent development, doubtless because until recently it was generally felt that its proceedings were confidential matters which it was owing to the President and to one's colleagues to keep secret, at least until posterity was on hand. Gideon Welles first breached this tradition in 1874, when he thought it essential to explode a strangely exaggerated view of Seward's importance in the Lincoln administration (no. 724), and in 1895 Horatio King, a minor official raised to cabinet rank by the seccession crisis, turned his light upon the troubled close of the Buchanan administration (no. 692). However, the cabinet memoir did not proliferate until the Wilson administration--in part because of the uncommon interest of the times, but in part, it is reasonable to suppose, because that President believed in taking the people more completely into his confidence than had any of his predecessors. Four members of Wilson's Cabinet have given us their versions of that stirring time: Robert Lansing in 1921 and again in 1935 (nos. 1150, 1166), William C. Redfield in 1924 (no. 1159), David F. Houston in 1926 (no. 1162), and Josephus Daniels in 1944 and 1946 (nos. 1173, 1177). From Wilson to Franklin Roosevelt there is only Harry A. Daugherty's attempt to palliate the scandals of the Harding administration (no. 1218), for the Wilbur-Hyde Hoover Policies (no. 1271) is not a memoir but the official apologia of the administration. From the Franklin Roosevelt Cabinet we have no fewer than five memoirists: James A. Farley in 1938 and 1948 (nos. 1310, 1321), Robert H. Jackson in 1941 (no. 1312), Frances Perkins in 1946 (no. 1316), Cordell Hull in 1948 (no. 1322), and Edward R. Stettinius a year later (no. 1325). Since 1945 there has been, as yet, only Ezra Taft Benson's justification of his agricultural policies in the Eisenhower administration (no. 1424). Biographies and correspondence of cabinet members are, of course, sources of information no less important, but rather more diffuse, and we could not extend this list to include them (save for no. 253). The lists at the end of the sketches in the Dictionary of American Biography will be the simplest way of coming at the older publications of this kind.

Records and narratives arising out of a President's family seldom afford detailed elucidation of his administration, but they may be valuable aids to a fuller knowledge of the man. Abigail Adams, the only wife of one President and mother of another, of course published nothing, but her extraordinary letters, first edited by her grandson (no. 375), give a unique dimension to her husband's career. The earliest First Lady to write memoirs for publication was Mrs. Taft (no. 1119), and this may be attributed to the same fact that stimulated her husband's ventures into authorship: the Tafts, on first leaving the White House, were distinctly hard up. In 1939 the second Mrs. Wilson followed in her footsteps, while Mrs. Eleanor Roosevelt combined autobiography and journalism for nearly a quarter of a century (nos. 1361, 1362, 1368, 1371, and 1374). Save in the Adams Family, the testimonies of Presidents' children have been rare. Late in life Jesse R. Grant published a volume of youthful recollections of his father (no. 895), while Elliot and James Roosevelt have both produced, 13 years apart, books on theirs (nos. 1317, 1353). Eleanor Wilson McAdoo wrote a very pleasant book on the home life of The Woodrow Wilsons down to her mother's death (no. 1167), while Alice Roosevelt Longworth and Margaret Truman Daniel have written author-centered memoirs (nos. 1097, 1395). In this connection should doubtless be mentioned the Memoirs of Washington by George Washington Parke Custis (no. 255), son of the President's stepson and an adoptive if disappointing son; our knowledge of Mount Vernon would be much thinner without it.

The contact between the press and the Presidency, always important for the publicizing of the President's views and policies (cf. no. 137), has become wider and closer in the present century as the corps of White House correspondents has multiplied. A harbinger of things to come was Noah Brooks's glimpses of Lincoln in the White House (no. 734). The first journalist admitted to the White House office so as to observe and record the President at his daily round was William Bayard Hale, toward the close of Theodore Roosevelt's administration (no. 1052); among his successors have been John Hersey under Truman (no. 1380) and Robert J. Donovan, whose privileged report on the first three Eisenhower years (no. 1413) is a unique development in the literature of the Presidency. A. Merriman Smith deserves mention here, since he has made the White House correspondent's job the basis for a whole series of instructive as well as entertaining volumes (nos. 190, 192, 1412, 1423).

Others who have contributed their special angles of vision to the knowledge of our Presidents--most of them in the present century--have been officials below cabinet rank (nos. 994, 995), chiefs of staff (no. 1328), special emissaries (no. 1161), Brain Trusters (nos. 1311, 1347), assistants to the President (no. 1422), political lieutenants (no. 1151), military aides (nos. 1064, 1114), physicians (nos. 1205, 1315), surgeons (no. 963), physical culture directors (no. 1118), speech-writers (no. 1427a), editors (no. 1336), housekeepers (no. 1323), and Secret Service men (no. 1318).

Only one of the Presidents, Chester A. Arthur, is quite without writings in this list, while one more, Franklin Pierce, has a single and rather dubious entry. The public and official writings of both, of course, will be found in The Messages and Papers of the Presidents (nos. 113, 114). The writings of the rest fall into two general classes: those published by themselves during their lifetimes, and those collected and edited, often but not invariably by scholars, after their decease. Mr. Jefferson made a few modest and anonymous publications during his lifetime, but the first President to publish copiously and in his own name was John Quincy Adams. Benjamin Harrison and Cleveland began, in a modest way, the practice of lecturing and publishing in retirement, which has been more intensively pursued by Taft (before he accepted the Chief Justiceship), Hoover, and Truman. Theodore Roosevelt and Wilson, historians both, were copious authors before they became even Presidential possibilities. One of the funniest cartoons of the 1912 campaign shows them disgustedly but desperately searching each other's writings for political ammunition. Theodore Roosevelt was indeed one of the most popular American writers of non-fiction in his day, while Wilson's books on American Government have had a continuing value, and both are in print as paperbacks at the present time. Franklin Roosevelt is the only President who has performed the exacting duties of an editor of historical texts (nos. 1295, 1300) or has written a campaign biography (no. 1294). President Kennedy has the distinction of having published his first book at the age of 23 (no. 1433), and of receiving the Pulitzer Prize in biography for his second (no. 1435).

Interesting and varied as this class of writings is, it is of considerably less importance than those assembled, usually by other hands, and after the President's death or retirement. This list points to an important priority for the four-volume set, Memoir, Correspondence, and Miscellanies, from the Papers of Thomas Jefferson (no. 380) which his grandson, T. J. Randolph, edited and had published at Charlottesville in 1829, only three years after his death. While the venture was doubtless prompted by the financial distress in which Jefferson left his heirs, Randolph did a quite workmanlike job, as is witnessed by the fact that his texts were good enough for most of them to be copied verbatim in the Washington or Congress edition of 1853-54, and reprinted thence in the Memorial edition of 1903-4 (no. 382)! Not until four years later did Jared Sparks get under way his edition of the writings of Washington, which at least had the merit of provoking a storm of controversy that served to make the principles of editorial competence and honesty better understood. It is not exactly a credit to American scholarship that a half-century was allowed to elapse before the job was competently redone (no. 225), although many of the papers themselves had come into public ownership as early as 1834, and the rest in 1849. Madison's invaluable records of the formation of the National Government were acquired in 1836 and published in 1840 by a competent editor from the Jacksonian entourage, Henry D. Gilpin (no. 503). After a decade Charles Francis Adams began publishing the works of his grandfather, according to an artificial scheme and with a very limited selection from the private correspondence; the world was nevertheless quite dependent upon the 10-volume set for 105 years after its completion in 1856 (no. 341). In 1853 Jared Sparks brought out four volumes of Correspondence of the American Revolution drawn from letters received by Washington (no. 235), and anyone who has no access to the original manuscripts is still dependent upon them and seems likely to remain so. Henry A. Washington's 7-volume edition of Jefferson, issued under Congressional auspices in 1853-54 (no. 385), amplified the work of T. J. Randolph, and a 4-volume one of the Letters of James Madison, carried out under the same authority by Philip R. Fendall, was completed before the Civil War broke out but had to wait until 1865 for publication.

The three antebellum decades therefore saw the establishment of a strong tradition in the publication of Presidential records, by both private and public enterprise; the next three would be nearly a complete blank were it not for the persistence of Charles Francis Adams--now an elder statesman himself--in publishing his father's great diary (no. 539), and the piety of a lifetime friend in collecting the addresses of Garfield (no. 935). A renaissance of historical editing with a new development of editorial commentary was at length brought about, not by the new and extremely self-satisfied guild of professional historians in the universities, but by the brothers Ford and the publishing house of Putnam. W. C. Ford's 14-volume edition of Washington, 1889-93 (no. 225), and P. L. Ford's 10-volume one of Jefferson, 1892-99 (no. 381), were followed by S. M. Hamilton's 7-volume edition of Monroe, 1898-1903 (no. 522), and Gaillard Hunt's 9-volume edition of Madison,1900-1910 (no. 504). Messrs. Putnam probably derived little profit from these 40 volumes but certainly performed a national service in supporting them. We cannot enumerate the many and important editions that have followed, save to note that the Federal Government resumed, after a 70-year interval, some responsibility in the field by supporting the Bicentennial edition of The Writings of George Washington in 1931-44 (no. 226), and that a new orientation was effected by The Papers of Thomas Jefferson (no. 383), which began publication in 1950 under the editorship of Julian P. Boyd and the joint sponsorship of the New York Times and Princeton University. Dr. Boyd's novel idea lay in the reassembling of a statesman's papers by procuring photocopies of all traceable manuscripts and publishing them more or less in extenso. Endorsed by President Truman and implemented by his appointment of a National Historical Publications Commission, the idea has now issued in monumental editions of The Adams Papers and The Madison Papers, both in process under diverse sponsorship and distinguished direction (nos. 342, 505). Editions of the papers of Polk, Johnson, and Wilson are on foot but have not yet reached publication (the movement and the editions in process are of course not limited to Presidential papers, nor even to persistent candidates like Clay and Calhoun, nor to statesmen).

Before we turn to biography, two or three other types of publications of Presidential writings deserve a brief notice. Some of our Presidents have become national oracles, and some emphatically have not. To some degreee their oracularity can be assessed by noting the number and date of volumes of selections from their writings. The earliest such book, I believe, was the Reverend John Frederick Schroeder's Maxims of Washington, Political, Social, Moral, and Religious, published in 1854 (no. 231). Although Washington was far from given to aphoristic expression, the work was reissued, with corrected texts and a new set of reference to the Bicentennial edition of the Writings, as late as 1942. With it we list five later compilations which are not so palpably aimed at edification (nos. 228-33). The other Presidents who have received like treatment are Jefferson, Lincoln, Cleveland, Theodore Roosevelt, Wilson, Coolidge (who has reversed the normal order; an oracle while alive, he has had few frequenters of his temple since his death), Franklin Roosevelt, Truman, and Eisenhower--and a compilation of the kind for Mr. Kennedy has been announced. The examples for John Adams and Madison are single, late, and special. An interesting development of this type, the factitious autobiography compiled from the subject's own writings, exists for Washington (no. 230), Jefferson (no. 387, which incorporates most of Jefferson's actual autobiography), Wilson (no. 1126), and Franklin Roosevelt (no. 1292). Its highest development is doubtless represented by the Jeffersonian and Theodore Roosevelt Cyclopedias, and the Lincoln Encyclopedia (nos. 384, 711, and 1106), in which the subject's views are minutely analyzed and presented under hundreds of subject headings alphabetically arranged. Only Washington and Lincoln have been made the subject of detailed daily chronologies (for Washington, nos. 260, 265, and 280; for Lincoln, no. 846), but one should not overlook the excellent if less exhaustive ones included in Elting E. Morison's edition of Theodore Roosevelt's Letters (no. 1005).

The development of Presidential biography is by no means closely synchronized with the publication of Presidential writings, for one type of biographer can get along nearly altogether without sources, while a higher type will make his way to the manuscripts. Ignoring the pious fabrications of Parson Weems, the first landmark in Presidential biography is by Chief Justice John Marshall, whose Life of George Washington in 6 volumes and an atlas appeared at Philadelphia in 1804-7. If no work of great erudition, it nevertheless set forth the double achievement of Washington in field and council in clear relief and paved the way for the greater work of Washington Irving just half a century later. A little volume of 1817, John H. Eaton's completion of a Life of Andrew Jackson begun by the General's aide, Major John Reid (no. 600), played its part in making its subject President, and the same can be said of the Historical Narrative of 1824 in which Moses Dawson of Cincinnati described the public services of his friend William Henry Harrison (no. 633). In 1837 George Tucker, Professor of Moral Philosophy at the University of Virginia, published two volumes (no. 422) which have been called the only Jeffersonian life of Jefferson, for no subsequent biographer has so completely shared the political outlook of the third President. In the 1850's, once more, we come upon compelling evidences of a new maturity in biographical writing: Irving's Washington, already noted, was followed by the memoir of John Adams begun by his son and finished by his grandson (nos. 341, 360), Henry S. Randall's 3-volume Jefferson (no. 424)--in its latter portions, still unreplaced--Josiah Quincy's Memoir of J. Q. Adams (no. 576), the first volume of William Cabell Rives' Madison (no. 511), and James Parton's masterly Life of Andrew Jackson in 3 volumes (no. 602), published on the very eve of the Civil War. The depressive effects of that struggle can be seen in biography as well as in the editing of sources: the next 25 years have nothing to offer comparable to these works of the 1850's, and not until Houghton Mifflin gets the American Statesmen series under way in the 1880's does Presidential biography resume a forward course which has continued to the present day. With the publication of Robert J. Rayback's Fillmore in 1959 and Philip S. Klein's Buchanan in 1962 (nos. 684, 703), it became possible to say that there is a good or excellent modern biography of every deceased President save one. The exception is Warren G. Harding, of whom an adequate life is not to be expected until the custodians of his papers elect to permit their use by competent investigators. It is also to be hoped that the final volume of Father Sievers' Benjamin Harrison (no. 985) will before long take its place beside the other two.

There is naturally a close relationship between the quantity and the specialization of the biographical literature. We have already noted that Presidents Arthur and Pierce cut the smallest figure as authors; they are equally behindhand as subjects, having but 7 entries between them. At the other end of the scale, Lincoln has 158 entries (and those quite without benefit of articles), followed by Jefferson with 122, Washington with 116, Theodore Roosevelt with 94, Wilson with 93, and Franklin Roosevelt with 88. Seventh, at a considerable remove, is J. Q. Adams with 59--and nearly two-thirds of this figure is made up by his own writings. The first six, therefore, can be judged the most interesting Presidents, and it is in their sections that we find such titles as George Washington and Rhode Island (no. 296), The Estate of George Washington, Deceased (no. 281), Jefferson and the Embargo (no. 446), Lawyer Lincoln (no. 765), Lincoln and the Tools of War (no. 826), Roosevelt and the Russo-Japanese War (no. 1066), The Economic Thought of Woodrow Wilson (no. 1171), and Champion Campaigner: Franklin D. Roosevelt (no. 1335). Are such minute monographs merely sterile exercises in hero-worship? Far from it; a conviction of the man's importance may provide the impetus to research and facilitate its publication, but the result is new knowledge in concrete detail which gets beneath the surface and enhances our understanding of the whole epoch. E. E. Prussing's analysis of Washington's will is of outstanding value for property-holding in Virginia toward the close of the 18th century, and the several studies of Lincoln as a lawyer are our best guides to the legal career in the older Middle West. Much the same can be said for each of the others.

A monographic approach of which one might expect to find more frequent examples is the study of a President as a President: how he conceived the role and performed in it. While few formal biographies ignore this angle, even fewer isolate it or strongly emphasize it. So far as I am aware, there is but one special study of the kind, and that a very recent one: Charles A. McCoy's Polk and the Presidency (no. 671), published in 1960. It is true that Polk in his Diary furnishes better materials for such a study than exist for most Presidents, but it is nevertheless to be hoped that Mr. McCoy will have imitators concerned with other administrations.

The 56 titles in our third section, Collective Biography, call for some consideration, save for the 6 containing collective writings (nos. 113, 114, 133, 151, 158 and 161), which have been sufficiently mentioned above. Collective biography proper--a series of briefer or longer lives of all the Presidents to the time of writing--seems to take its rise in the second term of Andrew Jackson, the seventh President, in a volume authored by an extremely obscure compiler, one Robert W. Lincoln, and including other matters such as sketches of the Signers of the Declaration of Independence (no. 111). By Fillmore's last year another hard-working hack, John Frost, was able to make a volume out of Presidential lives alone. Compilations of this kind have been in demand and in print for 130 years; they have seldom attracted scholars or top-drawer writers, but they manifestly meet a continuing national need and, when honestly and competently done, deserve our esteem. The late James Morgan's Our Presidents (no. 150) has been updated and kept in print for nearly forty years, since Coolidge's first term. Attention should certainly be called to Mr. Joseph N. Kane's extraordinary compendium of Presidential lore in concise and comparative form, Facts about the Presidents (no. 152), which has proved a boon to hard-pressed reference librarians. Such books have their graphic counterparts in a succession of pictorial volumes, mostly quite attractive, which may be limited to portraits (nos. 141, 164) but may also extend to pictures of every relevant kind (nos. 141, 164). There are also some pictorial volumes on individual Presidents, notably for Lincoln and for Theodore and Franklin Roosevelt (nos. 829, 1093 and 1356).

The remaining works in the section are of various special kinds. Two are genea-logical compendia, and another is of related interest (nos. 129, 136, and 147). A larger number are personal acquaintance narratives; they are as a class rather disappointing, and one can say of no. 118 that the most interesting thing about it is its title. There are a considerable number of special-angle volumes, some of which single out certain Presidents of a real or supposed class--"accidental," no. 139; "liberal," no. 140; "generals," no. 134--while others consider all the Presidents to the date of composition in a particular aspect--relations with the press, no. 137; in retirement, no. 142; health, nos. 154 and 159. Perhaps the most distinguished group consists of those which use the Presidents as the framework for an interpretation of American national history, as has been done, among others, by Herbert Agar, Charles A. Beard and son, the English historian Maurice Ashley, and a team assembled by Professor Morton Borden (nos. 127, 156, 138, and 157).

The nature of the fourth section, The White House, has been sufficiently indicated above, and here we may limit ourselves to noting that collective biography of the First Ladies makes its appearance in 1870, just 37 years after that of their husbands, and that we have no work of the kind between 1903 and 1948. Like a number of other titles in the section, such compilations would seem to appeal to a special curiosity, legitimate enough, rather than to assist in the interpretation of the national record. The earliest volume of White House memoirs (distinguished from those discussed earlier in that they seldom if ever have any light to throw upon matters of policy) is that of Thomas F. Pendel published in 1902 (no. 171); he had kept the door since the Civil War, and had opened it for Lincoln to go to Ford's Theater and for Garfield to go to the Pennsylvania Station.

We have at length worked our way back to the content of the first section, the literature on the office or the institution of the Presidency, in which we may point out a few landmarks. The first, which was also the earliest historical study published under the auspices of Harvard University, was E. C. Mason's The Veto Power, issued in 1891 (no. 3). A sterling specimen of the methods of the new discipline of political science, it dealt analytically and exhaustively with a single Presidential power in relative isolation, and became outmoded only by the accumulation of further uses of the veto since 1889. It should be pointed out that the evidence for the exercise of the veto lies primarily in the public and automatically published records of the Presidency, which is sufficient to account for the 26-year gap between this and the next monograph upon a particular Presidential power (no. 5). In 1912 H. B. Learned traced the origin of the cabinet offices; his work, as far as it goes, is still standard, and studies of the Cabinet's functioning did not make their appearance until 1959 and 1960 (nos. 4, 52, and 60). The only detailed account of the antecedents of the Presidential office during the first 14 and more or less executiveless years of our national existence is C. C. Thach's Johns Hopkins dissertation of 1922 (no. 7). Another Hopkins dissertation of 1932, Norman J. Small's Some Presidential Interpretations of the Presidency (no. 12), anticipates the later view that, within certain wide limits, the office is very much what the incumbent chooses and has the determination and ability to make it, and it has been extensively drawn upon by later writers. In 1937 came the first scholarly depiction of the Presidency in action on a wide canvas, by Wilfred E. Binkley (no. 72); the original edition bore the conventional title The Powers of the President, subsequent ones are renamed <u>President</u> <u>and</u> <u>Congress</u>. Three years later appeared the first edition of Edward S. Corwin's <u>The President, Office and Powers</u> (no. 45), which takes its departure from the rubrics of constitutional law but fills them out with matter so abundant and so concrete that, as expanded and improved in three revisions over 17 years, it is the one volume that all students of the subject agree in finding indispensable. George Fort Milton was no constitutional lawyer, but a journalist who took up history as a second line; his last book, <u>The Use of Presidential Power, 1789-1943</u> (no. 20), broke new ground in depicting the individual styles of the stronger Presidents. Lawrence Chamberlain's Columbia University study of 1946, <u>The President, Congress and Legislation</u> (no. 22), introduced the case history method of determining the respective shares of the executive and the legislature in statute-making and of exhibiting the process leading to the completed act. Leonard D. White's four volumes of administrative history from 1789 to 1901 appeared over the decade 1948-58 (nos. 25, 31, 36 and 50); they displayed the Presidency in its relation to the whole administrative machinery in a manner previously unapproached, as well as the large variations in supervision and innovation during different administrations. The writings of the last decade are too numerous and weighty to pass in review, but Clinton Rossiter's <u>The American Presidency</u>, first published in 1956 and continuously in print as a paperback (no. 65), deserves notice as a general treatment, both penetrating and popular, whose formulation of the President's functions has been widely adopted, both in journalism and in writing of greater permanence.

The general literature of Presidential Elections in our second section should be considered along with the titles on particular elections which are scattered through the sections on individual Presidents. Three main categories may be distinguished: descriptions of electoral machinery, histories of elections, and analyses of elections, with the line between the last two thin and wavering. The first-named type makes its appearance as early as 1878, with David A. McKnight's <u>The Electoral Machinery of the United States</u> (no. 74n), and reaches the monographic stage in 1926, with Louise Overacker's <u>The Presidential Primary</u> (no. 76). In recent years descriptions of machinery have usually been bound up with proposals of reform, as in Lucius Wilmerding's <u>The Electoral College</u> (no. 102).

Edward Stanwood's <u>History of Presidential Elections</u> first appeared in 1884 (no. 79), and was revised and updated by the author through the election of 1912. It is regrettable that the title was changed to the misleading <u>History of the Presidency</u>, and that Houghton Mifflin did not find a continuator who would adhere to the original form and scale, and so give it four more decades of currency and a usefulness which was little vitiated by the author's partiality for one of the major parties. The earliest study of a particular election, naturally of the most momentous of all, appeared in 1911: E. D. Fite's <u>The Presidential Campaign of 1860</u> (no. 740). The monographic study of less exciting ones was inaugurated in 1922 by S. R. Gammon's dissertation (no. 610) on Jackson's reelection, a canvass noteworthy for the emergence of the national party nominating convention.

The modern dissection of recently concluded campaigns makes its appearance in 1931, just three years after the fact, with <u>The 1928 Campaign, an Analysis</u>, by Roy J. Peel and Thomas C. Donnelly (no. 1265). The course of thought is revealed in the titles of two works by an amateur so successful that he turned professional: in 1940 _Ballot Behavior; a Study of Presidential Elections_, and eight years later _How to Predict Elections_ (nos. 80, 85), both by Louis H. Bean, late of the U. S. Department of Agriculture. In 1948 and 1954 the two volumes of Paul Lazarsfeld and Bernard Berelson, _The People's Choice_ and _Voting_ (nos. 87, 97), added a psychological dimension by seeking to penetrate into the voter's mind and reveal the actual process of decision. For the Eisenhower elections one finds such further-specialized studies as _Television and Presidential Politics_, _Press and Politics_, _Class Roles and Perspectives_, and a 5-volume study of _Presidential Nominating Politics in 1952_ (nos. 1409, 1418a, 1419, and 1425). Notwithstanding this extraordinary acceleration of election research, the electorate seems to retain the ability to confound prophet, pundit, and pollster. We have, nevertheless, achieved a new realization of the delicate complexity of motive, interest, and maneuver that enters into the final result of a 20th-century Presidential election.

A NOTE ON SYMBOLS

Three National Union Catalog symbols have been used here for five Presidential writings not in the Library of Congress:

NN   New York Public Library (nos. 566, 645, and 681)
Vi   University of Virginia, Charlottesville (no. 646)
InU   Indiana University, Bloomington (no. 1434)

RBD at the end of a call number signifies that the work is kept in the Rare Book Division.

Law in lieu of a call number signifies that the book is in the Law Library and is otherwise unclassified.

1

Woodward, Augustus B. The Presidency of
the United States. New York, D. Van
Veghten, 1825. 88 p.   JK516.W8 1825
    Some copies give the place of im-
print as Washington, where the articles
in the National Journal of which it was
composed had originally appeared. The
following year a 2d edition was printed
at Frederick-town by J. P. Thomson for
T. Taylor. The gifted territorial ju-
rist died the next year, 1827, but had
already established a long priority
among authors on the Presidency.

2

Presidential inability [by] Lyman Trumbull,
Thomas M. Cooley, Benjamin F. Butler
[and] Theodore W. Dwight. North American review, v. 133, Nov. 1881: 417-446.
                        AP2.N7, v. 133
    A symposium, arising out of Gar-
field's protracted illness, on a problem which remains unsolved 80 years
later.

3

Mason, Edward Campbell. The veto power;
its origin, development and function in
the Government of the United States
(1789-1889). Boston, Ginn, 1891.
232 p. (Harvard historical monographs,
no. 1)   JK586.M2 1891

4

Learned, Henry Barrett. The President's
Cabinet; studies in the origins, formation and structure of an American institution. New Haven, Yale University
Press, 1912.   JK611.L5

5

Corwin, Edward S. The President's control
of foreign relations. Princeton,
Princeton University Press, 1917.
216 p.   JK570.C6

6

Berdahl, Clarence A. War powers of the
Executive in the United States. Urbana,
University of Illinois [c1921] 296 p.
(University of Illinois studies in the
social sciences, v. 9, nos. 1-2)
                        JK558.B4
                H31.I4, v. 9, no. 1-2
    Bibliography: p. 271-281.

7

Thach, Charles Coleman. The creation of
the Presidency, 1775-1789; a study in
constitutional history. Baltimore,
Johns Hopkins Press, 1922. 182 p.
(Johns Hopkins University studies in
historical and political science,
ser. 40, no. 4)   JK511.T5
                H31.J6, ser. 40, no. 4

8

The ordinance making powers of the President of the United States. Baltimore,
Johns Hopkins Press, 1925. 339 p.
(Johns Hopkins University studies in
historical and political science,
ser. 43, no. 3)   JK516.H3 1925
                H31.J6, ser. 43, no. 3
    "Selected bibliography": p. 325-
332.

9

Corwin, Edward S. The President's removal
power under the Constitution. New York,
National Municipal League, 1927. xv,
70 p.   JK749.C75

10

Morganston, Charles E. The appointing and
removal power of the President of the
United States. Washington, U. S. Govt.
Print. Off., 1929. 224 p. (70th Cong.,
2d sess. Senate Document 172)
                        JK730.M6

11

Pepper, George Wharton. Family quarrels,
the President, the Senate, the House.
New York, Baker, Voorhis, 1931. 192 p.
                    JK585.P4
     Lectures at the University of Vir-
ginia on the William H. White Foundation.

12

Small, Norman J. Some Presidential interpretations of the Presidency. Baltimore, Johns Hopkins Press, 1932. 208 p.
(Johns Hopkins University studies in
historical and political science,
ser. 50, no. 2)   JK516.S6
                    H31.J6, ser. 50, no. 2

13

Larkin, John Day. The President's control
of the tariff. Cambridge, Mass., Harvard University Press, 1936. 207 p.
(Harvard political studies)   HF1753.L3

14

Tichelen, Joseph van. Le président de la
république et le problème de l'État;
étude de la situation juridique et
politique du chef de l'État aux États-
Unis, en France et dans le Deuxième
Reich. [Liége, Éditions Biblio, cover
1939] 877 p.   JF255.T5

15

Herring, Edward Pendleton. Presidential
leadership; the political relations of
Congress and the chief executive. New
York, Farrar and Rinehart [c1940]
173 p. (American government in action
series)   JK516.H4

16

Laski, Harold. The American Presidency,
an interpretation. New York, Harper
[c1940] 278 p.   JK516.L3 1940a
     "In the spring of 1939 Indiana Uni-
versity honored me with an invitation
to lecture there on the Patten Foundation; this volume is, substantially,
the course I delivered."

17

Humbert, Willard. The pardoning power of
the President. Foreword by W. W.
Willoughby. Washington, American Council on Public Affairs [c1941] 142 p.
                    JK584.B84

18

Jones, Harry Wilmer. The President, Congress, and foreign relations. California law review, v. 29, July 1941:
565-585.

19

Rich, Bennett Milton. The Presidents and
civil disorder. Washington, Brookings
Institution, 1941. 235 p. (The Institute for Government Research of the
Brookings Institution. Studies in administration, no. 42) JK562.R5 1941a

20

Milton, George Fort. The use of Presidential power, 1789-1943. Boston, Little,
Brown, 1944. 349 p.   JK516.M5
     "Bibliographical note"; p. 323-327.

21

Marcy, Carl Milton. Presidential commis-
sions. New York, King's Crown Press,
1945. 141 p.   JK516.M35 1945

22

Chamberlain, Lawrence. The President,
Congress and legislation. New York,
Columbia University Press, 1946. 478 p.
                    JK585.C5 1946a
                    H31.C7, no. 523

23

Patterson, Caleb Perry. Presidential
government in the United States; the
unwritten constitution. Chapel Hill,
University of North Carolina Press,
1947. 301 p.   JK516.P3

24

Morstein Marx, Fritz. The President and
his staff services. Chicago, 1947.
26 p. (Public Administration Service.
Publication no. 98)   JK516.M6

A concise summary of the range of Presidential responsibilities, the lack of any constitutional deputy, the findings of the President's Committee on Administrative Management (1937), and the development of the Executive Office of the President under the Reorganization Act of 1939. Pages 17-26 print Executive orders and other documents concerned with this development. No. 33 is a fuller and later treatment.

25
White, Leonard D. The Federalists; a study in administrative history. New York, Macmillan, 1948. 538 p.
JK161.A1W4

This and its three sequels (nos. 31, 36, and 50) are concerned with the whole Federal administration and not with the Presidency alone. However, they contain so much of value for the practical functioning of the Presidency, the greater part of which can be found nowhere else save in original sources, that we have departed from our rules in order to list them here.

26
Brownlow, Louis. The President and the Presidency. Chicago, Public Administration Service, 1949. 137 p.
JK516.B74

Lectures delivered at the University of Chicago on the Charles R. Walgreen Foundation.

27
The Presidency in transition. Journal of politics, v. 11, Feb. 1949: 1-256.
JA1.J6, v. 11

Contents.--Introduction, by R. S. Rankin.--The Presidency in perspective, by E. S. Corwin.--Presidential selection and democratic government, by C.A. Berdahl.--The President and party politics, by E. A. Helms.--The President and Congress, by W. E. Binkley.--The President and the Supreme Court, by C. H. Pritchett.--The President and labor disputes, by C. L. Rossiter.--Emergencies and the Presidency, by A. L. Sturm.--The President as Commander-in-Chief, by Charles Fairman.--The American President and foreign relations, by H. J. Laski.--The Presidency and world affairs: mobilization of assistance, by Wallace McClure.--The President as chief administrator, by C. P. Patterson.--Presidential succession and inability, by E. S. Brown and R. C. Silva.

28
Somers, Herman Miles. Presidential agency: OWMR, the Office of War Mobilization and Reconversion. Cambridge, Harvard University Press, 1950. 238 p. (Harvard political studies) HC106.4.S66

29
Rossiter, Clinton L. The Supreme Court and the Commander in Chief. Ithaca, N. Y., Cornell University Press, 1951. 145 p. (Cornell social studies) Law

30
Silva, Ruth. Presidential succession. Ann Arbor, University of Michigan Press, 1951. 213 p. (University of Michigan publications. History and political science, v. 18) JK609.S5 1951
Bibliography: p. 189-196.

31
White, Leonard D. The Jeffersonians; a study in administrative history, 1801-1829. New York, Macmillan, 1951. 572 p. JK180.W5

32
Harris, Joseph P. The advice and consent of the Senate; a study of the confirmation of appointments by the United States Senate. Berkeley, University of California Press, 1953. 457 p.
JK1274.H3

33
Hobbs, Edward H. Behind the President; a study of Executive Office agencies. Washington, Public Affairs Press [1954] 248 p. JK518.H6

34
Hyman, Sidney. The American President. New York, Harper [1954] 342 p.
JK516.H9

35

Neustadt, Richard E. Presidency and legislation: the growth of central clear-
ance. American political science review, v. 48, Sept. 1954: 641-671.
JA1.A6, v. 48

36

White, Leonard D. The Jacksonians; a
study in administrative history, 1829-
1861. New York, Macmillan, 1954.
593 p. JK201.W45

37

Fincher, Ernest Barksdale. The President
of the United States. New York, Abe-
lard-Schuman [1955] 192 p. JK516.F48

38

MacLean, Joan Coyne, ed. President and
Congress; the conflict of powers. New
York, H. W. Wilson, 1955. 218 p.
(The reference shelf, v. 27, no. 1)
JK585.M3
Bibliography: p. 207-218.

39

Neustadt, Richard E. Presidency and legislation: planning the President's
program. American political science
review, v. 49, Dec. 1955: 980-1021.
JA1.A6, v. 49

40

Seligman, Lester G. Developments in the
Presidency and the conception of political leadership. American sociological
review, v. 20, Dec. 1955: 706-712.
HM1.A7s, v. 20
Discusses, from the viewpoint of
social psychology, the relation of the
enlarged White House Office staff to
policy-making and to the President's
public image, and his use of them as
"presidential surrogates."

41

American Academy of Political and Social
Science, Philadelphia. The Office of
the American Presidency, edited by
Sidney Hyman. Philadelphia, 1956.
216 p. (Its Annals, v. 307)
H1.A4, v. 307
JK516.A7

42

Corwin, Edward S., and Louis W. Koenig.
The Presidency today. New York, New
York University Press, 1956. 138 p.
JK516.C62

43

Seligman, Lester G. The President is many
men. Antioch review, v. 16, Sept.
1956: 305-318. AP2.A562, v. 16
A principal task of the modern Presidents is to integrate their multiple
roles, and each does so in an individual manner.

44

The Presidential office. [Durham, N. C.]
School of Law, Duke University, 1956
[c1957] 608-752 p. (Law and contemporary problems, v. 21, no. 4) JK516.P7
Contents.--Foreword, by J. F. Pasch-
al.--The Presidency at mid-century, by
R. E. Neustadt.--Presidential succession and disability, by R. C. Silva.--
An historical review of plans for presidential staffing, by E. H. Hobbs.--The
Executive Office as administrative co-
ordinator, by J. R. Steelman and H. D.
Kreager.--The Executive Office and fis-
cal economic policy, by G. Colm.--The
Presidential office and the President
as party leader, by L. G. Seligman.--
The President as international leader,
by R. P. Longaker.

45

Corwin, Edward S. The President, office
and powers, 1787-1957; history and a-
nalysis of practice and opinion. 4th
rev. ed. New York, New York University
Press, 1957. 519 p. Law
First published 1940 (476 p.); rev.
ed. c1941; 3d rev. ed. 1948 (552 p.)
The Notes (p. 315-496) introduce leading cases and much previous literature.
It is generally regarded as the authoritative treatise on the Presidency from
the standpoint of constitutional law.

46
Linville, C. Edwin. The President of the
United States. New York, Oxford Book
Co., 1957. 92 p. (Oxford social studies pamphlets [24])   JK516.L5
     This modest and derivative but ade-
quate little study manual well displays
recent advances in the understanding of
the subject.

47
Schubert, Glendon A. The Presidency in
the courts. Minneapolis, University of
Minnesota Press [1957] 391 p. Law

48
Hamilton, Holman. White House images &
realities. Gainesville, University of
Florida Press, 1958. 98 p. E176.1.H2
     Lectures which summarily compare the
careers which have led the Presidents
to the White House, and seek to isolate
the elements involved in the attribu-
tion of greatness or failure to each,
together with the factors that go into
the making of "the Presidential image."

49
Plischke, Elmer. Summit diplomacy; personal diplomacy of the President of the
United States. College Park, Bureau of
Governmental Research, College of Business and Public Administration, University of Maryland, 1958. 125 p.
                         JK570.P58

50
White, Leonard D. The Republican era,
1869-1901; a study in administrative
history. With the assistance of Jean
Schneider. New York, Macmillan, 1958.
406 p.   JK231.W5

51
Binkley, Wilfred E. The man in the White
House: his powers and duties. Baltimore, Johns Hopkins Press [1959]
310 p.   JK516.B49
     Bibliography: p. 298-304.

52
Fenno, Richard F. The President's Cabi-
net; an analysis in the period from
Wilson to Eisenhower. Cambridge, Mass.,
Harvard University Press, 1959. 327 p.
(Harvard political studies) JK611.F4

53
Bell, Jack. The splendid misery; the
story of the Presidency and power politics at close range. Garden City,
N. Y., Doubleday, 1960. 474 p.
                         E806.B443
     Primarily concerned with the Presi-
dential campaigns from 1940 to 1960,
which Mr. Bell observed as a reporter
for the Associated Press, but also de-
tails a number of episodes during the
Truman and Eisenhower administrations.

54
Bolles, Blair. Men of good intentions;
crisis of the American Presidency.
Garden City, N. Y., Doubleday, 1960.
234 p.   JK421.B6

55
Brown, William Burlie. The people's
choice: the Presidential image in the
campaign biography. Baton Rouge, Louisiana State University Press [1960]
177 p.   JK528.B77

56
Coyle, David Cushman. Ordeal of the Pres-
idency. With illus. collected by M. B.
Schnapper. Washington, Public Affairs
Press [1960] 408 p.   E176.1.C8

58
Finer, Herman. The Presidency: crisis
and regeneration, an essay in possibilities. [Chicago] University of Chicago Press [1960] 374 p. JK516.F49

58
Heller, Francis H. The Presidency: a
modern perspective. New York, Random
House [1960] 114 p. (Studies in political science, PS33) JK516.H37

59
Henry, Laurin L. Presidential transitions.
Washington, Brookings Institution
[1960] xviii, 755 p.   E743.H4
     A study in great detail of the four
transitions from one Presidential administration to another in which a
change of party was involved, from
1912-13 to 1952-53. It considers equally the factors of continuity and of re-
sponsiveness to new leadership. The
first three were accomplished before
the 20th Amendment had reduced by nearly half the "lame-duck period" of nearly four months; but, as the author
points out, that Amendment does not
eradicate the difficulties, since the
real transition can still go on for
more than a full year.

60
Horn, John S. The Cabinet and Congress.
New York, Columbia University Press,
1960. 310 p.   JK616.H6

61
Johnson, Walter. 1600 Pennsylvania Ave-
nue; Presidents and the people, 1929-
1959. Boston, Little, Brown [1960]
390 p.   E743.J6
     "Selected bibliography": p. [353]-
373.
     A conspectus of 30 years of almost
continuous crisis in national affairs,
focused upon the role of presidential
leadership in reshaping the place of
Government in the economy and of the
Nation in world decisions.
     The author discussed a smaller facet
of his subject in his inaugural lecture'
as H. V. Harmsworth Professor of American History at Oxford: The American
President and the Art of Communication
(Oxford, Clarendon Press, 1958. 21 p.),
contrasting the mass-media images of
F. D. Roosevelt and Eisenhower, and the
political use to which each was put.

62
Koenig, Louis W. The invisible Presidency. New York, Rinehart, 1960.
438 p.   E176.K6

     An analysis of the influence exer-
cised upon the Presidents by their
closest advisers, or "favorites." After a preliminary survey of the kinds
of person who have achieved this favored position, and of the kind of
"palace politics" that has on occasion
gone on, seven examples are studied,
from Hamilton under Washington to
Sherman Adams under Eisenhower.

63
May, Ernest R., ed. The ultimate decision: the President as Commander in
Chief. New York, G. Braziller, 1960.
xvii, 290 p.   JK558.M3
     "Bibliographical notes": p. [259]-
269.
     A general essay by the editor is
followed by eight studies of individual Presidents in the role, from Madison to Eisenhower.

64
Neustadt, Richard E. Presidential power,
the politics of leadership. New York,
Wiley [1960] 224 p. JK516.N4
     An analytic study of how the Presi-
dent can effectively exercise the great
powers that are legally his in order to
make his choices and will prevail,
rather than others "from that maze of
personalities and institutions called
the government of the United States."
This theme is illustrated from a vari-
ety of concrete and well-documented
situations during the Truman and Eisenhower administrations.

65
Rossiter, Clinton L. The American Presi-
dency. [2d ed.] New York, Harcourt,
Brace [1960] 281 p. (A Harvest book,
HB35)   JK516.R6 1960
     Bibliography: p. 272-275.
     First published in 1956.

66
Smith, John Malcolm, and Cornelius P. Cotter. Powers of the President during
crises. Washington, Public Affairs
Press [1960] 184 p. JK516.S66

67

Tugwell, Rexford G. The enlargement of the Presidency. Garden City, N. Y., Doubleday, 1960. 508 p. JK516.T8

68

Coffey, Joseph I., _and_ Vincent P. Rock. The Presidential staff. Washington, National Planning Association, 1961. 102 p. (Planning pamphlet no. 112)
HC101.N352, no. 112

69

Fersh, Seymour H. The view from the White House; a study of the Presidential State of the Union Messages. Washington, Public Affairs Press [1961] 158 p. JK587.F4

70

Grundstein, Nathan D. Presidential delegation of authority in wartime. Pittsburgh, University of Pittsburgh Press, 1961. 106 p. Law

71

Longaker, Richard P. The Presidency and individual liberties. Ithaca, Cornell University Press, 1961. 239 p.
JK518.L6
Posits "a third major addition to presidential responsibility in the twentieth century--the constitutional obligation of the chief executive to protect individual liberty." The discussion, in quite abstract terminology, is illustrated by a number of situations since the War in which, the author considers, the President has more often than not failed to employ all his "available instruments for action" in upholding menaced constitutional liberties.

72

Binkley, Wilfred E. President and Congress. 3d rev. ed. New York, Vintage Books [1962] 403 p. JK516.B5 1962
First ed. published in 1937 under title: The powers of the President.

73

Dulce, Berton, _and_ Edward J. Richter Religion and the presidency. New York, Macmillan, 1962. 245 p. JK524.D78
The title claims more than the book performs. The first 80 pages deal sketchily with anti-Catholic agitation down to 1928, but effectively relate it to Presidential politics only in the campaigns of 1852 and 1884. After a chapter on the candidacy of Alfred E. Smith and a very miscellaneous one on F. D. Roosevelt, the remainder of the book (p. 120-221) traces the rise of John F. Kennedy in national politics.

74

Dougherty, John Hampden. The electoral
system of the United States; its history, together with a study of the
perils that have attended its operations, an analysis of the several efforts by legislation to avert these
perils, and a proposed remedy by amendment of the Constitution. New York,
Putnam, 1906. 425 p.   JK528.D7

The system having jogged along with
little change and fewer perils, no such
detailed analysis has been published
since. An earlier and even more detailed (and obsolete) one was David A.
McKnight's The Electoral System of the
United States (Philadelphia, Lippincott, 1878. 433 p.)

75

U. S. Library of Congress. Legislative
Reference Service. Election of the
President of the United States by the
House of Representatives, by George J.
Schulz. Washington, Govt. Print. Off.,
1925. 88 p. (68th Cong., 2d sess.
Senate. Document 227) JK528.A5 1925b

76

Overacker, Louise. The Presidential primary. New York, Macmillan, 1926.
308 p.   JK522.O8
Bibliography: p. 277-294.

77

Minnegerode, Meade. Presidential years,
1787-1860. New York, Putnam, 1928.
396 p.   E183.M67

78

Seitz, Don C. The "also rans"; great men
who missed making the Presidential
goal. New York, Crowell [c1928] xxiv,
356 p.   E176.S44
Eighteen sketches from Aaron Burr to
William Jennings Bryan

79

Stanwood, Edward. A history of the Presidency. New ed., rev. by Charles
Knowles Bolton. Boston, Houghton Mifflin [193-?] 2 v.   JK511.S7
Contents.--[v. 1] From 1788 to
1897.--[v. 2] From 1897 to 1916, with
additions and revisions to 1928.
First edition, 1898.
The title of the first four editions (1884-96), History of Presidential Elections, was considerably more
appropriate than the present one adopted for the edition of 1898. The work
deals thoroughly and systematically,
and in separate chapters, with each
Presidential election from 1788 to
1912. The later ones are documented
only in appendixes and tables supplied
by the reviser.

80

Bean, Louis H. Ballot behavior; a study
of Presidential elections. Introduction by Charles E. Merriam. Washington, American Council on Public Affairs
[c1940] 102 p.   JK1967.B4

81

Ewing, Cortez A. M. Presidential elections from Abraham Lincoln to Franklin D. Roosevelt. Norman, University
of Oklahoma Press, 1940. 226 p.
JK524.E94

82

Stein, Charles W. The third-term tradition; its rise and collapse in American politics. New York, Columbia University Press, 1943. xvi, 382 p.
JK550.S75
Bibliography: p. 353-364.
Its "collapse" was followed by its
triumphant reassertion in the 22d
Amendment, effective in 1951.

83

Stone, Irving. They also ran; the story
of the men who were defeated for the
Presidency. Garden City, N. Y.,
Doubleday, Doran, 1945. 427 p.
E176.S87 1945

84

Overacker, Louise. Presidential campaign
funds. With an introd. by Theodore
Francis Green. Boston, Boston University Press, 1946. 76 p. (The Gaspard
Bacon lectureship on the Constitution
of the United States, 1945)
JK1991.072

85

Bean, Louis H. How to predict elections.
New York, Knopf, 1948. 196 p.
JK2007.B4

86

Robinson, Edgar E. The Presidential vote,
1896-1932. Stanford University, Calif.,
Stanford University Press, 1947.
403 p. JK524.R6 1947

87

Lazarsfeld, Paul, Bernard Berelson, and
Hazel Gaudet. The people's choice; how
the voter makes up his mind in a presidential campaign. [2d ed.] New York,
Columbia University Press, 1948.
xxxiii, 178 p. JK524.L38 1948

88

Stoddard, Henry L. Presidential sweep-
stakes; the story of political conventions and campaigns. Edited by
Francis W. Leary. New York, Putnam
[1948] 224 p. E661.S86

89

Aly, Bower, ed. Presidential elections.
[Columbia? Mo., 1949] 2 v. (Debate
handbook, 23, 1949-1950)

JK528.A66
"Published under the auspices of the
Committee on Debate Materials and
Interstate Cooperation, the National
University Extension Association."
"Reading list": v. 1, p. 11-18.

A sourcebook for debaters on the
issue of the electoral college, with
essays for and against the several
reform proposals, some drawn from other
publications, but many written for use
in this handbook.

90

Johnsen, Julia Emily, comp. Direct election of the President. New York, H. W.
Wilson, 1949. 300 p. (The Reference
shelf, v. 21, no. 4) JK528.J7
Bibliography: p. 277-300.

91

Shannon, Jasper B., and Ruth McQuown.
Presidential politics in Kentucky,
1824-1948; a compilation of election
statistics and an analysis of political
behavior. Lexington, Bureau of Government Research, College of Arts and
Sciences, University of Kentucky, 1950.
129 p. JK5392.S48

92

Lorant, Stefan. The Presidency; a pic-
torial history of Presidential elec-
tions from Washington to Truman. New
York, Macmillan, 1951. 775 p.
E183.L65
Bibliography: p. 744-755.

93

Moos, Malcolm C. Politics, Presidents,
and coattails. Baltimore, Johns
Hopkins Press, 1952. xxi, 237 p.
JK1976.M6
The coattail theory considers that
the fate of a party's candidates for
Congress in alternate elections is
often determined by the showing of its
candidate for President. The author
analyzes 54 years of election results
without finding much confirmation for
the idea.

94

Aly, Bower, ed. Selecting the President.
[Columbia, Mo., Artcraft Press, 1953]
2 v. (Discussion and debate manual,
27, 1953-1954) JK528.A67

94
Aly, Bower, ed. Selecting the President. (cont.)
"Published under the auspices of the Committee on Discussion and Debate Materials and Interstate Cooperation, the National University Extension Association."

95
Daniels, Walter Machray, ed. Presidential election reforms. New York, H. W. Wilson, 1953. 200 p. (The Reference shelf, v. 25, no. 4)   JK528.D33
Bibliography: p. [190]-200.

96
Judah, Charles B. The presidential primary. Albuquerque, Division of Research, Dept. of Government, University of New Mexico, 1953. 31 p. JK2077.J8

97
Berelson, Bernard R., Paul F. Lazarsfeld, and William N. McPhee. Voting; a study of opinion formation in a presidential campaign. [Chicago] University of Chicago Press [1954] xix, 395 p.
JK526 1948.B4

98
Burnham, Walter Dean. Presidential ballots, 1836-1892. Baltimore, Johns Hopkins Press [1955] xix, 956 p.
JK524.B8

99
Butcher, Walter. Presidential election returns for Kansas, 1864-1952. Emporia, Kansas State Teachers College [1956] 1 v. (The Emporia State research studies, v. 5, no. 1)
JK524.B83

100
Roseboom, Eugene H. A history of presidential elections. New York, Macmillan, 1957. 568 p.   E183.R69

101
Nevada. Legislative Counsel Bureau. A study of the Presidential primary. Carson City, 1958. 89 p. (Its Bulletin no. 32)   JK2075.N2A5 1958

102
Wilmerding, Lucius. The electoral college. New Brunswick, N. J., Rutgers University Press, 1958. 224 p.
JK529.W64

103
Bain, Richard C. Convention decisions and voting records. Washington, Brookings Institution [1960] 327, [127] p. tables.   JK2255.B3

104
Bendiner, Robert. White House fever; an innocent's guide to principles and practices, respectable and otherwise, behind the election of American Presidents. New York, Harcourt, Brace [1960] 180 p.   JK528.B42

105
David, Paul T. The politics of national party conventions, by Paul T. David, Ralph M. Goldman [and] Richard C. Bain. [Washington] Brookings Institution [1960] 592 p.   JK2255.D39
A condensation to 274 p., edited by Kathleen Sproul, was issued the same year (JK2255.D39 1960a).

106
Hoyt, Edwin Palmer. Jumbos and Jackasses; a popular history of the political wars. Garden City, N. Y., Doubleday, 1960. 505 p.   E183.H855
Presidential politics from 1860 to 1960.

107
Moos, Malcolm C., and Stephen Hess. Hats in the ring. [New York] Random House [1960] 194 p.   JK2255.M65

108
U. S. Congress. Senate. Library. Nomination and election of the President and Vice President of the United States, including the manner of selecting delegates to National political conventions. Compiled under directions of Felton M. Johnson, secretary of the Senate, by Richard D. Hupman, Senate Library, and Samuel H. Still, Jr., Legislative Reference Service, Library

108
U. S. Congress. (cont.)
   of Congress. Washington, U. S. Govt.
   Print. Off., 1960. 258 p. forms,
   tables.   JK2063.A513

109
Blanchard, Robert, and others. Presidential elections, 1948-1960, by Robert
   Blanchard, Richard Meyer [and] Blaine
   Morley. Salt Lake City, Institute of
   Government, University of Utah, 1961.
   58 p. (Utah. University. Institute
   of Government. Research monograph
   no. 4)   JK524.B55
       Bibliography: p. 53-58.

110
Judah, Charles B., and George Winston
   Smith. The unchosen. New York,
   Coward-McCann, 1962. 377 p. JK2255.J8
       Narratives averaging 35 pages of the
   failure of nine aspirants to the Presi-
   dency eminent in their party to obtain
   its nomination for that honor: W. H.
   Seward in 1860, B. H. Bristow in 1876,
   John Sherman in three campaigns, Champ
   Clark in 1912, Frank Lowden in 1920,
   W. G. McAdoo in 1924, R. A. Taft in
   1952, Estes Kefauver in 1952, and L. B.
   Johnson in 1960.

111

Lincoln, Robert W. Lives of the Presidents of the United States, with biographical notices of the signers of the Declaration of Independence; sketches of the most remarkable events in the history of the country [etc.] Embellished with a portrait of each of the Presidents and 45 engravings. New York, N. Watson, 1833. 508 p.
E176.1.L46

New editions in 1839 and 1842 (New York, E. Kearny. 578 p.). Although the Presidents do not have the field to themselves, they engross the greater part of the text. Seems to be the first such compilation; later antebellum ones were put together by Edwin Williams (New York, 1849) and John Frost (Boston, 1852 and 1855). The indefatigable Frost may have the credit of being the first to omit extraneous matter.

112

Abbott, John S. C. Lives of the Presidents of the United States from Washington to the present time. Boston, B. B. Russell, 1867. 480 p.
E176.1.A24

The author deserted the Congregational ministry to become the most successful popular biographer of his day. He brought out expanded editions in 1869 and 1876, and after his death in 1877 Russell H. Conwell added the lives of new Presidents. The latest edition in LC is a 3-volume "Art edition" issued by J. M. Towers and Co. of Chicago, 1902. Some notice should be taken of two one-man libraries of Presidential biography: William O. Stoddard's The Lives of the Presidents in 10 volumes (New York, White, Stokes & Allen, 1886-1889) and John R. Ireland's The Republic in 16 (Chicago,

Fairbanks and Palmer, 1886-1888).

113

U. S. President. A compilation of the messages and papers of the Presidents, 1789-1897. Published, by authority of Congress, by James D. Richardson. Washington, Govt. Print. Off., 1896-99. 10 v.
J81.B96

Also issued as House misc. doc. no. 210, 53d Cong., 2d sess.

This is the original and official compilation and publication, which has been universally used and cited for over 60 years and has given general satisfaction, although it is not complete for the early Congresses and it does not reprint the papers which accompanied messages of transmission. Congressman Richardson of Tennessee was not paid for his labors, but received some 650 sets and a duplicate of the plates. The latter he disposed of to a commercial publishing house which first used the imprint: Washington, Bureau of National Literature and Art, and subsequently: New York, Bureau of National Literature. A number of supplements and at least 12 enlarged editions were issued under these auspices; an entry for the latest in LC follows.

114

----- A compilation of the messages and papers of the Presidents, prepared under the direction of the Joint Committee on Printing, of the House and Senate, pursuant to an Act of the 52d Congress of the United States (with additions and Encyclopedic index by private enterprise). New York, Bureau of National Literature [1927?] 20 v.

Encyclopedic index, v. 19-20. Vol. 18 concludes with a veto message of President Coolidge, Feb. 25, 1927

114
U. S. _President_. (cont.)
(p. 9675). However, there exists a
Supplement which includes all the messages of Coolidge's full term (1925-29)
and has the pagination 9481-9850.

115
Grosvenor, Charles H. The book of the
Presidents, with biographical sketches.
Washington, Continental Press, 1902.
193 p. 41 x 31 cm. E176.1.G87
The most imposing volume of its
kind, with text by an Ohio Congressman;
actual production by The Trow Print,
New York. Each sketch is preceded by a
full-page photogravure of a portrait or
photograph, opens with a rubricated
title and initial, and is set in bold-
face 20-point (or thereabouts) type.
The "Department of Autograph Letters"
(p. 127-161) reproduces a letter or
document signed by each President (but
Jefferson's and six others are not holographs). The "Department of Armorial
Bearings" (p. 165-193) consists of gen-
ealogical notes; Madison, Lincoln, and
six others are mercifully left without
coats of arms.

116
Wise, John S. Recollections of thirteen
Presidents. New York, Doubleday, Page,
1906. 284 p. E176.1.W81

117
Wilson, James Grant, _ed_. The Presidents
of the United States 1789-1914, by
John Fiske, Carl Schurz [and others]
New York, Scribner, 1914. 4 v.
E176.1.W762
Originally published by Appleton in
1 v., 1894, and based upon the articles
in Appletons' Cyclopaedia of American
Biography.

118
Hagner, Alexander B., 1826-1915. A personal narrative of the acquaintance of
my father [Peter Hagner, 1772-1850] and
myself with each of the Presidents of
the United States. Washington, W. F.
Roberts, 1915. 54 p. E176.1.H14

119
Wolf, Simon. The Presidents I have known
from 1860-1918. Washington, B. S.
Adams [1918] 459 p. E176.1.W85

120
Kohlsaat, Herman H. From McKinley to
Harding; personal recollections of our
Presidents. New York, Scribner, 1923.
235 p. E176.1.K75

121
Boyden, William L. Masonic Presidents,
Vice-Presidents and signers; the Masonic record of the Presidents of the
United States, Vice-Presidents and
signers of the Declaration of Independence. Washington, 1927. 71 p.
HS509.B6
A more recent accumulation of somewhat miscellaneous materials is Ray V.
Denslow's Freemasonry and the Presidency, U. S. A. ([Trenton? Mo.] 1952.
306 p.).

122
Stoddard, Henry L. As I knew them; Presidents and politics from Grant to Coolidge. New York, Harper, 1927. 571 p.
E176.1.S82

123
Thompson, Charles W. Presidents I've
known and two near Presidents. Indianapolis, Bobbs-Merrill [1929] 386 p.
E176.1.T45

124
White, William Allen. Masks in a pageant.
New York, Macmillan, 1929. 507 p.
E176.1.W583

125
Palmer, John Macaulay. Washington, Lincoln, Wilson; three war statesmen.
Garden City, N. Y., Doubleday, Doran,
1930. 417 p. E181.P17

126
Virginia born Presidents; addresses delivered on the occasions of unveiling the
busts of Virginia born Presidents at
old hall of the House of Delegates,

126

Virginia born Presidents ... (cont.)
Richmond, Virginia, compiled under the
auspices of and with an introd. by the
Hon. John Garland Pollard, Governor of
Virginia. New York, American Book Co.,
1932. 232 p.   E176.1.V72
    Eight addresses whose authors in-
clude Albert Bushnell Hart, John W.
Davis, Charles Evans Hughes, Charles P.
Summerall, Claude G. Bowers, and John
Barton Payne.

127

Agar, Herbert. The people's choice, from
Washington to Harding; a study in democracy. Boston, Houghton Mifflin,
1933. 337 p.   E187.A24
    Bibliography: p. 217-324.

128

Moran, Thomas F. American Presidents;
their individualities and their contributions to American progress. New ed.,
rev. and enl. by Louis Martin Sears.
New York, Crowell [1933] 318 p.
                        E176.1.M82 1933
    First edition 1917 (148 p.).

129

Henry, Reginald B. Genealogies of the
families of the Presidents. Rutland,
Vt., Tuttle, 1935. 340 p. CS69.H4
    Bibliography: p. 9-10.

130

Wilson, Fred Taylor. Pen pictures of the
Presidents. Nashville, Tenn., Southwestern Co., 1937. 574 p.
                        E176.1.W735 1937
    First edition 1932.

131

Stoddard, Henry L. It costs to be President. New York, Harper, 1938. 340 p.
                        JK511.S75

132

Pach, Alfred. Portraits of our Presidents;
the Pach collection. New York, Hastings House [1943] 68 p. E176.1.P3

133

Historical Records Survey, New York (City)
Presidential executive orders. Compiled by W. P. A. Historical Records
Survey. New York, Books, inc., distributed by Archives Pub. Co., a division of Hastings House [1944] 2 v.
                        J80.A72
    Introduction, v. 1, signed: Clif-
ford L. Lord.
    Contents.--v. 1. List.--v. 2. Index.

134

Goebel, Dorothy (Burne), and Julius
Goebel, Jr. Generals in the White
House. Garden City, N. Y., Doubleday,
Doran, 1945. 276 p.   E176.1.G63
    Contents.--American paradox.--The
pedigree of prejudice.--What makes a
general?--General Washington.--General
Jackson.--General William Henry Harrison.--General Taylor.--General Pierce.--
General Grant.--Generals Hayes, Garfield, and Benjamin Harrison.--Conclu-
sion.

135

Booth, Edward Townsend. Country life in
America, as lived by ten Presidents of
the United States. New York, Knopf,
1947. xviii, 264, xii p.
                        E176.1.B75
    Bibliography: p. 249-264.
    Eight from Washington to Lincoln,
and only Theodore Roosevelt and Coolidge since. The execution is as good
as the idea.

136

Perling, Joseph. Presidents' sons; the
prestige of name in a democracy. New
York, Odyssey Press [1947] 451 p.
                        E176.1.P4

137

Pollard, James E. The Presidents and the
press. New York, Macmillan, 1947.
866 p.   PN4888.P7P6

138

Ashley, Maurice P. Mr. President; an introduction to American history. London, J. Cape [1948] 448 p.
                        E176.1.A8

14

138
Ashley, Maurice P. Mr. President. (cont.)
Contents.--George Washington.--
Thomas Jefferson.--Andrew Jackson.--
Abraham Lincoln.--Theodore Roosevelt.--
Woodrow Wilson.--Epilogue: The United
States and Great Britain.

139
Levin, Peter R. Seven by chance: the
accidental Presidents. New York,
Farrar, Straus, 1948. 374 p.
E176.1.L38
Bibliography: p. 365-369.

140
Long, John C. The liberal Presidents; a
study of the liberal tradition in
the American Presidency. New York,
Crowell [1948] 226 p. E176.1.L85

141
Milhollen, Hirst D., and Milton Kaplan.
Presidents on parade. With a foreword
by Luther H. Evans, Librarian of Congress. New York, Macmillan, 1948.
425 p.   E176.1.M63
A collection of prints and photographs reproduced in part from material
in the Library of Congress, each with
brief commentary.

142
Martin, Asa Earl. After the White House.
State College, Pa., Penns Valley Publishers, 1951. 464 p. E176.1.M365
The ex-Presidents have lived periods
of varying duration after leaving the
White House, from less than 3 months
(Polk) to over 25 years (John Adams)
and even beyond that (Hoover). Professor Emeritus Martin has sketched out
just what each was thinking and doing
during these periods, which were by no
means all retirement.

143
Dietz, August. Presidents of the United
States of America; portraits and biog-
raphies. [3d ed.] Richmond, Dietz
Press [1953] 72 p. E176.1.D53 1953

144
Bowers, Claude G. Making democracy a
reality; Jefferson, Jackson, and Polk.
Memphis, Memphis State College Press,
1954. 170 p. (The J. P. Young lectures in American history) E176.1.B8

145
Donovan, Robert J. The assassins. New
York, Harper [1955] 300 p. HV6278.D6
Protection at last: p. 108-126,
describes the methods of the Secret
Service White House Detail and shows
how they would, in all probability,
have prevented the crimes of Booth,
Guiteau, and Czolgosz.

146
Three Presidents and their books; the
reading of: Jefferson [by] Arthur
Bestor; Lincoln [by] David C. Mearns;
Franklin D. Roosevelt [by] Jonathan
Daniels. Urbana, University of Illi-
nois Press, 1955. 129 p. (Fifth
annual Windsor lectures) E176.1.T48
Bibliography: p. 106-129.

147
Zorn, Walter Lewis. The descendants of
the Presidents of the United States of
America. 2d rev. ed. Monroe, Mich.,
1955. 182 p.   CS59.Z6 1955
First published in 1954 (149 p.).

148
Golterman, Guy. The book of the Presi-
dents: a gallery of famous portraits
of the Presidents of the United States.
Rev. ed. St. Louis, c1956. unpaged.
E176.1.G64 1956
First published in 1949 under title:
The White House collection of official
portraits of the Presidents.

149
McConnell, Jane (Tompkins), and Burt M.
McConnell. Presidents of the United
States; the story of their lives,
closely interwoven with the vast polit-
ical and economical changes of the
Nation. Ports. by Constance Joan Naar.
New York, Crowell [1957] 342 p.
E176.1.M15 1957

150

Morgan, James. Our Presidents; brief
biographies of our chief magistrates
from Washington to Eisenhower, 1789-
1958. 2d enl. ed. New York, Macmillan, 1958. 470 p. E176.1.M84 1958
    Began its prosperous career in
1924, with revisions or enlargements in
1926, 1935, and 1949.

151

U. S. President. Public papers of the
Presidents of the United States, containing the public messages, speeches,
and statements of the Presidents.
[Washington, U. S. Govt. Print. Off.,
1958-62] 10 v.   J80.A283
    This series of annual volumes, com-
piled by the Office of the Federal Reg-
ister in response to a recommendation
of the National Historical Publications
Commission, was initiated with the papers of 1957. The Eisenhower series
has been completed in 8 v., 1953-61,
and the Truman and Kennedy series begun
with volumes for 1945 and 1961.

152

Kane, Joseph Nathan. Facts about the
Presidents; a compilation of biograph-
ical and historical data. New York,
H. W. Wilson, 1959. 348 p. E176.1.K3

153

Armbruster, Maxim E. The Presidents of
the United States: a new appraisal.
New York, Horizon Press, 1960. 344 p.
                              E176.1.A75

154

Marx, Rudolph. The health of the Presidents. New York, Putnam [1961, ©1960]
376 p.   E176.1.M38
    An earlier and less comprehensive
assembling of medical data was Karl C.
Wold's Mr. President, How is Your
Health? (St. Paul, Bruce Pub. Co.,
1948. 214 p.).

155

U. S. Library of Congress. General Reference and Bibliography Division. Presidential inaugurations; a selected list
of references. Rev. ed. Washington,

155

U. S. Library of Congress. (cont.)
1960. 72 p.   Z1249.P7U6

156

Beard, Charles A. The Presidents in American history; brought forward since
1948 by William Beard. [Rev. ed.]
New York, Messner [1961] 182 p.
                    E176.1.B35 1961
    Thumbnail estimates of the personal-
ity and administration of each President, originally published in 1935, revised by the author in 1946, and since
kept up to date by his son. A "Biographical Digest" of dates, cabinets,
and election votes, which are not allowed to encumber the text, occupies
p. 151-182.

157

Borden, Morton, ed. America's ten great-
est Presidents. Chicago, Rand McNally
[1961] 269 p.   E176.1.B77
    "Selected reading list": p. 263-
269.
    Ten sketches by as many professors
of history on the Presidents who finished highest in the Schlesinger poll
of 1948. Each author seeks to explain
his subject's eminence.

158

Lott, Davis Newton, ed. The inaugural
addresses of the American Presidents,
from Washington to Kennedy. New York,
Holt, Rinehart, and Winston [1961]
299 p.   J81.C61

159

Roos, Charles A. Physicians to the Presidents, and their patients: a bio-
bibliography. In Medical Library Association. Bulletin, v. 49, July 1961:
p. 291-360.   Z765.M4M4, v. 49
    "Name index of [150] physicians to
the Presidents": p. 359-360.

160

Tobin, Richard L. Decisions of destiny.
Cleveland, World Pub. Co., 1961.
285 p.   E176.1.T6

160
Tobin, Richard L. Decisions ... (cont.)
    An experienced political journalist
sketches ten episodes in the adminis-
strations of as many Presidents from
Washington to Truman, all of which have
been significant for the course of national history and for the definition
of the Presidential office.

161
U. S. President. Inaugural addresses of
    the Presidents of the United States
    from George Washington, 1789, to John F.
    Kennedy, 1961. [Compiled by the Leg-
    islative Reference Service, Library of
    Congress] Washington, U. S. Govt.
    Print. Off., 1961. 270 p. (87th Cong.,
    1st sess. House document no. 218)
                          J81.C61a

162
Bergere, Thea. Homes of the Presidents.
    Illustrated by Richard Bergere. New
    York, Dodd, Mead [1962] 94 p. 19 x
    25 cm.   E159.B43
        Well, if a little darkly, executed
    pen-and-ink drawings of each home; es-
    sential information concerning it and
    a smaller sketch of the birthplace on
    facing pages.

163
Bruce, David K. E. Sixteen American Pres-
    idents. Indianapolis, Bobbs-Merrill
    [1962] 336 p.   E176.1.B887 1962
        A revision and expansion of Revolu-
    tion to Reconstruction, published in
    1939.

164
Durant, John, and Alice K. Rand Durant.
    Pictorial history of American Presi-
    dents. 2d rev. ed. New York, Barnes
    [1962] 340 p.   E176.1.D9 1962
        First published in 1955.

165
Jones, Cranston. Homes of the American
    Presidents. Photographer and picture
    editor: William H. Schleisner. New
    York, McGraw-Hill [1962] 232 p.
                          E159.J6

166
Wilson, Vincent. The book of the Presi-
    dents. Maps by Peter Guilday. Silver
    Spring, Md., American History Research
    Associates [1962] 75 p. E176.1.W785
        A neatly made booklet of portraits,
    one-page sketches, outline maps, and
    tabulated data.

167

Ellet, Elizabeth F. (Lummis) The court
circles of the Republic, or the beau-
ties and celebrities of the Nation; illustrating life and society under
eighteen Presidents; describing the
social features of the successive administrations from Washington to Grant.
Hartford, Conn., Hartford Pub. Co.,
1869. 586 p.   F194.E45

168

Langford, Laura C. H. The ladies of the
White House, by Laura Carter Holloway.
With 15 steel engravings. New York,
United States Pub. Co., 1870. 658 p.
E176.1.L27
    Appears to be the first book on the
First Ladies. LC has 9 editions, 1870-
1886, including one titled In the Home
of the Presidents. Second in the field
was Lydia L. Gordon's From Lady Wash-
ington [sic] to Mrs. Cleveland (Boston,
Lee and Shepard, 1889. 448 p.).

169

Upton, Harriet Taylor. Our early Presi-
dents: their wives and children. From
Washington to Jackson. Boston, D.
Lothrop [1891] 395 p.   E176.1.U71

170

Johnston, Frances B. The White House;
with thirty-six illustrations from Miss
Johnston's unique collection of recent
photographs of the Executive Mansion.
Washington, Gibson Bros., 1893. [4] p.
F204.W5J7

171

Pendel, Thomas F. Thirty-six years in the
White House. Washington, Neale Pub.
Co., 1902. 176 p.   F204.W5P3
    In addition to the story of his ex-
periences as door-keeper in the White
House during the administrations of

171

Pendel, Thomas F. Thirty-six ... (cont.)
nine Presidents, the author gives a
"List of furniture and bric-a-brac in
Executive Mansion, compiled from data
furnished ... by direction of Col.
F. A. Bingham, Apr. 5, 1898": p. 169-
176.

172

Woolfall, Lila G. A. Presiding Ladies of
the White House. Illustrated with symbolic borders and reproductions in
photogravure of the First Ladies of the
land. Washington, Bureau of National
Literature and Art [c1903] 137 p.
E176.1.W81
    A picture book, with text limited to
the area, on facing pages, within the
"symbolic borders." The faces of the
ladies' husbands may be detected in
small medallions on the lower stretch
of each border. The author's first issue of her material was in 1898, under
the nom-de-plume of Olga Stanley.

173

Smith, Margaret (Bayard) The first forty
years of Washington society portrayed
by the family letters of Mrs. Samuel
Harrison Smith (Margaret Bayard) from
the collection of her grandson J. Hen-
ley Smith. Edited by Gaillard Hunt.
New York, Scribner, 1906. 424 p.
F194.S65

174

Singleton, Esther. The story of the White
House. New York, McClure, 1907. 2 v.
F204.W5S6

175

Willets, Gilson. Inside history of the
White House; the complete history of
the domestic and official life in Washington of the Nation's Presidents and

175
Willets, Gilson. Inside ... (cont.)
their families. New York, Christian
Herald [c1908] 492 p.   F204.W5W7

176
Sage, Agnes C. The boys and girls of the
White House. New York, Frederick A.
Stokes [1909] 326 p.   E176.1.S13

177
Crook, William H. Memories of the White
House: the home life of our Presidents
from Lincoln to Roosevelt; being personal recollections. Compiled and
edited by Henry Rood. Boston, Little,
Brown, 1911. 308 p.   E176.1.C94

178
Hampton, William Judson. Our Presidents
and their mothers. Introd. by the
Honorable Walter E. Edge. Boston,
Cornhill Pub. Co. [1922] 255 p.
E176.1.H25

179
Colman, Edna M. (Hercher) Seventy-five
years of White House gossip; from Wash-
ington to Lincoln. Garden City, N. Y.,
Doubleday, Page, 1925. 334 p.
E176.1.C75

180
----- White House gossip, from Andrew
Johnson to Calvin Coolidge. Garden
City, N. Y., Doubleday, Page, 1927.
431 p.   E176.1.C76

181
Jaffray, Elizabeth. Secrets of the White
House. New York, Cosmopolitan Book
Corp., 1927. 200 p.   F204.W5J2
Mrs. Jaffray was housekeeper from
the days of Taft to Coolidge.

182
Chittenden, Cecil R. The White House and
its yesterdays; a narrative of an American home. Alexandria, Va., Washing-
ton-Mt. Vernon Memorial Book Corp.
[c1932] 155 p.   F204.W5C5

183
Hampton, Vernon B. Religious background

183
of the White House. Boston, Christopher
Pub. House [c1932] 416 p.
E176.1.H22
Bibliography: p. 396-407.

184
Hoover, Irwin H. Forty-two years in the
White House, by Irwin Hood (Ike) Hoo-
ver, chief usher. Boston, Houghton
Mifflin, 1934. 332 p.   E176.1.H78

185
Randolph, Mary. Presidents and First
Ladies. New York, D. Appleton-Century,
1936. 257 p.   E176.1.R24
The author was social secretary at
the White House through the Coolidge
and part of the Hoover administrations,
but includes material from the earlier
years of the century.

186
Lewis, Ethel. The White House; an informal history of its architecture, inte-
riors and gardens. New York, Dodd,
Mead, 1937. 330 p.   F204.W5L6

187
Sweetser, Kate D. Famous girls of the
White House. Rev. ed. New York,
Crowell [c1957] 303 p. E176.S96 1937
First edition 1930 (299 p.).
Contents: Nelly Custis; Dolly Madi-
son; Martha and Mary Jefferson; The
Monroe girls; "Lovely Emily"; Angelica
Singleton; Julia Gardiner; "Miss Betty";
Harriet Lane; Nellie Grant; Frances
Folsom; Alice Roosevelt; Helen Taft;
Three girls [Wilson] in the White House.

188
Hurd, Charles. The White House, a biogra-
phy; the story of the house, its occu-
pants, its place in American history.
New York, Harper [c1940] 339 p.
F204.W5H8

189
Crane, Katharine E. Blair House, past and
present, an account of its life and
times in the City of Washington, with
16 illustrations in gravure.

189
Crane, Katharine. Blair House ... (cont.)
    [Washington] U. S. Dept. of State,
    1945. 38 p. (U. S. Dept of State.
    [Publication 2361])   F204.B5C7

190
Smith, A. Merriman. Thank you, Mr. Presi-
    dent, a White House notebook. New
    York, Harper [1946] 304 p. E807.S57
    Impressions of the United Press's
    White House correspondent from his
    assignment in the fall of 1941 to the
    summer of 1946.

191
Starling, Edmund W. Starling of the White
    House; the story of the man whose Se-
    cret Service detail guarded five Pres-
    idents from Woodrow Wilson to Frank-
    lin D. Roosevelt, as told to Thomas
    Sugrue. New York, Simon and Schuster,
    1946. 334 p.   E748.S78A3

192
Smith, A. Merriman. A President is many
    men. New York, Harper, 1948. 269 p.
                                JK516.S65
    Comments on the multiplicity of a
    President's duties, the functions of
    his entourage, and the endless stream
    of his visitors, from the viewpoint of
    a reflective White House correspondent.

193
Whitton, Mary O. First First Ladies,
    1789-1865; a study of the wives of the
    early Presidents. New York, Hastings
    House [1948] 341 p.   E176.2.W5
    Bibliography: p. [333]-341.

194
Smith, Ira R. T. "Dear Mr. President ... "
    The story of fifty years in the White
    House mail room, by Ira R. T. Smith
    with Joe Alex Morris. New York,
    J. Messner [1949] 238 p. E176.1.S65

195
U. S. Commission on the Renovation of the
    Executive Mansion. Report ... Compiled
    under the direction of the Commission
    by Edwin B. Morris. [Washington, U. S.
    Govt. Print. Off., 1952] 109 p.

195
U. S. Commission ... (cont.)
                            F204.W5U52

196
Truett, Randle B. The White House, home
    of the Presidents. New York, Hastings
    House [1949] 81 p.   F204.W5T7

197
Furman, Bess. White House profile; a so-
    cial history of the White House, its
    occupants and its festivities. Indian-
    apolis, Bobbs-Merrill [1951] 368 p.
                            F204.W5F8
    Bibliography: p. 345-356.

198
Klapthor, Margaret (Brown). The dresses
    of the First Ladies of the White House,
    as exhibited in the United States Na-
    tional Museum, by Margaret W. Brown.
    Washington, Smithsonian Institution,
    1952. 149 p. (part col.) (Smithson-
    ian Institution, Publication 4060)
                            GT605.K55
----- Supplement. The gown of Mrs. Har-
    ry S. Truman, as displayed in the
    United States National Museum, Smith-
    sonian Institution. [Washington]
    Smithsonian Institution, 1954. [5] p.
    illus.   GT605.K55 Suppl.
----- Supplement. The gown of Mrs.
    Dwight D. Eisenhower, as displayed in
    the United States National Museum,
    Smithsonian Institution, 1954.
                            GT605.K55 Suppl. 2
    A full presentation of this unique
    collection, the brainchild of Mrs.
    Julian James of Washington. Mrs. W. H.
    Taft gave it official recognition in
    1912, and a hall in the Arts and Indus-
    tries Building of the Smithsonian was
    assigned for its display. For each
    unit there is a portrait or photo of
    the First Lady, a biographical sketch,
    a color photo of the dress on its plas-
    ter mannequin, a technical description
    of the dress, and a bibliographical
    reference or references. The two sup-
    plements follow the same scheme.

199

Leeming, Joseph. The White House in picture and story. New York, G. W. Stewart [1953] 95 p.   F204.W5L5
    Includes plans, and photographs of
the same room at different eras. The
text is closely related to the pictures.

200

Helm, Edith (Benham) The captains and the
kings. With a foreword by Mrs. Franklin D. Roosevelt. New York, Putnam
[1954] 307 p.   E176.1.H44 1954
    Autobiographical, with recollections
of her life as social secretary at the
White House under the Wilsons, the
Roosevelts, and the Trumans.

201

McConnell, Jane (Tompkins), and Burt
McConnell. The White House; a history
with pictures. New York, Studio Publications [1954] 80 p.   F204.W5M3
    Color photographs from Life show new
interior; black and white photographs
from National Park Service show new ex-
terior; and the text emphasizes the reconstruction of 1949-52 and the new
furnishings.

202

Prindiville, Kathleen. First Ladies.
[Rev. ed.] New York, Macmillan, 1954.
309 p.   E176.2.P88 1954

203

Truett, Randle B. The First Ladies in
fashion. With fashion notes by Philip
Robertson. New York, Hastings House
[1954] 80 p.   GT605.T7
    A presentation of the Smithsonian
collection of First Ladies' dresses,
with photographs and quite technical
descriptions of the dresses, by 2 cou-
turier.

204

Brown, Wilson. Aide to four Presidents.
American heritage, v. 6, Feb. 1955:
66-96.   E171.A43, v. 6
    Admiral Brown served as a naval aide
to Presidents Coolidge, Hoover, Roosevelt, and Truman. These extracts from
his memoirs give glimpses of life in

204

Brown, Wilson. Aide ... (cont.)
the White House and especially upon the
Presidential yacht Mayflower and its
successors.

205

Smithsonian Institution. The First Ladies
hall. [Washington, 1955] [12] p.
(Its Publication no. 4212) GT605.S55
    Photographs, with descriptive let-
terpress, of the eight period groups in
which the historic dresses, each displayed on a plaster mannequin, have
been arranged. Each case contains from
three to six figures, arranged against
a background representing an authentic
White House room of the time.

206

McConnell, Jane (Tompkins), and Burt
McConnell. Our First Ladies, from
Martha Washington to Mamie Eisenhower.
New York, Crowell [1957] 342 p.
          E176.2.M3 1957
    First published in 1953 under title:
First Ladies.
    Bibliography: p. 333-337.

207

Rysavy, Francois. White House chef, as
told to Frances Spatz Leighton. New
York, Putnam [1957] 286 p.   TX731.R9
    Mr. Rysavy, a naturalized Czech, was
recruited for White House service early
in 1955, and remained through the
spring of 1957, cooking in French style
for the company and in American for the
family. He gives many White House
menus and recipes.

208

Eberlein, Harold D., and Cortlandt Van D.
Hubbard. Historic houses of George-
Town & Washington City. Pref. by
Richard H. Howland. Richmond, Dietz
Press [1958] 480 p.   F195.E2
    The White House: p. 180-247; Blair
House: p. 292-300; The Octagon: p.
301-316; 2017 I Street, N. W. [Monroe
House]: p. 330-341; Corn Rigs-Anderson
House [in the grounds of Soldiers' Home,
used as a summer residence by President
Lincoln and perhaps by President

208

Eberlein <u>and</u> Hubbard. Historic ... (cont.)
Buchanan]: p. 465-468.
    The text consists of documented
sketches of the owners or occupants,
social use, and associations, rather
than the architectural features, of
18th- and early 19th-century houses.
The sketch of the White House is much
the longest, and extends from its occupation by John Adams to the death of
President Lincoln.

209

Esperancilla, Irineo. I served four Presidents. Edited by Eugene Gonda. Look,
v. 23, Oct. 27, 1959: 134, 136, 138-
139.   AP2.L79, v. 23
    A navy steward assigned to President
Hoover's camp on the Rapidan, the author spent nearly 25 years in personal
attendance on Hoover, F.D.R., Truman,
and Eisenhower, at the White House, on
Presidential yachts and trains, and at
"Shangri-La" or Camp David.

210

Allen, George E. Presidents who have
known me. New York, Simon and Schuster
[1960] 290 p.   E748.A195A3 1960
    First published in 1950 (254 p.).

211

Jeffries, Ona Griffin. In and out of the
White House, from Washington to the
Eisenhowers; an intimate glimpse into
the social and domestic aspects of the
Presidential life. New York, W. Funk
[1960] 404 p.   E176.1.J4

212

Fields, Alonzo. My 21 years in the White
House. New York, Coward-McCann [1961]
223 p.   F204.W5F5

213

Haskin Service, <u>Washington, D. C.</u> The
Presidents and their wives, from Washington to Kennedy. [Washington, 1961]
66 p.   E176.1.H343 1961
    First published in 1953.

214

Parks, Lillian (Rogers) My thirty years
backstairs at the White House [by]
Lillian Rogers Parks in collaboration
with Frances Spatz Leighton. New York,
Fleet Pub. Corp. [1961] 346 p.
                            E176.1.P37
    Mrs. Parks was the daughter of a
White House maid, Maggie Rogers, and
although handicapped by polio, herself
served as White House maid and seam-
stress for over 30 years (1929-60).
Since her mother's recollections went
back to the Taft administration, the
book, written in journalese, spans half
a century.

215

Jensen, Amy La Follette. The White House
and its thirty-three families. Howard
C. Jensen, art editor. New enl. ed.
New York, McGraw-Hill [1962] 292 p.
                       F204.W5J4 1962
    First edition 1958.
    The lavish and clearly reproduced
illustrations from contemporary prints
and photographs rather outmatch the
slender and undocumented text.

216

Rigdon, William M. White House sailor
[by] William M. Rigdon, with James
Derieux. Garden City, N. Y., Doubleday, 1962. 298 p.   E806.R5

217

White House Historical Association, <u>Wash-
ington, D. C.</u> The White House; an
historic guide. Washington, 1962.
129 p.   F204.W5W6
    A sound and informative text lavish-
ly illustrated in color, and including
most of the recently added antique
furnishings.

218

Wolff, Perry S. A tour of the White House
with Mrs. John F. Kennedy. Garden
City, N. Y., Doubleday, 1962. 258 p.
                          F204.W5W73
    Based on the television program of
the same name, with additional information, photographs, and sketches.

219
Hatch, Louis Clinton. A history of the
    Vice-Presidency of the United States.
    Revised and edited by Professor Earl L.
    Shoup. New York, American Historical
    Society, 1934. 437 p.   E176.H35

220
Young, Klyde H., and Lamar Middleton.
    Heirs apparent, the Vice Presidents of
    the United States. New York, Prentice-
    Hall [1948] 314 p.   E176.Y7
        The 34 sketches, from John Adams to
    Harry S. Truman, include the ten who
    succeeded to or were subsequently
    elected to the Presidency.

221
Williams, Irving G. The American Vice-
    Presidency: new look. Garden City,
    N. Y., Doubleday, 1954. 82 p. (Dou-
    bleday short studies in political
    science, SSPS 10)   JK609.5.W55

222
Waugh, Edgar Wiggins. Second consul, the
    Vice Presidency: our greatest polit-
    ical problem. Indianapolis, Bobbs-
    Merrill [1956] 244 p. JK609.5.W3

223
Williams, Irving G. The rise of the Vice
    Presidency. Introd. by Edward R. Mur-
    row. Washington, Public Affairs Press
    [1956] 266 p.   JK609.5.W56

224
Tompkins, Dorothy Louise (Campbell) Culver.
    The office of Vice President; a selec-
    ted bibliography. Berkeley, Bureau of
    Public Administration, University of
    California, 1957. 19 p. Z1249.P7T6

GEORGE WASHINGTON

Writings

225
Washington, George. Writings; collected
and edited by Worthington Chauncey
Ford. New York, Putnam, 1889-93.
14 v.   E312.7 1889
    Until the appearance of this edi-
tion, of which only 750 sets were
printed, the world had to depend upon
the edition of Jared Sparks, originally
published in 12 v. at Boston, 1833-37,
and several times reprinted. Sparks
felt at liberty to "improve" his author when he considered his manuscripts
to be incorrect or inadequate in expression.

226
----- The writings of George Washington
from the original manuscript sources,
1745-1799; prepared under the direction
of the United States George Washington
Bicentennial Commission and published
by authority of Congress: John C.
Fitzpatrick, editor. Washington, U. S.
Govt. Print. Off. [1931-44] 39 v.
                         E312.7 1931
    "George Washington bicentennial edi-
tion."
    "General index by David M. Matteson":
v. 38-39.
    Exhaustive for letters sent; but
does not include the Diaries, which Dr.
Fitzpatrick had already edited under
different auspices.

227
----- Diaries, 1748-1799, edited by John
C. Fitzpatrick. Published for the
Mount Vernon Ladies' Association of the
Union. Boston, Houghton Mifflin, 1925.
4 v.   E312.8 1748-99
    Contents.--v. 1. 1748-1770.--v. 2.
1771-1785.--v. 3. 1786-1788.--v. 4.
1789-1799.

228
----- Writings; edited with an introd.
and notes by Lawrence B. Evans. New
York, Putnam, 1908. lxix, 567 p.
                         E312.72 1908

229
----- Washington speaks for himself, by
Lucretia Perry Osborn. New York,
Scribner, 1927. xxii, 323 p.
                         E312.72 1927

230
----- The autobiography of George Washington, 1753-1799, arr. and edited by
Edward C. Boykin. New York, Reynal &
Hitchcock [°1935] 119 p. illus.
                         E312.W72 1935
    Selections from Washington's dia-
ries, letters, addresses and state papers arranged as an autobiographical
narrative.

231
----- Maxims of Washington, political,
social, moral, and religious. Collected and arr. by John Frederick Schroeder. [Rev. ed.] Mount Vernon, Va.,
The Mount Vernon Ladies' Association
[1942] xxvii, 348 p.
                    E312.79.W3127 1942
    First published in 1854.

232
----- Basic writings of George Washington, edited with an introd. and notes,
by Saxe Commins. New York, Random
House, 1948. xvii, 697 p.
                         E312.72 1948

233
----- The Washington papers; basic selections from the public and private writings of George Washington, edited and
arr., with an introd., by Saul K. Padover. New York, Harper [1955] 430 p.

233
----- The Washington papers ... (cont.)
                    E312.72 1955
    Bibliography: p. 417-418.

234
----- Letters from His Excellency George
    Washington, President of the United
    States, to Sir John Sinclair, Bart.
    M. P., on agricultural and other inter-
    esting topics. Engraved from the orig-
    inal letters [by S. J. Neele] London,
    W. Bulmer, 1800. 57 p. E312.75.A25
        Sinclair, author of the Statistical
    Account of Scotland and first President
    of the Board of Agriculture, was re-
    sponsible for this unusual publication
    which he dedicated to the people of
    America. Eight letters, 1792-97, are
    fully reproduced in facsimile (p. 17-
    51). This publication doubtless stim-
    ulated another, not in facsimile, of
    letters to Arthur Young, the famous
    traveling observer of agricultural
    methods now secretary to Sinclair's
    Board of Agriculture: Letters from His
    Excellency General Washington to Arthur
    Young containing an Account of His Hus-
    bandry (London, W. J. and J. Richardson
    [etc.] 1801. 172 p.) Some half-cen-
    tury later the two were combined in an
    American publication edited by Franklin
    Knight: Letters on Agriculture from
    His Excellency George Washington, Pres-
    ident of the United States (Washington,
    The Editor, 1847. 198 p.), in which
    the letters to Sinclair are still given
    in engraved facsimile, and with the
    original page numbers.

235
Sparks, Jared, ed. Correspondence of the
    American Revolution: being letters of
    eminent men to George Washington, from
    the time of his taking command of the
    Army to the end of his Presidency.
    Boston, Little, Brown, 1853. 4 v.
                    E203.S73
        While no text printed by Sparks can
    be given complete trust, he was at
    least less apt to meddle with the let-
    ters of Washington's correspondents
    than with those of Washington. No one
    has ever attempted to replace this

235
Sparks, Jared. Correspondence ... (cont.)
    edition of vastly useful material (over
    2,000 pages) from the main body of
    Washington Papers. The postwar period
    is not reached until v. 4, p. 57. Let-
    ters not addressed to Washington are
    printed in appendixes, in smaller type.

236
Washington, George. The Washington-Craw-
    ford letters, being the correspondence
    between George Washington and William
    Crawford, from 1767 to 1781, concerning
    western lands. Edited by C[onsul] W.
    Butterfield. Cincinnati, R. Clerke,
    1877. 107 p.   E312.75.O37
        Crawford, a Virginian who took up
    his residence on the Youghiogeny in
    territory then claimed by Virginia but
    eventually incorporated in Pennsylva-
    nia, acted as agent for Washington's
    trans-Appalachian lands before the
    Revolution. An appendix contains sim-
    ilar letters from Valentine Crawford,
    William's brother, to Washington during
    1774-75.

237
----- Washington-Irvine correspondence;
    the official letters which passed be-
    tween Washington and Brig.-Gen. William
    Irvine and between Irvine and others
    concerning military affairs in the West
    from 1781 to 1783. Edited by C[onsul]
    W. Butterfield. Madison, Wis., D. At-
    wood, 1882. 430 p.   E203.B98
        General Irvine was placed in command
    at Fort Pitt in the latter part of
    1781. His correspondence with Washing-
    ton fills p. 71-152; 13 Appendixes are
    devoted to his correspondence with
    other Continental and state officials,
    and with his wife, presumably drawn
    from the body of his papers now in the
    Historical Society of Pennsylvania.

238
----- George Washington and Mount Vernon;
    a collection of Washington's unpub-
    lished agricultural and personal let-
    ters, edited with historical and gene-
    alogical introd. by Moncure Daniel Con-
    way. Brooklyn, N. Y., Long Island

238
----- George Washington ... (cont.)
Historical Society, 1889. xcii, 352 p.
(Memoirs of the Long Island Historical
Society, v. 4)   F116.L87, v. 4
                        E312.5.W3

239
The Spurious letters attributed to Washington. With a bibliographical note by
Worthington Chauncey Ford. Brooklyn,
Priv. print., 1889. 166 p.
                        E312.77 1889
      In May or June 1777 a London book-
seller, J. Bew, published a 73-page
pamphlet purporting to print seven letters of June 12-July 22, 1776, from
Washington to his overseer, Lund Washington, and to his wife and stepson.
They were reprinted in New York and
Philadelphia by Tory journals and as a
pamphlet; and they were resurrected in
1795-96 by the opponents of Jay's
Treaty. They were all forgeries, but
done by one who knew Washington's
household and some of his criticisms of
Congress. Washington guessed that it
was John Randolph (1728?-84), late
attorney general of Virginia, father of
his aide Edmund Randolph, and now an
exile in England. No one has offered
a plausible substitute.

240
Boston Athenaeum. A catalogue of the
Washington Collection in the Boston
Athenaeum; compiled and annotated by
Appleton P. C. Griffin. [Cambridge,
University Press for] The Boston Athenaeum, 1897. 566 p.   Z8950.B75
      Part 1, "Books from the Library of
General George Washington," describes
the collection which Henry Stevens
bought from George Corbin Washington
about 1847, and resold to the Athenaeum. An Appendix by William Coolidge
Lane deals with the other books in the
inventory of Washington's estate, and
traces the later descent of many. An
85-page Index was separately published
in 1900.

241
Hamilton, Stanislaus Murray, ed. Letters
to Washington and accompanying papers
[1752-July 1, 1775] Published by the
Society of the Colonial Dames of America. Boston, Houghton Mifflin, 1898-
1902. 5 v.   E312.2.H22
      Texts, lightly annotated, of prac-
tically all the early in-letters in
the main collection of Washington papers, then in the State Department and
now in the Library of Congress.

242
Jenkins, Charles Francis. Washington in
Germantown. Philadelphia, W. J. Campbell, 1905. xvi, 318 p. illus.
                        E312.29.J45
      Germantown has long since been ab-
sorbed into the city of Philadelphia,
but in 1793-94 was still a rustic sub-
urb. Philadelphia having not yet
emerged from its epidemic of yellow
fever, Washington took up his residence
there in November 1793, at first lodg-
ing with the Rev. Frederick Herman and
then taking over the house of Col.
Isaac Franks, now known as the Morris
House. Washington returned there in
August and September 1794. The book
gets its bulk from printing Washington's correspondence during these
months, with many supplementary documents.

243
Washington, George. Masonic correspondence as found among the Washington
papers in the Library of Congress, compiled under the direction of the Committee on Library of the Grand Lodge of
Pennsylvania, by Julius F. Sachse.
Philadelphia [Lancaster, Pa., New Era
Printing Co.] 1915. 144 p. E312.75.M4
                        HS511.W3A4
      Contains 15 exchanges from 1782 to
1798, of which the greater part are
complimentary addresses from Masonic
lodges and Washington's replies. There
are numerous facsimiles, and idenifi-
cations and portraits of a number of
Washington's Masonic contemporaries.

244

----- George Washington's accounts of
expenses while Commander-in-Chief of
the Continental Army, 1775-1783, reproduced in facsimile, with annotations
by John C. Fitzpatrick. Boston, Houghton, Mifflin, 1917. 154 p.
                              E312.81 1917
    "The accounts of the expenses of the
Commander-in-Chief of the Continental
Army were kept in duplicate by Washington himself. One he transmitted, at
the close of the war, to the Board of
Treasury of the Continental Congress
for auditing ... the other he retained,
and it is from this document, now in
the Library of Congress, that the accounts are now reproduced in photographic facsimile."--Pref. note.

245

----- The agricultural papers of George
Washington, edited by Walter Edwin
Brooke. Boston, R. G. Badger [c1919]
145 p.   E312.75.A2
    Includes 15 letters from Washington
to various persons on agricultural subjects, extracts from his diaries, farm
accounts, etc.

246

----- Rules of civility and decent behav-
iour in company and conversation, edited with an introd. by Charles Moore;
with frontispiece and facsimiles. Boston, Printed for Houghton Mifflin by
the Riverside Press, Cambridge, 1926.
xv, 64 p.   E312.78 1926
    The "Rules of Civility" occupy the
last ten pages of Washington's second
school exercise book, and are imper-
fect, some of the margins having come
off. They have been printed a number
of times since 1886; this is much the
best edition. Moore shows that they
are a selection and a simplification
from Francis Hawkins' Youth's Behav-
iour, of which nine editions appeared
between 1640 and 1672; and that this
derived from a French Jesuit treatise
of 1595.

247

----- Farewell address, in facsimile,
with transliterations of all the drafts
of Washington, Madison, & Hamilton, together with their correspondence and
other supporting documents; edited,
with a history of its origin, reception
by the Nation, rise of the controversy
respecting its authorship, and a bibliography, by Victor Hugo Paltsits. New
York, New York Public Library, 1935.
xvi, 360 p.   E312.95 1935
    "Bibliography of the farewell ad-
dress": p. [305]-360.

248

----- Washington, sa correspondence avec
d'Estaing. Paris, Fondation nationale
pour la reproduction des manuscrits
precieux et pièces rares d'archives
[D. Jacomet & Cie., 1937] 65 p.
                              E312.74 1937
    Introduction signed Ch[arles] de la
Roncière; superb facsimiles of two of
Washington's letters signed (July 22
and 26, 1778) which the editor took to
be holographs; letters from d'Estaing
followed by English translations, p.
1-29; letters from Washington, not
transcribed with complete accuracy, p.
31-45; overall dates, July 4-Oct. 27,
1778; originals in the Archives Na-
tionales, Marine B^4 146.

249

----- Correspondence concerning the Society of the Cincinnati, edited by Lt.-
Col. Edgar Erkine Hume. Baltimore,
Johns Hopkins Press, 1941. xliv,
472 p.   E312.75.S6

250

Lafayette, Marie-Joseph-Paul du Motier,
marquis de. The letters of Lafayette
to Washington, 1777-1699, edited by
Louis Gottschalk. New York, Priv.
print. by Helen F. Hubbard, 1944.
xxxvi, 417 p.   E207.L2L185

251
Washington, George. The journal of Major
    George Washington; an account of his
    first official mission, made as emissa-
    ry from the Governor of Virginia to the
    commandant of the French forces on the
    Ohio, October 1753-January 1754. Fac-
    sim. ed. Williamsburg, Va., Colonial
    Williamsburg; distributed by Holt, New
    York [1959]   E312.8 1753ag
        xi p., facsim.: (28 p.), [31]-41 p.
        "Introduction and notes are by James
    R. Short and Thaddeus W. Tate, Jr."

252

Marshall, John. The life of George Washington, Commander in Chief of the American forces, during the war which established the independence of his country, and first President of the United States. Philadelphia, C. P. Wayne, 1804-7. 5 v. and atlas. E312.M33

Frequently reprinted, abridged, etc. The latest edition in LC is New York, Walton Book Co., 1930.

For criticism, see William A. Foran, "John Marshall as a Historian," American Historical Review, v. 43, Oct. 1937: 51-64.

253

Gibbs, George. Memoirs of the administrations of Washington and John Adams, edited from the papers of Oliver Wolcott, Secretary of the Treasury. New York, Printed for the subscribers, 1846. 2 v. E311.G44

Wolcott became Auditor, the third position in the new Treasury Department, in Sept. 1789, was promoted to Comptroller in 1791, and became Secretary on Hamilton's resignation. These extracts from his correspondence, thinly stitched together by Gibbs, have always been a primary source for the first three administrations.

254

Irving, Washington. Life of George Washington. New York, Putnam, 1855-59. 5 v. E312.I6

Frequently reprinted, abridged, etc. The latest edition in LC is New York, Crowell [1916?].

255

Custis, George Washington Parke. Memoirs of Washington, by his adopted son. With a memoir of the author, by his daughter; and illustrative and explana-

255

Custis, George. Memoirs ... (cont.) tory notes, by Benson J. Lossing. [Philadelphia] Edgewood Pub. Co. [1859] 644 p. E312.15.C957

Editions of 1860 and 1861 have the title: Recollections and private memoirs of Washington.

256

Baker, William S. The engraved portraits of Washington, with notices of the originals and brief biographical sketches of the painters. Philadelphia, Lindsay & Baker, 1880. 212 p. E312.43.B155

The painters are in a chronological order, according to the earliest date at which Washington sat to them, and engravings 1-397 are placed under the appropriate painter, alphabetically by engravers. There is an Index of engravers. Nos. 398-434 are silhouettes, memorial designs, and fictitious portraits.

257

----- Medallic portraits of Washington, with historical and critical notes and a description catalogue of the coins, medals, tokens and cards. Philadelphia, R. M. Lindsay, 1885. 252 p. E312.43.B164

258

----- Character portraits of Washington as delineated by historians, orators, and divines, selected and arranged in chronological order with biographical notes and references. Philadelphia, R. M. Lindsay, 1887. 351 p. E312.17.B16

Selections range from Dr. James Thacher's diary in October 1778 to Robert C. Winthrop's oration on the completion of the Washington monument in 1885. This is an anthology of

258
Baker, William S. Character ... (cont.)
eulogy (Senator Maclay is not included)
which still retains much of interest.

259
Ford, Worthington Chauncey. Washington as
an employer and importer of labor.
Brooklyn, N. Y., Priv. print., 1889.
78 p.   E312.17.F69
    Largely the texts of a number of
economic documents, of great intrinsic
interest.

260
Baker, William S. Itinerary of General
Washington from June 15, 1775, to December 23, 1783. Philadelphia, Lippincott, 1892. 334 p.   E312.27.B16
    The Commander-in-Chief's whereabouts
and principal actions on nearly every
day from his election by the Continental Congress to his resignation of his
commission into their hands at Annapo-
lis.

261
Bowen, Clarence Winthrop, ed. The history
of the centennial celebration of the
inauguration of George Washington as
first President of the United States.
New York, Appleton, 1892. xviii, 673 p.
illus. (incl. facsims.)
                          E312.6.B785
    A monumental compilation, particu-
larly distinguished by its wealth of
illustrations.

262
Toner, Joseph M. George Washington as an
inventor and promoter of the useful
arts. An address delivered at Mount
Vernon, April 10, 1891. Washington,
Gedney & Roberts, 1892. 69 p.
                          E312.17.T66
    Washington's inventions, naturally,
were nearly all of agricultural appa-
ratus and included several kinds of
plow, one "a drill or Barrel plow"
which would sow grain as it plowed; but
he also thought up "the graceful and
convenient device of the dinner wine
coaster."

263
Ford, Paul Leicester. The true George
Washington. Philadelphia, Lippincott,
1896. 319 p.   E312.F63
    Later printings have the title:
George Washington.

264
Wilson, Woodrow. George Washington.
Illustrated by Howard Pyle. New York,
1896. 333 p.   E312.W75
    Very pleasantly written but much
fuller for the early years--Washington
assumes command of the Continental Army
on p. 180 and becomes President on
p. 270.

265
Baker, William S. Washington after the
Revolution, 1784-1799. Philadelphia,
Lippincott, 1898. 416 p. E312.29.B14

266
Carrington, Henry B. Washington the soldier. Boston, Lamson, Wolffe, 1898.
xx, 431 p.   E312.35.C31
    The author, who rendered distin-
guished service as adjutant-general of
Ohio (and, by loan, of Indiana) during
the Civil War, took a lifelong interest
in military history, and, when a young
teacher, had his interest directed to
Washington by Washington Irving. The
text is rewritten from his Battles of
the American Revolution (1876) and the
maps reduced from his Battle Maps and
Charts of the American Revolution
(1881). The narrative of operations is
considerably richer in detail than
Frothingham's (no. 286); in the other
aspects of war it is less satisfactory.

267
Lodge, Henry Cabot. George Washington.
Rev. ed. Boston, Houghton Mifflin,
1898. 2 v. (American Statesmen)
                          E312.L82
    Originally published in 1889 and
frequently reprinted; the latest edition in LC is 1924.

268

Ford, Paul Leicester. Washington and the theatre. New York, Dunlap Society, 1899. 68 p. (Its Publications. new ser., no. 8)   E312.17.F67
                         PN2016.D7, new ser., no. 8

269

U. S. Dept. of State. Calendar of applications and recommendations for office during the Presidency of George Washington, prepared by Gaillard Hunt. Washington, U. S. Govt. Print. Off., 1901. 146 p.   E311.U62
     The application files of the State Department (now in Record Group 69, the National Archives) are most important during the early administrations when they hold the papers for all Federal offices and not merely for those in the Department. This Calendar is arranged in an alphabetical order of officeseekers (recommendations being filed under the person recommended). Hunt commented upon its unique conspectus in "Office-seeking during Washington's Administration," American Historical Review, v. 1, Jan. 1896: 270-283.

270

Hart, Charles Henry. Catalogue of the engraved portraits of Washington. New York, Grolier Club, 1904. xxv, 406 p.
                         E312.43.H32

271

Wister, Owen. The seven ages of Washington; a biography. New York, Macmillan, 1907. 263 p.   E312.W8
     Frequently reprinted.
     Less a biography than a charming essay in appreciation, embellished with well-chosen quotations from the sources.

272

Belote, Theodore T. Descriptive catalogue of the Washington relics in the United States National Museum. In U. S. National Museum. Proceedings, v. 49, 1916: 1-24. illus.   Q11.U55, v. 49
     Statues, paintings, and engravings; furniture; candelabra, lamps and candlesticks; table furnishings; chinaware; glassware; personal relics

272

Belote, Theodore. Descriptive ... (cont.) (including his Continental uniform, tents with poles and pegs, camp mess chest and its furnishings, surveyor's compass, and portable writing case) and miscellaneous relics. The largest group is comprised by the Lewis Collection, which passed from Martha Washington to Mrs. Lawrence Lewis in 1802 and was purchased from her heirs by Act of Congress, June 20, 1878.

273

New York. Public Library. Washington eulogies; a checklist of eulogies and funeral orations on the death of George Washington, December, 1799-February, 1800, comp. by Margaret Bingham Stilwell. [New York] 1916. 68 p.
                         Z8950.N55
     Will give a sufficient idea of this unprecedented outburst of public mourning; those wishing to go further will find a large sample in the two volumes compiled by Franklin B. Hough: Washingtoniana, or Memorials of the Death of George Washington (Roxbury, Mass., Woodward, 1865).

274

Fielding, Mantle. Gilbert Stuart's portraits of George Washington. Philadelphia, Printed for the subscribers, 1923. 264 p.   E312.43.F54
     After abundant introductory matter, catalogs 124 Stuart portraits of Washington--mostly, of course, replicas-- and reproduces 31 of them.

275

Henderson, Archibald. Washington's southern tour, 1791. Boston, Houghton Mifflin, 1923. xxviii, 340 p. E312.27.H47
     This beautiful volume could be called a definitive treatment of its subject--the President's progress to Savannah and Augusta, Ga., and return, in the spring of 1791--if it had been provided with an index.

276

Haworth, Paul L. George Washington, country gentleman; being an account of his

276
Haworth, Paul L. (cont.)
   home life and agricultural activities.
Indianapolis, Bobbs-Merrill, 1925.
336 p.   E312.17.H392

277
Hughes, Rupert. George Washington. New
   York, W. Morrow, 1926-30. 3 v.
                          E312.H924
      Contents.--[v. 1] The human being &
the hero, 1732-1762.--[v. 2] The rebel
& the patriot, 1762-1777.--[v. 3] The
savior of the States, 1777-1781.
      No more published.
      "Books consulted and quoted": v. 1,
p. 565-572; v. 2, p. 675-683; v. 3, p.
796-810.

278
Moore, Charles. The family life of George
   Washington. With an introd. by Mrs.
Theodore Roosevelt. Boston, Houghton
Mifflin, 1926. 250 p.   E312.M75

279
Woodward, William E. George Washington,
   the image and the man. New York, Boni
& Liveright, 1926. 460, xiii-xxxv p.
      Bibliography: p. xiii-xxvi.
      Reissued by the Liveright Publishing
Corporation in 1946.

280
Fitzpatrick, John C. George Washington,
   colonial traveller, 1732-1775. Indianapolis, Bobbs-Merrill, [c1927] 416 p.
                          E312.27.W3
      Completes William S. Baker's two
compilations (nos. 260 and 265) by
tracing Washington's daily whereabouts
and activities during his first 43
years, largely from his diaries and
ledgers.

281
Prussing, Eugene E. The estate of George
   Washington, deceased. Boston, Little,
Brown, 1927. 512 p.   E312.5.P98
      A definitive commentary on Washing-
ton's will, the properties of which it
disposed, and the beneficiaries under
it.

282
Sawyer, Joseph Dillaway. Washington.
   Profusely illustrated. New York, Macmillan, 1927. 2 v. (640, 619 p.)
                          E312.S27
      The text is undocumented, derivative,
and flat, but the illustrations are
the largest corpus yet assembled for
the first President. Unfortunately
they are meanly reproduced and without
indication of source.

283
King, Grace. Mount Vernon on the Potomac;
   history of the Mount Vernon Ladies'
Association of the Union. New York,
Macmillan, 1929. 491 p. E312.5.K54
      A history of the organization which
in 1858 undertook the restoration of
Washington's home, then in a semi-ruin-
ous state, and has ever since made it
available to all Americans. A briefer
and more popular account is Gerald W.
Johnson's Mount Vernon: the Story of a
Shrine (New York, Random House, 1953.
122 p.), of which p. 67-116 consist
of extracts from Washington's letters
and diaries dealing with his "Home
House."

284
Little, Shelby (Melton) George Washington. New York, Minton, Balch, 1929.
481 p.   E312.L78
      Bibliography: p. 465-473.

285
Corbin, John. The unknown Washington:
   biographic origins of the Republic.
New York, Scribner, 1930. 454 p.
                          E312.C76
      "Authorities cited": p. 431-439.

286
Frothingham, Thomas G. Washington, Com-
   mander in Chief. Boston, Houghton
Mifflin, 1930. 404 p. E312.25.F94

287
Knox, Katharine (McCook) The Sharples,
   their portraits of George Washington
and his contemporaries; a diary and an
account of the life and work of James
Shaples and his family in England and

287
Knox, Katharine. The Sharples ... (cont.)
America. New Haven, Yale University
Press, 1930. xvi, 133 p. ND497.S445K6

288
Wilstach, Paul. Mount Vernon, Washing-
ton's home and the nation's shrine.
Illustrations from photographs by Henry
H. Saylor and others. Indianapolis,
Bobbs-Merrill [c1930] 301 p.
E312.5.W746

289
Fay, Bernard. George Washington, repub-
lican aristocrat. Boston, Houghton
Mifflin, 1931. 297 p. E312.F32

290
Morgan, John Hill, and Mantle Fielding.
The life portraits of Washington and
their replicas. Philadelphia, Printed
for the subscribers [Lancaster, Pa.,
Lancaster Press, c1931] xxiii, 432 p.
E312.43.M85
N7268.W3M6

291
Nolan, James Bennett. George Washington
and the town of Reading in Pennsylvania. [Reading, Pa.] Chamber of Commerce of Reading, 1931. 162 p.
E312.27.N76

292
Ritter, Halsted L. Washington as a business man. New York, Sears Pub. Co.,
1931. 308 p. E312.17.R66

293
Van Dyke, Paul. George Washington, the
son of his country, 1732-1775. New
York, Scribner, 1931. 310 p.
E312.2.V24
    "This book tries briefly to untangle
what came to him from environment and
what in him was superior to environment ..."

294
Delaware. Public Archives Commission.
George Washington and Delaware; pre-
pared for the Delaware State George
Washington Bicentennial Commission.

294
Delaware. Public ... (cont.)
Dover, Del., 1932. 56 p. E312.27.D43

295
Eisen, Gustav. Portraits of Washington
[by] Gustavus A. Eisen. New York,
R. Hamilton & Associates, 1932. 3 v.
(1021 p.) illus. E312.43.E37
    Bibliography: v. 3, p. 969-989.
    Contents.--Portraits in oil painted
by Gilbert Stuart, by G. A. Eisen assisted by C. J. Dearden.--2. Portraits
in oil painted by Charles Willson Peale
and others; also miniatures, crayons,
charcoal and line drawings by James
Sharples, C. B. J. F. de Saint Mémin
and others, by G. A. Eisen.--3. Sculp-
tured portraits, including statues,
busts, reliefs, and masks, in wax,
marble, and plaster, by G. A. Eisen
assisted by W. S. Conrow.

296
Haley, John Williams. George Washington
and Rhode Island. Published by the
state of Rhode Island. [Providence,
Printed by Haley & Sykes Co.] 1932.
40 p. E312.27.H24

297
Helderman, Leonard C. George Washington,
patron of learning. New York, Century
Co., 1932. 187 p. E312.17.H48
    Studies of Washington's bequests to
a national university and to Liberty
Hall, now Washington and Lee Universi-
ty; and of his influence upon the U. S.
Military Academy, Washington College,
Md., and Alexandria Academy.

298
Ives, Mabel (Lorenz) Washington's headquarters. Upper Montclair, N. J., L.
Fortune, 1932. xv, 336 p. E312.25.I95
    "This is a book about those of Wash-
ington's Revolutionary headquarters
that are still standing and open to
visitors," from Cambridge, Mass., to
Williamsburg, Va.

299
Knox, Dudley W. The naval genius of
George Washington. Boston, Houghton
Mifflin, [ᶜ1932] 137 p. E312.25.K67
"In this realm he attained a pro-
ficiency worthy of the highest admira-
tion and comparable to that reached by
the most eminent naval leaders in all
history."

300
Morison, Samuel Eliot. The young man
Washington. Cambridge, Harvard University Press, 1932. 43 p. E312.17.M86
An address delivered at Sanders Theatre, Cambridge, February 22, 1932.
Reprinted with some corrections in
the author's By Land and by Sea; Essays
and Addresses (New York, Knopf, 1953.
p. 161-180), but unfortunately without
the valuable notes (p. 35-43).

301
Page, Elwin L. George Washington in New
Hampshire. Boston, Published for the
George Washington Bicentennial Commis-
sion of New Hampshire by Houghton Miff-
lin, 1932. xv, 95 p. E312.27.P19
A minute account of five days: Oct.
31-Nov. 4, 1789.

302
Preston, Howard W. Washington's visits to
Rhode Island, gathered from contempora-
ry accounts. [Rhode Island] State
Bureau of Information. Providence
[Oxford Press] 1932. 28 p.
F76.R334, no. 5

303
Sears, Louis M. George Washington. New
York, Crowell, 1932. 560 p. E312.S44

304
Showalter, William Joseph. The travels of
George Washington; dramatic episodes in
his career as the first geographer of
the United States. Washington, National Geographic Society, 1932. 63 p.
illus. E312.27.S49
Noteworthy for the large colored
folding map of Washington's routes,
with insets, the map on p. 40 of the
chain of forts Washington set up in

304
Showalter, William. The travels ... (cont.)
1756, and the many and excellent photographs of the 1932 state of sites vis-
ited by Washington. An extract from
The National Geographic Magazine, v.
61, Jan. 1932: 1-63.

305
Tatsch, Jacob Hugo. The facts about
George Washington as a Freemason. 3d
ed. New York, Macoy Pub. and Masonic
Supply Co., 1932. xvi, 100 p.
E312.17.T294
Slightly enlarged from the 1st edi-
tion published the year before. About
as big a book as the subject will af-
ford; the large tomes of Charles H.
Callahan, Washington, the Man and the
Mason (Washington, Gibson Bros., ᶜ1913.
366 p.) and William Moseley Brown,
George Washington, Freemason (Richmond,
Garrett & Massie, 1952. xxvi, 542 p.)
are in fact miscellanies of Washington-
iana and Masonica.

306
U. S. George Washington Bicentennial Commission. History of the George Washington bicentennial celebration. Literature series. Washington, United
States George Washington Bicentennial
Commission, 1932. 3 v. E312.6.U58
The Bicentennial Commission, under
the energetic direction of Representative Sol Bloom, went into action on
March 1, 1930, and these huge volumes
reprint nearly everything which it published during the next two years or
more. They are a mixture of materials
of lasting interest with such ephemera
as press releases and prize-winning
school orations. Among the former are
the 15 topical pamphlets edited by Albert Bushnell Hart under the general
title, "Honor to George Washington and
Reading about George Washington" (v. 1,
p. 1-199), of which no. 15 is a "Classified Washington Bibliography: (v. 1,
p. 184-199); the unique "George Washington Atlas," edited by Lawrence Martin (v. 1, p. 371-444); David M. Matteson's exhaustive compilation of "Religious References in the Writings" of

306

U. S. George Washington ... (cont.)
Washington (v. 1, p. 499-522); and a
group of miscellaneous pieces conclud-
ing v. 3, p. 289-716. Among the last,
a section of "Questions and Answers"
(v. 3, p. 641-688), which is not listed
in the table of contents, brings together much precise information not easily found elsewhere.

307

Decatur, Stephen. Private affairs of
George Washington, from the records and
accounts of Tobias Lear, esquire, his
secretary. Boston, Houghton Mifflin,
1933. 356 p.   E312.29.D32

308

[Dutcher, George Matthew] George Washington and Connecticut in war and peace.
[New Haven] Published for the [Connec-
ticut] Tercentenary Commission by the
Yale University Press, 1933. 36 p.
                          E312.27.D76

309

Fitzpatrick, John C. George Washington
himself; a common-sense biography
written from his manuscripts. Indianapolis, Bobbs-Merrill, 1933. 544 p.
                          E312.F52

310

Smith, Harold Clifford. Sulgrave Manor
and the Washingtons; a history and
guide to the Tudor home of George Washington's ancestors. London, J. Cape
[1933] 259 p.   E312.195.S62
    Sulgrave, in southwest Northampton-
shire, is in the heart of England, a
few miles from Banbury and not far from
Stratford-on-Avon and Oxford. The
Washington family originated in Washington (originally Wessington) in Durham. In 1539 one Lawrence Washington
(d. 1584) purchased the manor of Sulgrave which had just fallen to the
Crown on the dissolution of the Priory
of St. Andrew's and soon afterward
built the present Manor House. His son
lived there until 1619, and descendants
of a different surname until 1659.
Another Lawrence Washington, father of

310

Smith, H. C. Sulgrave Manor ... (cont.)
the emigrants to Virginia, was presuma-
bly born there about 1602. In 1914 the
Manor House was purchased by the British Committee for the Celebration of
the Hundred Years' Peace between England and America, and restored in 1920.
Open to the public since June 1921, it
has become the principal Washington
shrine outside the United States.

311

Whittemore, Frances Davis. George Washington in sculpture. Boston, Marshall
Jones, 1933. 203 p.   E312.4.W47
    47 photographs reproduced in half-
tone show nearly as many statues,
busts, reliefs, medals and memorial
structures, all in the United States
save two, in Buenos Aires and Rio de
Janeiro, and ranging in time from the
work of Duvivier and Houdon to the
Bicentennial medal. The text is undocumented and unindexed, but otherwise
informative enough.

312

Bemis, Samuel Flagg. Washington's Farewell address: a foreign policy of independence. American historical review, v. 39, Jan. 1934: 250-268.
                       E161.A57, v. 39
    Sets the foreign-affairs sections
of the Address against their proper
background of the Anglo-French maritime
war that began in March 1793, and shows
that its immediate purpose "was to
strike a powerful blow against French
intermeddling in American affairs" and
using "the lever of a political opposition to overthrow any government that
stood in the way of French policy."
Its assertion of independence and national sovereignty has, however, come
to be construed as a policy of isolation.

313

De La Bedoyère, Michael. George Washington; an English judgment. London, Har-
rap, 1935. 309 p.   E312.D45

313
De La Bedoyère. Washington ... (cont.)
The American edition of the same
year (Philadelphia, Lippincott) has the
title: George Washington.

314
Ambler, Charles H. George Washington and
the West. Chapel Hill, University of
North Carolina Press, 1936. 270 p.
E312.A62
"Select bibliography": p. 249-259.

315
Mayo, Katherine. General Washington's di-
lemma. New York, Harcourt, Brace
[c1938] 323 p.   E312.25.M38
Bibliography: p. 313-318.
A detailed and thoroughly documented
narrative of a case which occupied
Washington's attention during much of
1782. A Loyalist unit had hanged Cap-
tain Joshua Huddy of New Jersey on
April 12, and retaliation was demanded
upon a group of captive British offi-
cers, the youngest of whom, Captain
Charles Asgill, son of a Lord Mayor of
London, was chosen by lot. Congress
did not authorize Washington to release
Asgill until Nov. 7, after the Court of
France had interceded for him.

316
Bankers Trust Company, New York. Wall &
Nassau; an account of the inauguration
of George Washington in Federal Hall at
Wall and Nassau Streets, April 30, 1789.
New York, Bankers Trust Co., [c1939]
81 p.   E311.B35

317
Hutchins, Frank, and Cortelle Hutchins.
Washington and the Lafayettes. Illus-
trated by W. Merritt Berger. New York,
Longmans, Green, 1939. 211 p.
E312.17.H97
A pleasant narrative, designed for
junior readers but not unduly "Juven-
ile" in style, of President Washing-
ton's tutelage of his namesake, George
Washington Lafayette, during the lat-
ter's exile in America, 1795-97.

318
Chinard, Gilbert, ed. George Washington
as the French knew him; a collection
of texts, edited and translated, with
an introd. by Gilbert Chinard.
Princeton, Princeton University Press,
1940. xviii, 161 p.   E312.17.C5
From Lafayette in 1777 to Guizot in
1839.

319
Knollenberg, Bernhard. Washington and the
Revolution, a reappraisal; Gates, Con-
way, and the Continental Congress.
New York, Macmillan, 1940. xvi, 269 p.
E312.25.K64
Bibliography: p. 232-251.

320
Stephenson, Nathaniel Wright, and Waldo
Hilary Dunn. George Washington. New
York, Oxford University Press, 1940.
2 v.   E312.S82
After the death of Dr. Stephenson
in 1935, the incomplete work was revised, and the last seven chapters
written by W. H. Dunn.
Contents.--v. 1. 1732-1777.--v. 2.
1778-1799.

321
Leduc, Gilbert F. Washington and "the
murder of Jumonville." Published under
the auspices of La Société Historique
Franco-americaine. Boston, 1943.
235 p.   E312.23.L43
Bibliography: p. [229]-235.
Argues against the claim, made by
French authorities in 1755 and repeated
by Canadian historians 180 years later,
that "le Sieur de Jumonville fut assas-
iné par le Colonel Wemcheston [sic] et
sa troupe."

322
Freeman, Douglas Southall. George Washington, a biography. New York, Scribner, 1948-57. 7 v. illus. E312.F82
Contents.--v. 1-2. Young Washington.--v. 3. Planter and patriot.--v. 4.
Leader of the Revolution.--v. 5. Victory with the help of France.--v. 6.
Patriot and President.--v. 7. First in
peace.

323
Hart, James. The American Presidency in
action, 1789; a study in constitutional
history. New York, Macmillan, 1948.
xv, 256 p.   JK511.H3

324
Albert, Alphaeus Homer. Washington historical buttons; Washington inaugural
buttons, and other buttons bearing the
portrait of Washington or alluding to
him and his administration. Highstown,
N. J., 1949. 82 p.   NK3670.A55

325
Duke, Jane Taylor. Kenmore and the Lew-
ises. Foreword by Harry Flood Byrd.
Garden City, N. Y., Doubleday, 1949.
xvi, 268 p.   E312.19.D84
    Washington's only sister, Elizabeth
or Betty Washington (1733-97) married
Col. Fielding Lewis (1725-81) in 1750;
their house, which has received the
name "Kenmore" since they lived in it,
was built on the outskirts of Freder-
icksburg, Va., about 1752. Here was
born their 9th child, Lawrence Lewis,
who in 1799 married Martha Washington's
granddaughter, Eleanor Parke Custis.
The house was well cared for in the
19th century, has been completely restored, and open to the public since
1932.

326
Bellamy, Francis Rufus. The private life
of George Washington. New York, Crowell [1951] 409 p.   E312.B45
        Bibliography: p. 387-401.

327
Nettels, Curtis P. George Washington and
American independence. Boston, Little,
Brown, 1951. 338 p.   E312.25.N4
    Bibliography: p. [313]-324.
    A detailed narrative of events from
the meeting of the Second Continental
Congress to the Declaration of Independence, which exhibits Washington as
the pivotal figure in arriving at that
outcome.

328
Bryan, William Alfred. George Washington
in American literature, 1775-1865.

328
Bryan, William. (cont.)
New York, Columbia University Press,
1952. 280 p.   PS169.W3B7

329
Swiggett, Howard. The great man: George
Washington as a human being. Garden
City, N. Y., Doubleday, 1953. 491 p.
                              E312.S9
    The first 350 pages are a detailed
commentary on the events, personalities, and issues of the Revolutionary
War, taking for granted an extensive
knowledge of the campaigns, but empha-
sizing and illustrating Washington's
essential rightness and greatness in
contrast to contemporary opponents and
latter-day critics.

330
Smelser, Marshall. George Washington and
the Alien and Sedition Acts. American
historical review, v. 59, Jan. 1954:
322-334.   E171.A57, v. 59
    Biographers and historians have
largely ignored Washington's complete
approval of these acts and the other
Federalist policies with which they
were linked. Here that approval is
easily demonstrated, but the author
points out that Washington was neither
pro-British nor opposed to an accommo-
dation with Revolutionary France.

331
Tebbel, John W. George Washington's America. New York, Dutton, 1954. 478 p.
fold. map.   E312.27.T4
    "This book ... is the story of Wash-
ington's travels over the face of America, how he looked to the nation, and
how the nation looked to him." Nec-
essarily it places Washington against
his urban background in New York and
Philadelphia, but it has little to say
about life at Mount Vernon.

332
Cleland, Hugh. George Washington in the
Ohio Valley. Pittsburgh, University of
Pittsburgh Press, 1955. 405 p. (West-
ern Penna. series)   E312.C62

333
Hudson, J. Paul. George Washington Birthplace National Monument, Virginia.
Washington, 1956. 44 p. (U. S. National Park Service. Historical handbook series, no. 26)   E312.5.H87
Bibliography: p. 44.

334
Stetson, Charles Wyllys. Washington and
his neighbors. Richmond, Garrett and
Massie [1956] 342 p.   E312.17.S82
Bibliography: p. 314-319.
This presentation of Washington as
a gentleman planter of northern Virginia has interest in systematically introducing the other prominent inhabitants of the area in Washington's lifetime.

335
Wright, Esmond. Washington and the American Revolution. London, English Universities Press, 1957. 192 p. (Teach
yourself history)   E312.25.W73

336
Cunliffe, Marcus. George Washington, man
and monument. Boston, Little, Brown
[1958] 234 p.   E312.C88
Bibliography: p. 217-223.

337
Sears, Louis M. George Washington & the
French Revolution. Detroit, Wayne
State University Press, 1960. 378 p.
E312.29.S4
Bibliography: p. 355-359.

338
Bemis, Samuel Flagg. Washington and Lafayette, the prisoner in Europe. In
his American foreign policy and the
blessings of liberty, and other essays.
New Haven, Yale University Press, 1962.
p. 209-239.   E183.7.B44
Originally published in the Daughters of the American Revolution Magazine, v. 58, June-Aug. 1924.

338a
Boller, Paul F. George Washington & religion. Dallas, Southern Methodist University Press [1963] 235 p.
E312.17.B74
"Selected bibliography": p. 219-
227.
At long last a thoroughly critical
and discriminating treatment. "Broadly
speaking, of course, Washington can be
classified as a Deist," but one whose
quite personal views differed from
those of Jefferson, Franklin, and
Paine.

339
Wharton, Anne Hollingsworth. Martha Washington. New York, Scribner, 1897.
306 p. (Women of colonial and revolutionary times)   E312.19.W95W5

340
Thane, Elswyth. Washington's lady. New
York, Dodd, Mead, 1960. 268 p.
E312.19.W95T48

Writings

341
Adams, John. The works of John Adams,
second President of the United States;
with a life of the author, notes and
illustrations, by his grandson, Charles
Francis Adams. Boston, Little, Brown,
1850-56 [v. 1, 1856] 10 v. E302.A26

342
----- Diary and autobiography. L. H.
Butterfield, editor, Leonard C. Faber
and Wendell D. Garrett, assistant editors. Cambridge, Belknap Press of
Harvard University Press, 1961. 4 v.
(His Papers. Series 1: Diaries)
                                E322.A3
     Contents.--v. 1. Diary, 1755-1770.--
v. 2. Diary, 1771-1781.--v. 3. Diary,
1782-1804. Autobiography to October
1776.--v. 4. Autobiography, 1777-1780.

343
----- The selected writings of John and
John Quincy Adams, edited and with an
introd. by Adrienne Koch and William
Peden. New York, Knopf, 1946. xxxix,
413, xxix p.   E302.A28

344
----- The political writings of John
Adams: representative selections.
Edited with an introd. by George A.
Peek, Jr. New York, Liberal Arts
Press [1954] 223 p.   JC176.A3

345
[Adams, John] Thoughts on government,
applicable to the present state of the
American colonies. In a letter from a
gentleman to his friend [George Wythe]
Philadelphia, J. Dunlap, 1776. 28 p.
                         E187.C82, v. 16

346
Adams, John. A collection of state-pa-
pers, relative to the first acknowl-
edgment of the sovereignity [sic] of
the United States of America, and the
reception of their minister plenipotentiary, by their high mightinesses the
States-General of the United Nether-
lands. At the Hague, 1782. 96 p.
                         E249.A21
     Published the same year at London
by J. Fielding.

347
----- Twenty-six letters, upon interesting subjects, respecting the revolution of America. Written in Holland,
in the year 1780. [London] Printed for
the subscribers [1786] 89 p.
                         E211.A214
     John Fenno, issuing a New York edi-
tion in 1789, claimed, as was tech-
nically correct, that the letters were
"never before published."

348
----- A defence of the constitutions of
government of the United States of
America. London, printed for C. Dilly,
1787-88. 3 v.   JK171.A2 1787
     Volume 1 only was reprinted at Phil-
adelphia in 1787 and at Boston in 1788.
J. Stockdale brought out a 2d London
edition in 1794, but the whole set was
not published in America until 1797,
when Budd and Bartram of Philadelphia
reprinted it for William Cobbett.

349
[Adams, John] Discourses on Davila. A
series of papers, on political history.
Written in the year 1790, and then published in the Gazette of the United
States. By an American citizen. Boston, Printed by Russell and Cutler,
1805. 248 p.   JK171.A23

349
[Adams, John] Discourses ... (cont.)
     The subject of Adams' discourses was
Enrico Caterino Davila's Italian history of the civil wars of France, originally published in 1630.

350
----- Correspondence of the late President Adams. Originally published in
  the Boston Patriot. In a series of
  [63] letters [Apr. 10, 1809--Feb. 10,
  1810] Boston, Everett and Munroe,
  1809[-10] 572 p.   E322.A515
     Messrs. Everett and Munroe did not
  mean that John Adams was dead, but only
  that he was out of office.

351
----- Novanglus, and Massachusettensis;
  or, Political essays, published in the
  years 1774 and 1775, on the principal
  points of controversy, between Great
  Britain and her colonies. The former
  by John Adams, the latter by Jonathan
  Sewall. To which are added, a number
  of letters, lately written by President
  Adams to the Honourable William Tudor;
  some of which were never before published. Boston, Hews & Goss, 1819.
  312 p.   E211.A195
     Between Dec. 12, 1774, and Apr. 3,
  1775, the Massachusetts Gazette published a series of 17 letters in defense of the case of the British Crown
  and signed Massachusettensis. From
  Jan. 23 to Apr. 17, 1775, the Boston
  Gazette published a series of 12 letters in reply, signed Novanglus, who
  was John Adams. Adams believed at the
  time that Massachusettensis was his
  friend Jonathan Sewall, and still did
  in 1819, as his preface here testifies
  (p. iii-vii). Documents since come to
  light prove that he was mistaken; his
  opponent was Daniel Leonard, then a
  fugitive in Boston from the Whigs of
  Taunton. The Novanglus letters were
  published in abridged form at London
  in 1784 as History of the Dispute with
  America from its Origin in 1784; here
  they are given in full (p. 9-139), followed by those of Massachusettensis
  (p. 141-227). Adams' letters to Tudor

351
----- Novanglus ... (cont.)
  (p. 229-312) cover Jan. 14-Sept. 23,
  1818, and originally appeared in the
  Boston Daily Advertiser. They include
  two each to Hezekiah Niles and William
  Wirt, and are concerned with James Otis
  and his priority in introducing the
  typical arguments of the American Revolution. William Tudor's Life of James
  Otis appeared in 1823.

352
----- Correspondence between the Hon.
  John Adams and the late William Cunningham, esq., beginning in 1803, and
  ending in 1812. Boston, E. M. Cunningham, 1823. 219 p.   E210.A21
     Adams' candid and confidential pro-
  nouncements on the politics of the day,
  published out of spite and in the hope
  of blasting his son's Presidential
  prospects.

353
----- Deeds and other documents relating
  to the several pieces of land, and to
  the library presented to the town of
  Quincy, by President Adams, together
  with a catalogue of the books. Cambridge, Hilliard and Metcalf, 1823.
  67 p.   Z997.A214

354
----- Familiar letters of John Adams and
  his wife Abigail Adams, during the
  Revolution. With a memoir of Mrs.
  Adams. By Charles Francis Adams. New
  York, Hurd and Houghton, 1876. xxxii,
  424 p.   E322.A518

355
Old family letters: copied from the orig-
  inals for Alexander Biddle. Series A.
  Philadelphia, Lippincott, 1892. 479 p.
                    E302.1.044, v. 1
     The content is principally a long
  series of letters from John Adams to
  Dr. Benjamin Rush, 1778-1813.

356
Adams, John, and others. Warren-Adams
    letters, being chiefly a correspondence
    among John Adams, Samuel Adams, and
    James Warren, 1743-1814. Boston, Mas-
    sachusetts Historical Society, 1917-25.
    2 v. (Massachusetts Historical Soci-
    ety Collections, v. 72-73)
                          F61.M41, v. 72-73

357
Adams, John. Statesman and friend; cor-
    respondence of John Adams with Benjamin
    Waterhouse, 1784-1822, edited by Worth-
    ington Chauncey Ford. Boston, Little,
    Brown, 1927. 178 p.   E322.A519

358
----- The Adams-Jefferson letters; the
    complete correspondence between Thomas
    Jefferson and Abigail and John Adams.
    Edited by Lester J. Cappon. Chapel
    Hill, Published for the Institute of
    Early American History and Culture at
    Williamsburg, Va., by the University of
    North Carolina Press [1959]
    2 v. (11, 638 p.)   E312.A516

                Biography

359
A Selection of [19] eulogies, pronounced
    in the several states, in honor of
    those illustrious patriots and states-
    men, John Adams and Thomas Jefferson.
    Hartford, D. F. Robinson, 1826. 426 p.
                          E322.S46

360
Adams, Charles Francis. The life of John
    Adams. Begun by John Quincy Adams.
    Completed by Charles Francis Adams.
    Rev. and cor. Philadelphia, Lippin-
    cott, 1871. 2 v.   E322.A52
        Originally published as v. 1 of The
    Works of John Adams, 1856.

361
Morse, John T. John Adams. Boston,
    Houghton Mifflin, 1885. 338 p. (Amer-
    ican statesmen)   E176.A53, v. 6
                          E322.M88

362
Hunt, Gaillard. Office-seeking during the
    administration of John Adams. American
    historical review, v. 2, Jan. 1897:
    241-261.
        A continuation of his article for
    the Washington administrations (no.
    269), and like it based upon the ap-
    plication files of the State Depart-
    ment. The close of Adams' term saw the
    dissipation of the central file, the
    appointive power having been delegated
    to the departments and the papers hav-
    ing gone with it.

363
Walsh, Dorrea Moylan. The political sci-
    ence of John Adams; a study in the
    theory of mixed government and the
    bicameral system. New York, Putnam,
    1915. 374 p.   JK171.A3W3

364
Adams, James Truslow. The Adams family.
    Boston, Little, Brown, 1930. 364 p.
                          E176.A23

365
Chinard, Gilbert. Honest John Adams.
    Boston, Little, Brown, 1933. 359 p.
                          E322.C47

366
Adams, Henry, 2d. The Adams mansion, the
    home of John Adams and John Quincy
    Adams, Presidents of the United States.
    Quincy, Mass., Printed for the Adams
    Memorial Society, 1935. 42 p.
                          F74.Q7A5
        Reprinted, with additions, from
    Old-Time New England.

367
Butterfield, Lyman H. The dream of Ben-
    jamin Rush: the reconciliation of John
    Adams and Thomas Jefferson. Yale re-
    view, v. 40, winter 1951: 297-319.
                          AP2.Y2, v. 40
        In a letter to Adams, Oct. 17, 1809,
    Rush described a fictive dream of the
    reconciliation and subsequent corre-
    spondence of the two elder statesmen.
    Largely as a result of this and his
    other hints to each, Rush's dream

367
Butterfield, Lyman. The dream ... (cont.)
became a reality at the beginning of
1812.

368
Haraszti, Zoltán. John Adams & the proph-
ets of progress. Cambridge, Harvard
University Press, 1952. 362 p.
E322.H3

369
Iacuzzi, Alfred. John Adams, scholar.
New York, S. F. Vanni (Ragusa) [1952]
306 p. E322.I15

370
Dauer, Manning J. The Adams Federalists.
Baltimore, Johns Hopkins Press, 1953.
xxiii, 381 p. E321.D23
Bibliography: p. 351-373.

371
Butterfield, Lyman H. The papers of the
Adams Family: some account of their
history. In Massachusetts Historical
Society. Proceedings. v. 71; 1953-57.
Boston, p. 328-356. F61.M38, v. 71
Contains much of great interest that
is not repeated in the author's introduction to v. 1 of Diary and Autobiography of John Adams (no. 342), especially concerning the accumulation of the
family archive, the uses made of it,
and the attitudes of various members of
the family to it and to each other.

372
Kurtz, Stephen G. The Presidency of John
Adams; the collapse of Federalism,
1795-1800. Philadelphia, University of
Pennsylvania Press [1957] 448 p.
E321.K8

373
Quincy Historical Society, Quincy, Mass.
The President John Adams and President
John Quincy Adams birthplaces, Quincy,
Massachusetts; their origin, early his-
tory, and changes down to the present
time. Prepared for the Quincy Histor-
ical Society by Waldo Chamberlain
Sprague. [Quincy] 1959. unpaged
F74.Q7Q78

374
Smith, Page. John Adams. Garden City,
N. Y., Doubleday, 1962. 2 v. (xx,
1170 p.) E322.S64
Contents.--v. 1. 1735-1784.--v. 2.
1784-1826.

375
Adams, Abigail (Smith) Letters of Mrs.
John Adams, the wife of John Adams.
With an introductory memoir by her
grandson, Charles Francis Adams. 4th
ed., rev. and enl. Boston, Wilkins,
Carter, 1848. 472 p. E322.1.A32

376
Bobbé, Dorothie (De Bear) Abigail Adams,
the second First Lady. New York, Minton, Balch, 1929. 336 p. E322.1.B66

377
Adams, Abigail (Smith) New letters of
Abigail Adams, 1788-1801; edited with
an introd. by Steward Mitchell. Bos-
ton, Houghton Mifflin, 1947. xliii,
281 p. E322.1.A37
Letters written to the author's sis-
ter, Mary Cranch, reprinted from the
Proceedings of the American Antiquarian
Society, v. 55, p. [95]-232; [299]-444.

378
Whitney, Janet Payne. Abigail Adams.
Boston, Little, Brown, 1947. 357 p.
E322.1.W5
Bibliography: p. [343]-348.

379
Adams, Abigail (Smith) The Adams family
in Auteuil, 1784-1785; as told in the
letters of Abigail Adams. With an
introd. and notes by Howard C. Rice,
Jr. Boston, Massachusetts Historical
Society, 1956. 31 p. E322.1.A33

Writings

380

Jefferson, Thomas. Memoir, correspondence, and miscellanies, from the papers of Thomas Jefferson. Edited by Thomas Jefferson Randolph. Charlottesville, Va., F. Carr, 1829. 4 v.
E302.J458

There followed a London edition of the same year, a Boston one of 1830, and a 2-volume French abridgment of 1833.

No other of the Founding Fathers had so representative and respectably edited a selection from his papers in print within three years of his death, for which T. J. Randolph deserves more credit than he has usually been given.

381

Jefferson, Thomas. Writings [1760-1826]. Collected and edited by Paul Leicester Ford. New York, Putnam, 1892-99. 10 v. E302.J466

Reissued in 12 v., 1904-5, as the "Federal edition."

382

----- Writings. Memorial ed., containing his Autobiography, Notes on Virginia, parliamentary manual, official papers, messages and addresses, and other writings, official and private, now collected in their entirety for the first time. With numerous illustrations and a comprehensive analytical index. Andrew A. Lipscomb, editor-in-chief; Albert Ellery Bergh, managing editor. Washington, Thomas Jefferson Memorial Association of the United States, 1903-4. 20 v. E302.J47

Achieved its inclusiveness by incorporating in extenso Henry A. Washington's edition of the Writings, published by order of the Joint Committee of Congress on the Library (Washington, Taylor & Maury, 1853-54. 7 v.).

383

----- Papers [1760-July 4, 1790]. Julian P. Boyd, editor; Lyman H. Butterfield and [others] associate editors. Princeton, University Press, 1950-61. 16 v. E302.J463
----- ----- Index, volumes 1-12. Compiled by Elizabeth J. Sherwood and Ida T. Hopper. Princeton, Princeton University Press, 1954-58. 2 v.
E302.J463 Index

Should eventually supplant all other editions, collected and invidual, but but it has not maintained the announced rate of publication.

384

----- The Jeffersonian cyclopedia; a comprehensive collection of the views of Thomas Jefferson classified and arranged in alphabetical order under nine thousand titles relating to government, politics, law, education, political economy, finance, science, art, literature, religious freedom, morals, etc.; edited by John P. Foley. New York, Funk & Wagnalls, 1900. 1009 p.
JK113.J4 1900

385

----- The best letters of Thomas Jefferson, selected and edited by J. G. de Roulhac Hamilton. Boston, Houghton Mifflin, 1926. 300 p. E302.J443

386

----- Jeffersonian principles; extracts from the writings of Thomas Jefferson, selected and edited by James Truslow Adams. Boston, Little, Brown, 1928. xxii, 161 p. E302.J484

Contents.--Introduction.--Chronology.--Political principles and practice.--Education and religion.--The art of living.

387

----- Jefferson himself, the personal narrative of a many-sided American, edited by Bernard Mayo. Boston, Houghton Mifflin, 1942. 384 p.   E332.J464

388

----- The complete Jefferson, containing his major writings, published and unpublished, except his letters, assembled and arranged by Saul K. Padover, with illustrations and analytic index. New York, Duell, Sloan & Pearce [1943] 1322 p.   E302.J4564

389

----- The life and selected writings of Thomas Jefferson, edited, and with an introd., by Adrienne Koch & William Peden. New York, The Modern Library [1944] xliv, 730 p.   E332.J47

390

----- Basic writings. Edited by Philip S. Foner. Garden City, N. Y., Halcyon House [1950, ^{c}1944] xviii, 816 p.   E302.J442 1950

391

----- Political writings: representative selections. Edited with an introd. by Edward Dumbauld. New York, Liberal Arts Press [1955] xlii, 204 p. (American heritage series, no. 9)   JC176.J4
      Bibliography: p. xxxvii-xl.

392

----- A Jefferson profile as revealed in his letters. Selected and arr. with an introd. by Saul K. Padover. New York, J. Day [1956] xxiv, 359 p.   E332.J466

393

----- Crusade against ignorance; Thomas Jefferson on education. Edited, with an introd. and notes, by Gordon C. Lee. New York, Bureau of Publications, Teachers College, Columbia University [1961] 167 p.   LB695.J36 1961
      (Classics in education, no. 6)

394

[Jefferson, Thomas] A summary view of the rights of British America. Set forth in some resolutions intended for the inspection of the present delegates of the people of Virginia, now in convention. By a native, and member of the House of Burgesses. Williamsburg, Printed by Clementina Rind [1774] 23 p.   E211.J44
      Reprinted the same year at London, for G. Kearsley (xvi, 44 p.). A facsimile of the original edition, with editorial matter by Thomas P. Abernethy, was issued by Scholars' Facsimiles and Reprints, New York, 1943.

395

----- Notes on the State of Virginia. Illustrated with a map. London, J. Stockdale, 1787. 382 p.   F230.J41
      This was the first public edition. The work was originally printed at Paris in 1784-85, in an edition of 200 copies which TJ himself distributed. The first American edition was published in 1788 by Prichard and Hall, Philadelphia (244 p.).

396

----- Notes on the State of Virginia; edited with an introd. and notes by William Peden. Chapel Hill, Published for the Institute of Early American History and Culture, Williamsburg, Va., by the University of North Carolina Press, 1955 [^{c}1954] xxv, 315 p. maps (1 fold.)   F230.J5102 1955

397

U. S. **Dept of State**. Report of the Secretary of State, on the subject of establishing a uniformity in the weights, measures and coins of the United States. Published by order of the House of Representatives. New York, Childs and Swaine, 1790. 49 p.   QC89.U5A5 1790
      AC901.M5, v. 1076
      A commentary on this epoch-making report is provided by C. Doris Hellman's "Jefferson's Efforts towards the Decimalization of the United States Weights and Measures," in Isis, v. 16, Nov. 1931: 266-314.

398

Jefferson, Thomas. A manual of parliamentary practice. For the use of the Senate of the United States. Washington City, S. H. Smith, 1801. 199 p.

JK 1091 1801

The fruit of Jefferson's four years of presiding over the Senate, which has developed into those perennial documents, the Senate Manual and the House Manual.

399

----- The proceedings of the Government of the United States, in maintaining the public right to the beach of the Mississippi, adjacent to New Orleans, against the intrusion of Edward Livingston. Prepared for the use of counsel, by Thomas Jefferson. New York, Ezra Sergeant, 1812. 80 p. F379.N5J4

AC901.M5,v.1076

The controversy between the United States and Livingston over his claim to a part of the New Orleans waterfront broke out in 1807 and was not finally settled until 1830; there is a detailed narrative in William B. Hatcher's Edward Livingston (Louisiana State University Press, 1940. chapter 8, p. 139-189). Jefferson's pamphlet was a response to the suit against him for trespass and $100,000 damages which Livingston had brought in the Federal Circuit Court at Richmond.

400

Virginia (Colony) General Court. Reports of cases determined in the General Court of Virginia. From 1730, to 1740; and from 1768 to 1770. By Thomas Jefferson. Charlottesville, Va., F. Carr, 1829. 145 p.   Law

The later cases were reported by Jefferson himself, the earlier ones came from manuscript notes which he had acquired.

401

Jefferson, Thomas. An essay towards facilitating instruction in the Anglo-Saxon and modern dialects of the English language. For the use of the University of Virginia.

401

Jefferson, Thomas. An essay ... (cont.) New York, J. F. Trow, 1851. 43 p.

PE123.J3

"Printed by order of the Board of Trustees for the University of Virginia."

402

----- The Jefferson Papers [1770-1826]. In Massachusetts Historical Society. Collections; ser. 7, v. 1. Boston, 1900. xxxvii, 389 p.

F61.M41, ser. 7, v. 1

Selections from the collection of the more private papers which had been presented to the Society in the previous year by Thomas Jefferson Coolidge.

403

----- The complete anas [1791-1809] of Thomas Jefferson; edited by Franklin B. Sawvel. New York, Round Table Press, 1903. 283 p.   E310.J45

404

Bible. N. T. Gospels. Selections. The life and morals of Jesus of Nazareth, extracted textually from the Gospels in Greek, Latin, French, and English, by Thomas Jefferson. With an introd. [by Cyrus Adler]. Washington, Govt. Print. Off., 1904. p. 7-18, facsim. (82 numb. 1.)   BS2549.J3 1904

Jefferson's simplified Gospels, put together with scissors and paste from two copies each (necessary so as to have either side of the page) of three printed Bibles or New Testaments, in 1819 or soon after. One of the three contained both Greek and Latin texts. The original was acquired by the Smithsonian Institution in 1895, and on May 13, 1902, Congress, by concurrent resolution, authorized the present facsimile edition "by photolithographic process." It was also incorporated into the last volume of the Lipscomb and Bergh edition (1903-4).

405

Jefferson, Thomas. Jefferson's Germantown letters, together with other papers relating to his stay in Germantown [Pa.] during the month of November, 1793. Edited by Charles Francis Jenkins. Philadelphia, W. J. Campbell, 1906. 194 p.   E332.J46

Similar to the editor's Washington in Germantown (no. 242 above).

406

----- Autobiography of Thomas Jefferson, 1743-1790, together with a summary of the chief events in Jefferson's life, an introd. and notes by Paul Leicester Ford, and a foreword by George Haven Putnam. New York, Putnam, 1914. 162 p
                        E332.J44

Jefferson put this curious and composite but extremely interesting fragment together in 1821, and his grandson included it in his collection of 1829. The above is extracted from P. L. Ford's edition of Jefferson's Writings (no. 381).

407

----- Thomas Jefferson, architect; original designs in the collection of Thomas Jefferson Coolidge, Junior, with an essay and notes by Fiske Kimball. Boston, Printed for private distribution at the Riverside Press, Cambridge, 1916. 205 p. 233 facsim. on 50 l.
                        E332.J48
                        NA737.J4A3

"The Jefferson papers, by Worthington Chauncey Ford": p. [1]-9.

"The architectural books owned by Thomas Jefferson": p. 90-101.

"Known drawings among Jefferson papers outside the Coolidge collection": p. 200-205.

408

----- Thomas Jefferson correspondence, printed from the originals in the collections of William K. Bixby, with notes by Worthington Chauncey Ford. Boston, 1916. 322 p.   E302.J57

409

----- The commonplace book of Thomas Jefferson, a repertory of his ideas on government, with an introd. and notes by Gilbert Chinard. Baltimore, Johns Hopkins Press, 1926. 403 p. (Johns Hopkins studies in Romance literatures and languages, extra v. 2) E302.J454

A manuscript volume of 158 leaves begun when Jefferson was studying law; the earlier parts consist entirely of legal extracts and references, and there is much of legal relevance in the later ones.

410

----- The literary Bible of Thomas Jefferson, his commonplace book of philosophers and poets; with an introd. by Gilbert Chinard. Baltimore, Johns Hopkins Press; Paris, Les Presses universitaires de France, 1928. 210 p. (Semi-centennial publications of the Johns Hopkins University, 1876-1926)
                        E302.J456

411

Virginia. Governor. Official letters of the governors of the State of Virginia. v. 2. The letters of Thomas Jefferson [June 1, 1779--June 3, 1781]. H. R. McIlwaine, general editor. Richmond, Virginia State Library, 1928. 567 p.   F221.V6, v. 2

412

Lafayette, Marie J. P. Y. R. Gilbert du Motier, marquis de. The letters of Lafayette and Jefferson, with an introd. and notes by Gilbert Chinard. Baltimore, Johns Hopkins Press, 1929. (The Johns Hopkins studies in international thought) 443 p. E207.L2L18

413

----- The correspondence of Jefferson and [Pierre S.] Du Pont de Nemours, with an introd. on Jefferson and the physiocrats, by Gilbert Chinard. Baltimore, Johns Hopkins Press, 1931. cxxiii, 293 p.   E302.J4572

An edition of the same correspondence by Dumas Malone (Boston, Houghton Mifflin, 1930. xxv, 210 p.) has

413
----- The correspondence ... (cont.) translations of Du Pont's French letters by Ernest Linwood Lehman.

414
Jefferson, Thomas. Thomas Jefferson and his unknown brother Randolph. Twenty-eight letters exchanged between Thomas and Randolph Jefferson ... during the years 1807 to 1815; now for the first time put into print, together with an introd. by Bernard Mayo. Charlottesville, Tracy W. McGregor Library, University of Virginia, 1942. 41 p.
E332.A15

415
----- Thomas Jefferson's Garden book, 1766-1824, with relevant extracts from his other writings, annotated by Edwin Morris Betts. Philadelphia, American Philosophical Society, 1944. (Memoirs of the American Philosophical Society, v. 22) 704 p. SB479.J4
"Books and pamphlets on agriculture, gardening, and botany in the library of Thomas Jefferson": p. 655-662.
Bibliography: p. 663-666.

416
----- Correspondence of Thomas Jefferson and Francis Walker Gilmer, 1814-1826. Edited, with an introd., by Richard Beale Davis. Columbia, University of South Carolina Press, 1946. 163 p.
E332.J447

417
----- Thomas Jefferson and the National Capital; containing notes and correspondence exchanged between Jefferson, Washington, L'Enfant, Ellicott, Hallet, Thornton, Latrobe, the commissioners, and others, relating to the founding, surveying, planning, designing, constructing, and administering of the city of Washington, 1783-1818. Pref. by Harold L. Ickes. Edited by Saul K. Padover. Washington, U. S. Govt. Print. Off., 1946. xxxvi, 522 p. (U. S. National Park Service. Source book series, no. 4) E160.U629, no. 4

418
----- Jefferson's ideas on a university library; letters from the founder of the University of Virginia to a Boston bookseller. Edited by Elizabeth Cometti. Charlottesville, Tracy W. McGregor Library, University of Virginia, 1950. 49 p. Z733.V72J4
Letters to William Hilliard and to Cummings, Hilliard and Co., Boston, 1824-26.

419
U. S. Library of Congress. Jefferson Collection. Catalogue of the library of Thomas Jefferson. Compiled with annotations by E. Millicent Sowerby. Washington, Library of Congress, 1952-59. 5 v. Z881.U5 1952J

420
Jefferson, Thomas. Thomas Jefferson's Farm book, with commentary and relevant extracts from other writings; edited by Edwin Morris Betts. [Princeton] Published for the American Philosophical Society by Princeton University Press, 1953. xxii p., facsim. (178 (i. e. 168) p.), 552 p. (Memoirs of the American Philosophical Society, v. 35) S451.V8J4

421
----- The Jefferson-Dunglison letters. Edited by John M. Dorsey. Charlottesville, University of Virginia Press [1960] 120 p. E332.88.D75

Biography

422
Tucker, George. The life of Thomas Jefferson, third President of the United States. With parts of his correspondence never before published, and notices of his opinions on questions of civil government, national policy, and constitutional law. Philadelphia, Carey, Lea & Blanchard, 1837. 2 v.
E332.T89

423

[Cabell, Nathaniel F., ed.] Early history of the University of Virginia, as contained in the letters of Thomas Jefferson and Joseph C. Cabell, hitherto unpublished. Richmond, J. W. Randolph, 1856. xxxvi, 528 p.   LD5678.3.C2

424

Randall, Henry S. The life of Thomas Jefferson. New York, Derby & Jackson, 1858. 3 v.   E332.R18
    Reissue: Philadelphia, Lippincott, 1888.

425

Pierson, Hamilton W. Jefferson at Monticello; the private life of Thomas Jefferson, from entirely new materials. New York, Scribner, 1862. 138 p.
    E332.P62
    The Rev. Mr. Pierson recorded the reminiscences of the venerable Edmund Bacon, who had been Jefferson's overseer at Monticello from 1806 to October 1822, when he moved to Kentucky.

426

Randolph, Sarah N. The domestic life of Thomas Jefferson, compiled from family letters and reminiscences by his great-granddaughter. New York, Harper, 1871. 432 p.   E332.25.R2 1871
    Reprinted by the University Press of Cambridge, Mass., 1939 (383 p.), and by F. Ungar of New York, 1958 (432 p.), but the valuable materials which it includes still remain unindexed.

427

Parton, James. Life of Thomas Jefferson, third President of the United States. Boston, J. R. Osgood, 1874. 764 p.
    E332.P27
    Latest printing in LC is Boston, Houghton Mifflin, 1902.

428

Adams, Herbert B. Thomas Jefferson and the University of Virginia. Washington, Govt. Print. Off., 1888. 308 p. (U. S. Bureau of Education. Contributions to American educational history, edited by Herbert B. Adams, no. 2)

428

Adams, Herbert. Thomas ... (cont.)
    LA201.A3
    LD5678.3.A18

429

Boutell, Lewis Henry. Thomas Jefferson, the man of letters. Chicago, Priv. print. [press of S. Thompson] 1891. 73 p.   E332.B77
    "Read before the Phi Beta Kappa Society at the Northwestern University, Evanston, Illinois, June 23d, 1891."

430

Schouler, James. Thomas Jefferson. New York, Dodd, Mead, 1893. 252 p. (Makers of America)   E332.S39

431

Callender, James Thomson. Thomas Jefferson and James Thomson Callender, 1798-1802. Edited by Worthington Chauncey Ford. Brooklyn, Historical Print. Club, 1897. 45 p.   E321.C16
    Chiefly Callender's letters to Jefferson, 1797-1801.

432

Donaldson, Thomas. The house in which Thomas Jefferson wrote the Declaration of Independence. Philadelphia, Avil Printing Co., 1898. 119 p.
    E221.D67
    By a Philadelphian who watched 700 Market Street being torn down to make way for the Penn National Bank Building in March 1883, and proposed to rebuild it in Washington, on the grounds of the Smithsonian Institution.

433

Hunt, Gaillard. Office-seeking during Jefferson's administration. American historical review, v. 3, Jan. 1898: 270-291.   E171.A57, v. 3

434

Curtis, William E. The true Thomas Jefferson. Philadelphia, Lippincott, 1901. 395 p. (The "true" biographies)
    E332.C97

435

Patton, John S. Jefferson, Cabell and the University of Virginia. New York, Neale Pub. Co., 1906. 380 p.
LD5678.P3

436

Lambeth, William Alexander, and Warren H. Manning. Thomas Jefferson as an architect and a designer of landscapes. Boston, Houghton Mifflin, 1913. 121 p. 23 plates.
E332.L22

437

Muzzey, David Saville. Thomas Jefferson. New York, Scribner, 1918. 319 p. (Figures from American history)
E332.M94

438

Gray, Francis Calley. Thomas Jefferson in 1814, being an account of a visit to Monticello, Virginia, with notes and introd. by Henry S. Rowe and T[homas] Jefferson Coolidge, Jr. Boston, Club of Odd Volumes, 1924. 84 p.
E332.G77

439

Bowers, Claude G. Jefferson and Hamilton; the struggle for democracy in America. Boston, Houghton Mifflin, 1925. xvii, 531 p.
E311.B652
Bibliography: p. 513-518.

440

Chinard, Gilbert.. Jefferson et les idéologues d'après sa correspondance inédite avec Destutt de Tracy, Cabanis, J.-B. Say et Auguste Comte. Baltimore, Johns Hopkins Press, 1925. 295 p. (The Johns Hopkins studies in Romance literatures and languages, extra v. 1)
F332.C53
PC13.J62, v. 1
"Ouvrages consultés": p. [288]-291.

441

Wilstach, Paul. Jefferson and Monticello. Garden City, N. Y., Doubleday, Page, 1925. 258 p.
E332.W75
The revision of the 2d edition (Doubleday, Doran, 1927. 262 p.) extended only to the lists in the appendixes;

441

Wilstach, Paul. Jefferson ... (cont.) text remained unchanged in the 5th edition of 1935.
A pleasant narrative of Jefferson's residences at Monticello.

442

Hirst, Francis W. Life and letters of Thomas Jefferson. New York, Macmillan, 1926. 588 p.
E332.H65

443

Nock, Albert Jay. Jefferson. New York, Harcourt, Brace [c1926] 340 p.
E332.N75
Frequently reissued, and available as a paperback from Hill & Wang, New York (AC 34).

444

Philips, Edith. Louis Hue Girardin and Nicholas Gouin Dufief and their relations with Thomas Jefferson; an unknown episode of the French emigration in America. Baltimore, Johns Hopkins Press, 1926. 75 p. (The Johns Hopkins studies in Romance literatures and languages, extra v. 3)
DC146.G4P5
PC13.J62, v. 3

445

Chinard, Gilbert. Trois amitiés françaises de Jefferson, d'après sa correspondance inédite avec Madame de Bréhan, Madame de Tessé et Madame de Corny. Paris, Société d'édition "Les Belles lettres," 1927. 242 p.
E332.C54

446

Sears, Louis Martin. Jefferson and the embargo. Durham, N. C., Duke University Press [c1927] 340 p.
E336.5.S42
Bibliography: p. 321-324.

447

Woolery, William Kirk. The relation of Thomas Jefferson to American foreign policy, 1783-1793. Baltimore, Johns Hopkins Press, 1927. 128 p. (Johns Hopkins University studies in historical and political science, ser. 45, no. 2)

447
Woolery. The relation ... (cont.)
                    E332.W92
                    H31.J6, ser. 45
                        no. 2
        Bibliography: p. 123-125.
        A concise and careful review of the
principal issues of the decade during
which Jefferson was primarily concerned
with foreign affairs.

448
Arrowood, Charles Flinn, ed. Thomas Jef-
    ferson and education in a republic.
    New York, McGraw-Hill, 1930. 184 p.
                    E332.A77

449
Chinard, Gilbert, ed. Houdon in America;
    a collection of documents in the Jef-
    ferson Papers in the Library of Con-
    gress. Baltimore, Johns Hopkins Press,
    1930. xxvi, 51 p. (Institut francais
    de Washington. Historical documents,
    cahier 4)   NB553.H8C5

450
Honeywell, Roy J. The educational work of
    Thomas Jefferson. Cambridge, Harvard
    University Press, 1931. xvi, 295 p.
    (Harvard studies in education, v. 16)
                    E332.H77
        Bibliography: p. 289-295.

451
Malone, Dumas. Polly Jefferson and her
    father. Virginia quarterly review,
    v. 7, Jan. 1931: 81-95. AP2.V76, v. 7
        A sympathetic sketch of Jefferson's
younger daughter, Maria (1778-1804)--
beautiful, shy and untalented, and
never quite at home with her Olympian
papa.

452
Bowers, Claude G. Jefferson in power; the
    death struggle of the Federalists.
    Boston, Houghton Mifflin, 1936. xix,
    538 p.   E331.B75

453
Halsey, Robert H. How the President,
    Thomas Jefferson, and Doctor Benjamin
    Waterhouse established vaccination as a
    public health procedure. New York,
    The Author, 1936. 58 p. (History of
    medicine series, issued under the aus-
    pices of the Library of the New York
    Academy of Medicine, no. 5)
                    RM787.H23

454
Kimball, Marie (Goebel) Thomas Jeffer-
    son's cook book. Richmond, Garrett &
    Massie, 1938. 111 p. TX715.K498
        After an initial essay on "The
    Epicure of Monticello," Mrs. Kimball
    prints recipes from the manuscript
    transcribed from household originals
    by Jefferson's granddaughter, Martha
    Randolph Trist, which had lately been
    acquired by the Thomas Jefferson Memor-
    ial Foundation. The recipes are trans-
    posed for latter-day quantities, stoves,
    and, on occasion, materials (such as
    junket instead of chicken gizzard).

455
Adams, Randolph G. Thomas Jefferson, li-
    brarian. In his Three Americanists.
    Philadelphia, University of Pennsylva-
    nia Press, 1939. p. 69-96.
                    Z1206.A2A2
        Presents Jefferson as a collector
    and reader of books with "a perfect
    passion for the systematic and orderly
    arrangement of data so as to make it
    most readily available for actual use."

456
Chinard, Gilbert. Thomas Jefferson, the
    apostle of Americanism. 2d ed., rev.
    Boston, Little, Brown, 1939. xviii,
    548 p.   E332.C536 1939
        First published in 1929.

457
Kimball, Marie (Goebel) The furnishing of
    Monticello. [Philadelphia? c1940]
    32 p.   F234.M7K5

458

Betts, Edwin M., and Hazlehurst Bolton Perkins. Thomas Jefferson's flower garden at Monticello. Photographs by Benjamin Runk and Edwin H. Robbins. Richmond, Dietz Press, 1941. 56 p. E332.B48

459

Bullock, Helen C. (Duprey) The papers of Thomas Jefferson. Charlottesville, Va., 1941. [237]-249 p. E302.J85B8
    Reprinted from the American Archivist, v. 4, Oct. 1941.

460

Mayo, Barbara. Twilight at Monticello. Virginia quarterly review, v. 17, autumn 1941: 502-516. AP2.V76, v. 17
    A vivid evocation of the last eight years at Monticello, based on the letters of Virginia Randolph, Jefferson's granddaughter, to her fiancé, Nicholas P. Trist.

461

Padover, Saul K. Jefferson. New York, Harcourt, Brace [1942] 459 p.
                            E332.P12
    Bibliography: p. 435-447.

462

American Philosophical Society, Philadelphia. Thomas Jefferson. Papers read before the American Philosophical Society in celebration of the bicentennial of Thomas Jefferson, third president of the society. Annual meeting April 22, 23, and 24, 1943. Philadelphia, 1943. 199-389 p. (Its Proceedings, v. 87, no. 3, July 14, 1943]
                    Q11.P5, v. 87, no. 3
    Contents.--Introduction to the Jefferson bicentennial program, by E. G. Conklin.--What is still living in the political philosophy of Thomas Jefferson? By Carl Becker.--Jefferson as a lawyer, by R. S. Morris.--Thomas Jefferson--farmer, by M. L. Wilson.--Thomas Jefferson and the classics, by L. B. Wright.--Notes on Thomas Jefferson as a natural philosopher, by Harlow Shapley.--Jefferson and the arts, by Fiske Kimball.--The old political philosophy and the new, by John Dickinson.--

462

American Philosophical Society ... (cont.) Jefferson and the American Philosophical Society, by Gilbert Chinard.--The beginnings of the American Philosophical Society, by Carl Van Doren.

463

Browne, Charles A. Thomas Jefferson and the scientific trends of his time. Waltham, Mass., Chronica Botanica Co., 1943. 63 p. illus. (Chronica Botanica reprints, no. 1) E332.B9

464

Edwards, Everett E., comp. Jefferson and agriculture; a sourcebook. [Washington, 1943] 92 p. (U. S. Bureau of Agricultural Economics. Agricultural history series, no. 7)
                    HD1751.A9145, no. 7

465

Kimball, Marie (Goebel) Jefferson, the road to glory, 1743 to 1776. New York, Coward-McCann [1943] 358 p. E332.K5

466

Koch, Adrienne. The philosophy of Thomas Jefferson. New York, Columbia University Press, 1943. 208 p. (Columbia studies in American culture, no. 14)
                            E332.K6
    Bibliography: p. 191-199.

467

Mott, Frank L. Jefferson and the press. Baton Rouge, Louisiana State University Press, 1943. 65 p. (Journalism monographs, no. 2) PN4853.J6, no. 2
                            E332.M925

468

Caldwell, Lynton K. The administrative theories of Hamilton & Jefferson; their contribution to thought on public administration. Chicago, University of Chicago Press [1944] 244 p. (Studies in public administration) JK171.A1C3

469
Kimball, Fiske. The life portraits of
Jefferson and their replicas. In American Philosophical Society, Philadelphia. Proceedings. v. 88; 1944.
Philadelphia. p. 497-534.
Q11.P5, v. 88

470
Bowers, Claude G. The young Jefferson,
1743-1789. Boston, Houghton Mifflin,
1945. xxx, 544 p.   E332.B78
Bibliography: p. 525-530.

471
Boyd, Julian P. The Declaration of Independence; the evolution of the text as
shown in facsimiles of various drafts
by its author, Thomas Jefferson.
Princeton, Princeton University Press,
1945. 46 p. facsims.   JK128.B66
                        Z663.D38
An earlier version of this work published by the Library of Congress in
1943 has a briefer text, but much superior facsimiles.

472
Bullock, Helen C. (Duprey) My head and my
heart, a little history of Thomas Jefferson and Maria Cosway. New York,
Putnam [1945] xvii, 235 p. E332.B95
Bibliography: p. 210-219.

473
Dumbauld, Edward. Thomas Jefferson, American tourist, being an account of his
journeys in the United States of America, England, France, Italy, the Low
Countries, and Germany. Norman, University of Oklahoma Press, 1946. xv,
266 p.   E332.D8
Bibliography: p. 241-260.

474
Berman, Eleanor Davidson. Thomas Jefferson among the arts; an essay in early
American esthetics. New York, Philosophical Library [1947] xviii, 305 p.
                        E332.B47
Bibliography: p. 273-281.

475
Foote, Henry Wilder. Thomas Jefferson,
champion of religious freedom, advocate
of Christian morals. Boston, Beacon
Press, 1947. 70 p.   E332.F65

476
Kimball, Marie (Goebel) Jefferson, war
and peace, 1776 to 1784. New York,
Coward-McCann [1947] E322.K52

477
Lehmann-Hartleben, Karl. Thomas Jefferson, American humanist. New York,
Macmillan, 1947. 273 p. E333.L45

478
Boorstin, Daniel J. The lost world of
Thomas Jefferson. New York, Holt
[1948] 306 p.   B878.B6

479
Koch, Adrienne, and Harry Ammon. The Virginia and Kentucky resolutions: an
episode in Jefferson's and Madison's
defense of civil liberties. William
and Mary quarterly, 3d ser., v. 5,
Apr. 1948: 145-176.
                F221.W71, ser. 3, v. 5
Disentangles the circumstances, the
successive texts, and the part which
Jefferson and Madison had in each.
Madison "used his considerable influence to tone down Jefferson's feverpitch impatience."

480
Malone, Dumas. Jefferson and his time.
Boston, Little, Brown, 1948-62. 3 v.
illus.   E332.M25
"Select critical bibliography":
v. 1, p. [457]-470; v. 2, p. [494]-504.
Contents.--v. 1. Jefferson the
Virginian.--v. 2. Jefferson and the
rights of man.--v. 3. Jefferson and
the ordeal of victory [to Feb. 1801].

481
Rice, Howard C. L'Hôtel de Langeac, Jefferson's Paris residence. Résidence de
Jefferson à Paris, 1785-1789. Paris,
H. Lefebvre; Monticello, Va., Thomas
Jefferson Memorial Foundation, 1947
[i. e. 1948] 25 p. NA7348.P2R5 1948

481
Rice, Howard C. L'Hôtel ... (cont.)
    "A by-product of research undertaken
by the author in France for the editorial board of The papers of Thomas Jefferson."--p. 23.

482
Beloff, Max. Thomas Jefferson and American democracy. New York, Macmillan,
1949. 271 p. (Teach yourself history
library)   E332.B43 1949

483
Dumbauld, Edward. The Declaration of Independence and what it means today.
Norman, University of Oklahoma Press
[1950] 194 p.   JK128.D3
    Bibliography: p. 161-189.

484
Frary, Ihna T. Thomas Jefferson, architect and builder. [3d ed.] Richmond,
Garrett and Massie [1950] 154 p.
110 plates (incl. plans, facsim.)
                        E332.F84 1950
                        NA737.J4F7 1950
    Bibliography: p. 151.
    First published in 1931.

485
Kimball, Marie (Goebel) Jefferson, the
scene of Europe, 1784 to 1789. New
York, Coward-McCann [1950] 357 p.
                        E332.K513 1950

486
Koch, Adrienne. Jefferson and Madison;
the great collaboration. New York,
Knopf, 1950. xv, 294, xiv p.
                        E332.K58 1950

487
Jefferson, Isaac. Memoirs of a Monticello
slave, as dictated to Charles Campbell
in the 1840's by Isaac, one of Thomas
Jefferson's slaves. Edited by Rayford
W. Logan. Charlottesville, Published
by the University of Virginia Press for
the Tracy W. McGregor Library, 1951.
45 p.   E444.J4

488
Martin, Edwin T. Thomas Jefferson: sci-
entist. New York, H. Schuman [1952]
289 p.   E332.M33

489
Patterson, Caleb Perry. The constitutional principles of Thomas Jefferson.
Austin, University of Texas Press,
1953. 211 p.   E332.P32
    Bibliography: p. 191-199.

490
Rosenberger, Francis Coleman, ed. Jefferson reader, a treasury of writings
about Thomas Jefferson; illustrated
with 15 life portraits of Jefferson.
New York, Dutton, 1953. 349 p.
                            E332.R63

491
Dos Passos, John. The head and heart of
Thomas Jefferson. Garden City, N. Y.,
Doubleday, 1954. 442 p. E332.D6

492
Klapthor, Margaret (Brown) The story of
the Declaration of Independence desk
and how it came to the National Museum.
In Smithsonian Institution. Annual report, 1953. Washington, 1954. p. 455-
462.   Q11.S66 1953
    Bibliography: p. 462.

493
Schachner, Nathan. Thomas Jefferson, a
biography. New York, T. Yoseloff
[1957] 1070 p.   E332.S32 1957
    Bibliography: p. 1049-1060.
    First published in 2 v. in 1951.

494
Peterson, Merrill D. The Jefferson image
in the American mind. New York, Oxford
University Press, 1960. 548 p.
                        E332.2.P4
    "Guide to sources": p. 459-522.

495
Conant, James B. Thomas Jefferson and the
development of American public education. Berkeley, University of California Press, 1962. 164 p. LB695.J4C6

496

Burr, Aaron. Memoirs of Aaron Burr, with
    miscellaneous selections from his cor-
    respondence. By Matthew L. Davis.
    New York, Harper, 1836-37. 2 v.
                              E302.6.B9B9
        Reissued in 1855.

497

Parton, James. The life and times of
    Aaron Burr. Enl. ed. Boston, J. R.
    Osgood, 1872. 2 v.   E302.6.B9P282
        Originally published in 1 v., 1858.

498

Wandell, Samuel H., and Meade Minnigerode.
    Aaron Burr; a biography compiled from
    rare, and in many cases unpublished,
    sources. New York, Putnam, 1925.
    2 v.   E302.6.B9W2
        Bibliography: v. 1, p. xxvii-xxxiv.

499

Schachner, Nathan. Aaron Burr, a biogra-
    phy. New York, A. Stokes, 1937.
    565 p.   E302.6.B9S3
        Bibliography: p. 547-553.
        Reissued in paperback form by A. S.
    Barnes and Co., N. Y. (Perpetua books
    P4028).

500

Spaulding, Ernest Wilder. His Excellency
    George Clinton, critic of the Constitu-
    tion. New York, Macmillan, 1938.
    325 p.   E302.6.C6S7
        "Bibliographical note": p. 305-309.

501

Abernethy, Thomas Perkins. The Burr con-
    spiracy. New York, Oxford University
    Press, 1954. 301 p.   E334.A6
        Bibliography: p. 276-284.

Writings

502

Madison, James. The papers of James Madison, purchased by order of Congress; being his correspondence and reports of debates during the Congress of the Confederation, and his reports of debates in the Federal Convention; now published from the original manuscripts, deposited in the Department of State, by direction of the Joint Library Committee of Congress, under the superintendence of Henry D. Gilpin. Washington, Langtree & O'Sullivan, 1840. 3 v.   JK111.M2

    Madison took notes on debates in Congress during Nov. 4, 1782-June 21, 1783, and Feb. 19-Apr. 25, 1787. His famous notes on the Constitutional Convention of 1787, which supply the greatest part of our knowledge of what went on in that unique body, have been several times reedited, notably by Gaillard Hunt below, and by Max Farrand in The Records of the Federal Convention (New Haven, Yale University Press, 1911. 3 v.).

503

----- Letters and other writings [1769-1836]. Published by order of Congress. Philadelphia, Lippincott, 1865. 4 v.
                    E302.M18

    Edited by Philip R. Fendall. It contains a number of items which do not appear in Hunt's otherwise considerably superior edition.

504

----- The writings of James Madison, comprising his public papers and his private correspondence, including numerous letters and documents now for the first time printed. Edited by Gaillard Hunt. New York, Putnam, 1900-10. 9 v.
                    E302.M22

504

----- The writings ... (cont.)
Contents.--v. 1. 1769-1783.--v. 2. 1783-1787.--v. 3-4. 1787. The Journal of the Constitutional Convention.--v. 5. 1787-1790.--v. 6. 1790-1802.--v. 7. 1803-1807.--v. 8. 1808-1819.--v. 9. 1819-1836.

505

----- Papers. Edited by William T. Hutchinson and William M. E. Rachal. Editorial staff: Jean Schneider [and others. Chicago] University of Chicago Press [1962] 2 v.   JK111.M24
    Contents.--v. 1. 16 Mar. 1751-16 Dec. 1779.--v. 2. 20 Mar. 1780-23 Feb. 1781.

506

----- The complete Madison; his basic writings, edited and with an introd. by Saul K. Padover. New York, Harper [1953] 361 p.   E302.M17
    A curious title for a volume of topically arranged selections, the largest part of which comes from Madison's contributions to The Federalist (no. 507).

507

The Federalist; a collection of essays, written in favour of the new Constitution, as agreed upon by the Federal Convention, September 17, 1787. New York, J. & A. M'Lean, 1788. 2 v.
               JK154 1788

    The first complete edition of the 85 essays which had begun to appear on Oct. 27, 1787, in the New York Independent Advertiser and were finished only in time for the publication of volume 2 on May 28, 1788. Of the 85, at least 24 are from Madison's pen, and 29 may well be. Of the others, 5 are John Jay's and the remainder Alexander Hamilton's. Three recent editions are

507

The Federalist ... (cont.)
improvements upon their numerous predecessors: by Benjamin Fletcher Wright
(Cambridge, Mass., Belknap Press of
Harvard University Press, 1961, 672
p.), by Jacob E. Cooke (Middletown,
Conn., Wesleyan University Press, 1961.
xxx, 672 p.), and an inexpensive paperback by Clinton Rossiter (New York, New
American Library, 1961. 559 p. A Men-
tor book, MT328).

508

[Madison, James.] Letters of Helvidius:
written in reply to Pacificus, on the
President's proclamation of neutrality.
Published originally in the year 1793.
Philadelphia, S. H. Smith, 1796. 48 p.
E312.H22

The letters first appeared in the
Gazette of the United States, Aug. 24-
Sept. 18, 1793, in answer to Alexander
Hamilton, whose Pacificus letters had
appeared earlier in the same paper.
Helvidius argued that Pacificus and the
proclamation unduly favored Britain as
against France.

509

----- An examination of the British doctrine, which subjects to capture a neu-
tral trade, not open in time of peace.
[Philadelphia? 1806?] 204 p.
JX5316.M26

The Secretary of State's "shilling
pamphlet hurled against eight hundred
ships of war" (John Randolph). It was
several times reprinted during the next
two years, including a London edition.

510

Madison, James. An address delivered before the Agricultural Society of Albe-
marle, on Tuesday, May 12, 1818. By
Mr. Madison, President of the society.
Richmond, Shepherd & Pollard, 1818.
31 p. S523.M18

Biography

511

Rives, William Cabell. History of the
life and times of James Madison. Boston, Little, Brown, 1859-68. 3 v.
E342.R62

Solemn and ponderous but reliable
enough, this first attempt to write
Madison's life from his papers had only
reached 1797 when it was cut off by the
author's death in 1868. The publishers
printed a second edition in 1873.

512

Hunt, Gaillard. The life of James Madison. New York, Doubleday, Page, 1902.
402 p. E342.H943

513

Smith, Abbot Emerson. James Madison:
builder; a new estimate of a memorable
career. New York, Wilson-Erickson,
1937. 366 p. E342.S55

514

Burns, Edward McNall. James Madison,
philosopher of the Constitution. New
Brunswick, Rutgers University Press,
1938. 212 p. (Rutgers University
studies in history, v. 1) E342.B87
Bibliography: p. 201-206.

515

Brant, Irving. James Madison. Indianapolis, Bobbs-Merrill [1941-61] 6 v.
E342.B7

Contents.--]1] The Virginia revolu-
tionist.--[2] The nationalist, 1780-
1787.--[3] Father of the Constitution,
1787-1800.--[4] Secretary of State,
1800-1809.--[5] The President, 1809-
12.--[6] Commander in Chief, 1812-
1836.

516

Austin, James T. The life of Elbridge
Gerry. With contemporary letters. To
the close of the American Revolution.
Boston, Wells and Lilly, 1828-29.
2 v. E302.6.G37A9

517
Madison, Dorothy (Payne) Todd. Memoirs
    and letters of Dolly Madison, wife of
    James Madison, President of the United
    States, edited by her grandniece [Lu-
    cia B. Cutts] Boston, Houghton Miff-
    lin, 1886. 210 p.   E342.1.M18

518
Goodwin, Maud Wilder. Dolly Madison. New
    York, Scribner, 1896. 287 p. (Women
    of colonial and revolutionary times)
                        E342.1.G65

519
Clark, Allen C. Life and letters of Dolly
    Madison. Washington, W. F. Roberts
    Co., 1914. 517 p.   E342.1.C5
        Valuable for the letters and papers
    quoted at length; otherwise inchoate.

520
Dean, Elizabeth L. Dolly Madison, the
    Nation's hostess. Boston, Lothrop,
    Lee & Shepard Co. [c1928] 250 p.
                        E342.1.D28

521
Anthony, Katharine S. Dolly Madison, her
    life and times. Garden City, N. Y.,
    Doubleday, 1949. 426 p. E342.1.A58

JAMES MONROE

Writings

522
Monroe, James. Writings. Edited by Stanislaus Murray Hamilton. New York, Putnam, 1898-1903. 7 v. E302.M74

523
----- A view of the conduct of the executive, in the foreign affairs of the United States, connected with the mission to the French Republic, during the years 1794, 5, & 6. By James Monroe, late Minister Plenipotentiary to the said Republic. Philadelphia, B. F. Bache, 1797. lxvi, 407 p. E313.M76
JX1412.M7

524
----- The memoir of James Monroe, esq., relating to his unsettled claims upon the people and government of the United States. Charlottesville, Gilmer, Davis, 1828. 60 p. E372.M76

525
----- The people the sovereigns; being a comparison of the government of the United States with those of the republics which have existed before, with the causes of their decadence and fall. Edited by Samuel L. Gouverneur. Philadelphia, Lippincott, 1867. 274 p.
JC212.M75

A work which Monroe began in 1825 but left incomplete, deciphered and given to the press by his grandson with the encouragement of George Bancroft. A first chapter gives "A Comparative Elementary View of Government and of Society"; the second is said to compare the Government of the United States with Athens, Lacedemon and Carthage, but in fact merely summarizes ancient authors' description of these republics.

526
----- Monroe's defense of Jefferson and Freneau against Hamilton, edited by Philip M. Marsh. Oxford, Ohio, 1948. 56 p. E311.M63

When Secretary Hamilton, under various pseudonyms, began attacking Secretary Jefferson and his translating clerk, Philip Freneau, in the Gazette of the United States, Senator Monroe rallied to his defense and, with assistance from Congressman Madison, contributed a series of six letters, "The Vindication of Mr. Jefferson," to John Dunlap's American Daily Advertiser, Sept. 22-Dec. 31, 1792. They are reprinted here (p. 27-51), preceded by an introduction and excerpts from Hamilton's Gazette letters.

527
----- Autobiography. Edited, and with an introd., by Stuart Gerry Brown, with the assistance of Donald G. Baker. [Syracuse] Syracuse University Press [1959] 236 p. E372.A3

The first publication of an uncompleted manuscript which had long been available in the Monroe papers in the New York Public Library, but little used largely because Monroe's crabbed hnnd is so difficult to decipher. After 35 preliminary pages on his career down to 1794, it is thereafter concerned with his first mission to France (p. 57-147) and his subsequent ones to France, Britain, and Spain, 1803 to 1805, when it breaks off. It was doubtless intended to support the claim for further compensation Monroe presented to Congress in 1828 (no. 524).

Biography

528

A Narrative of a tour of observation, made during the summer of 1817, by James Monroe, President of the United States, through the north-eastern and north-western departments of the Union: with a view to the examination of their several military defenses. Philadelphia, S. A. Mitchell & H. Ames, 1818. 228, xxvi p. E371.N23

The same junket inspired two other publications: Samuel Putnam Waldo's The Tour of James Monroe (Hartford, 1818. 2d ed., Hartford, S. Andrus, 1820. 348 p.) and The President's Tour; a Collection of Addresses made to James Monroe, etc. (New-Ipswich, N. H., 1822. 76 p.).

529

[Wolfe, Udolpho] Grand civic and military demonstration in honor of the removal of the remains of James Monroe, fifth President of the United States, from New York to Virginia. New York, U. Wolfe, 1858. 324 p. E372.W85

530

Gilman, Daniel C. James Monroe in his relations to the public service during half a century, 1776 to 1826. Boston, Houghton Mifflin, 1883. 287 p. (American statesmen) E176.A5, v. 14
E372.G48

"Bibliography of Monroe, and the Monroe Doctrine," by John Franklin Jameson: p. 253-280.
Reprinted, 1898 and 1911.

531

Bond, Beverly W. The Monroe mission to France, 1794-1796. Baltimore, Johns Hopkins Press, 1907. 104 p. (Johns Hopkins University studies in historical and political science, ser. 25, no. 2-3) H31.J6, ser. 25, no. 2-3
JX1412.B7

532

Morgan, George. The life of James Monroe. Boston, Small, Maynard [1921] 484 p. E372.M84

533

Hall, Edward Hagaman. The Monroe house, a landmark history of the house in New York City in which President James Monroe died on July 4, 1831, with biographical notes concerning some of the owners. In American Scenic and Historic Preservation Society. Annual report. 28th; 1922-23. Appendix C, p. 251-266. E151.A51, v. 28

534

Perkins, Dexter. The Monroe Doctrine, 1823-1826. Cambridge, Harvard University Press, 1927. 280 p. (Harvard historical studies, v. 29)
JX1425.P385

Reprinted in 1932.
The Doctrine which has kept Monroe's name continuously before the public was the product of collaboration, his Secretary of State, John Quincy Adams, being the most important formulator. This monograph has remained the fullest and most authoritative reconstruction of its genesis.

535

Pratt, Julius W. James Monroe, Secretary of State, November 25, 1811, to March 3, 1817 (ad interim, April 3 to November 25, 1811) In Bemis, Samuel Flagg, ed. The American secretaries of state and their diplomacy. v. 3. New York, Knopf, 1927. p. 199-277, 294-303.
E183.7.B46, v. 3

536

Cresson, William P. James Monroe. Chapel Hill, University of North Carolina Press [1946] 577 p. E372.C7
"List of references": p. 549-559.

536
Cresson, W. P. James Monroe. (cont.)
     Cresson died in 1932, but left this
biography in so advanced a state that
it could ultimately be got through the
press. It is particularly good for
foreign affairs, where Cresson's own
career had been. Arthur Styron's The
Last of the Cocked Hats: James Monroe
and the Virginia Dynasty (Norman, University of Oklahoma Press, 1945. 480
p.) is an interpretation of Monroe's
era rather than a biography.

537
Wilmerding, Lucius. James Monroe, public
   claimant. New Brunswick, N. J., Rutgers University Press [1960] 144 p.
                    E372.W5
     A detailed examination, by a student
of American public finance, of Monroe's
claim, presented to Congress in the
last months of his Presidency, for
$53,836, in principal and interest over
a long period, as owing to him for his
past diplomatic and other services. He
received $29,500 from Congress in 1826,
and a further $30,000 in 1830, the year
before his death "in wretchedness and
beggary."

Writings

538
Adams, John Quincy. Writings [1779-1823],
edited by Worthington Chauncey Ford,
New York, Macmillan, 1913-17. 7 v.
E337.8.A21
No more published.

539
----- Memoirs ... comprising portions of
his diary from 1795 to 1848. Edited
by Charles Francis Adams. Philadelphia, Lippincott, 1874-77. 12 v.
E377.A19

540
----- Diary, 1794-1845; American diplo-
macy and political, social, and intel-
lectual life from Washington to Polk.
Edited by Allan Nevins. New York,
Scribner, 1951. xxxv, 586 p.
E377.A213
A selection, originally published
in 1928, from the preceding 12-volume
edition.

541
[Adams, John Quincy] An answer to Pain's
Rights of man. By John Adams, esq.
London, Printed for J. Stockdale, 1793.
48 p.   JC177.H5 1793
Seven of a series of eleven letters
originally published in the Columbian
Centinel, June-July 1791, under the
pseudonym of "Publicola," and at the
time commonly ascribed to John Adams,
Vice-President of the United States,
but in reality the work of his son,
then a young lawyer in Boston.

542
Adams, John Quincy. Letters on Silesia,
written during a tour through that
country in the years 1800, 1801. Embellished with a new map. London,
J. Budd, 1804. 387 p. DD491.S44A2
Originally published in the Port

542
Adams, John Quincy. Letters ... (Cont.)
folio, of Philadelphia.

543
----- An inaugural oration, delivered at
the author's installation, as Boylston's professor of rhetorick and oratory, at Harvard University, in Cambridge, Massachusetts, on Thursday, 12
June, 1806. Published at the request
of the students. Boston, Monroe &
Francis, 1806. 28 p. PN4130.A25

544
----- A letter to the Hon. Harrison Gray
Otis, a member of the Senate of Massachusetts, on the present state of
our national affairs; with remarks on
Mr. Pickering's letter to the Governor
of the Commonwealth. Boston, Oliver
and Munroe, 1808. 32 p.
AC901.B3, v. 3

545
----- American principles. A review of
the Works of Fisher Ames, compiled by
a number of his friends. Boston,
Everett and Munroe, 1809. 56 p.
E302.A57

546
----- Lectures on rhetoric and oratory,
delivered to the classes of senior
and junior sophisters in Harvard University. Cambridge, Hilliard and Metcalf, 1810. 2 v.   PN175.A4

547
U. S. Dept. of State. Report upon weights
and measures, by John Quincy Adams,
Secretary of State of the United
States. Prepared in obedience to a
resolution of the Senate of the third
March, 1817. Washington, Gales &
Seaton, 1821. 245 p. 3 fold. tables.

547

U. S. <u>Dept. of State</u>. (Cont.)

QC88.A22

     Also issued as 16th Cong., 2d sess. Senate Document 119; and House Document 109.

548

Adams, John Quincy. The duplicate letters, the fisheries and the Mississippi. Documents relating to the transactions at the negotiation of Ghent. Collected and published by John Quincy Adams. Washington, Davis and Force, 1822. 256 p.

E358.A21

SH229.A21

549

----- Correspondence between John Quincy Adams, esquire, President of the United States, and several citizens of Massachusetts concerning the charge of a design to dissolve the Union alleged to have existed in that State. Boston, Press of the Boston Daily Advertiser, 1829. 80 p.

E357.6.A2

550

----- An eulogy: on the life and character of James Monroe, fifth President of the United States. Delivered at the request of the Corporation of the City of Boston. Boston, J. H. Eastburn, city printer, 1831. 100 p.

E372.A21

551

----- Dermot MacMorrogh, or, The conquest of Ireland; an historical tale of the twelfth century. In four cantos. Boston, Carter, Hendee, 1832. 108 p.

PS1005.D4 1832

552

U. S. <u>Congress</u>. <u>House</u>. <u>Committee on Manufactures</u>. Report of the minority of the Committee on Manufactures, submitted to the House of Representatives of the United States, February 28, 1833. By John Quincy Adams and Lewis Condict. Boston, J. H. Eastburn, 1833. 37 p.

HF1754.A17 1833

553

Adams, John Quincy. Oration on the life and character of Gilbert Motier de Lafayette. Delivered at the request of both houses of the Congress of the United States ... on the 31st of December, 1834. Washington, D. Green, 1835. 96 p.

E207.L2A202

554

----- An eulogy on the life and character of James Madison ... delivered at the request of the mayor, aldermen, and Common Council of the City of Boston. Boston, J. H. Eastburn, City Printer, 1836. 90 p.

E342.A21

555

----- Letters from John Quincy Adams to his constituents of the twelfth Congressional District in Massachusetts. To which is added his speech in Congress delivered February 9, 1837. Boston, J. Knapp, 1837. 72 p.

E449.A214

     This publication, in which Adams explained his defense of the right of petition against the "Gag Rule," has a preface by John Greenleaf Whittier and concludes with two of his poems (p. 66-72).

556

----- An oration delivered before the inhabitants of the town of Newburyport, at their request, on the sixty-first anniversary of the Declaration of Independence, July 4th, 1837. Newburyport, Mass., Morss and Brewster [1837] 68 p.

E286.N64 1837

557

----- The jubilee of the Constitution. A discourse delivered at the request of the New York Historical Society. New York, S. Colman, 1839. 136 p.

JK119.A4

558

----- A discourse on education, delivered at Braintree, Thursday, Oct. 24, 1839. Boston, Perkins & Marvin, 1840. 36 p.

LB695.A23

559

----- Argument, before the Supreme Court of the United States, in the case of the United States, appellants, vs. Cinque, and others, Africans, captured in the schooner Amistad, by Lieut. Gedney, delivered on the 24th of February and 1st of March, 1841. New York, S. W. Benedict, 1841. 135 p.
                                    E447.A21

560

----- Address to his constituents of the Twelfth Congressional District, at Braintree, September 17th, 1842. Boston, J. H. Eastburn, 1842. 63 p.
                            AC901.W3, v. 119

561

----- The social compact, exemplified in the constitution of the Commonwealth of Massachusetts; with remarks on the theories of divine right of Hobbes and of Filmer, and the counter theories of Sidney, Locke, Montesquieu, and Rousseau ... a lecture, delivered before the Franklin Lyceum, at Providence, R. I., November 25, 1842. Providence, Knowles and Vose, 1842. 32 p.
                                    JK3119.A6

562

----- The New England Confederacy of MDCXLIII. A discourse delivered before the Massachusetts Historical Society, at Boston, on the 29th of May, 1843; in celebration of the second centennial anniversary of that event. Boston, Little, Brown, 1843. 47 p.
                                    F7.A23

    Also published in the Society's Collections, 3d ser., v. 9 (Boston, 1846) p. 189-223.

563

----- An oration delivered before the Cincinnati Astronomical Society, on the occasion of laying the corner stone of an astronomical observatory, on the 10th of November, 1843. Cincinnati, Shepard, 1843. 72 p.   QB51.A23
                                    QB82.C54

564

----- Letters on the Masonic institution. Boston, T. R. Marvin, 1847. xl, 284 p.
                                    HS527.A2

565

----- Letters of John Quincy Adams to his son, on the Bible and its teachings. Auburn, J. M. Alden, 1850. 128 p.   BS538.A3
    Originally published as an appendix to Letters of Mrs. Adams, the wife of John Adams, 4th ed. (Boston, Wilkins, Carter, 1848. p. 421-472).

566

----- Poems of religion and society, with notices of his life and character by John Davis and T. H. Benton. New York, W. H. Graham, 1850. 116 p.
                                    NN
    First published in 1848. Includes a version of the 13th satire of Juvenal and number of verse paraphrases of the Psalms.

567

Adams, Henry, ed. Documents relating to New England Federalism, 1800-1815. Boston, Little, Brown, 1877. 437 p.
                                    JK2306.A3
    The most important single item is J. Q. Adams's "Reply to the Appeal of the Massachusetts Federalists" (p.107-329) which he completed in 1829 but decided not to publish. Even in 1877 his grandson preferred to omit some of the bitterest paragraphs on Harrison Gray Otis.

568

Adams, John Quincy. Life in a New England town: 1787, 1788. Diary of John Quincy Adams while a student in the office of Theophilus Parsons at Newburyport. Boston, Little, Brown, 1903. 204 p.   F74.N55A2

569

----- [Address to the Massachusetts Historical Society, November 22, 1841, on the Opium War between Great Britain and China, edited by Charles Francis Adams] In Massachusetts Historical

569

----- [Address to ... (Cont.)
Society. Proceedings. 2d ser., v. 43;
1910. Boston. p. 295-325.
                F61.M38, 2d ser., v. 43
    Originally written for the North
American Review, whose editor, John
Gorham Palfrey, declined to publish it
after discovering that J. Q. Adams
blamed the war upon Chinese insolence.
The Address proper: p. 303-325.

570

----- Letters of John Quincy Adams to
Alexander [Hill] Everett, 1811-1837.
American historical review, v. 11,
Oct. 1905: 88-116; Jan. 1906: 332-
354.   E171.A57, v. 11
    26 letters from originals in the
Library of Congress; introductory note
signed Andrew C. McLaughlin.

571

----- Correspondence of John Quincy
Adams, 1811-1814, edited by Charles
Francis Adams. In American Antiquarian Society, Worcester, Mass. Proceedings. New ser., v. 23; 1913. Worcester. p. 110-169.
            E172.A35, new ser., v. 23
    Extracts from J. Q. Adams' letters
from St. Petersburg to his mother and
brother.

572

----- A catalogue of the books of John
Quincy Adams deposited in the Boston
Athenaeum, with notes on books, Adams
seals and book-plates by Henry Adams,
with an introd. by Worthington
Chauncey Ford. Boston, The Athenaeum,
1938. 152 p.   Z997.A2145

573

Wieland, Christoph Martin. Oberon, a
poetical romance in twelve books,
translated from the German of Wieland
(1799-1801) by John Quincy Adams; edited with an introd. and notes by
A[lbert] B. Faust. New York, Crofts,
1940. xcii, 340 p.
                PT2568.A3022 1940
    Adams learned German and completed
this translation while resident in

573

Wieland, Christoph Martin. (Cont.)
Berlin as U. S. Minister to Prussia.
He did not publish it because of the
appearance of William Sotheby's trans-
lation. Wieland himself judged
Sotheby's to be the more poetic, but
Adams' the more faithful to the orig-
inal.

574

Adams, John Quincy. Parties in the United States. Foreword by Charles True
Adams. New York, Greenberg, 1941.
136 p.   E302.1.A28

575

----- Ten unpublished letters of John
Quincy Adams, 1796-1837, edited by
Edward H. Tatum, Jr. Huntington Li-
brary quarterly, v. 4, Apr. 1941:
369-388.   Z733.S24Q, v. 4
    Save for 3 brief notes, includes
all of the miscellaneous group of
Adams' letters then in the Huntington
Library.

Biography

576

Quincy, Josiah. Memoir of the life of
John Quincy Adams. Boston, Phillips,
Sampson, 1858. 429 p. E377.Q7
    Prepared at the request of the Mas-
sachusetts Historical Society.

577

Morse, John T. John Quincy Adams. Boston, Houghton Mifflin, 1882. 315 p.
(American statesmen) E176.A53, v. 15

578

Ford, Worthington Chauncey. John Quincy
Adams, his connection with the Monroe
Doctrine (1823-1842) by W. C. Ford,
and with emancipation under martial
law (1819-1842) by Charles Francis
Adams. Cambridge, J. Wilson, 1902.
113 p.   E377.F71
    "Reprinted from the Proceedings of
the Massachusetts Historical Society,
for Jan. 1902."

579
Adams, Charles Francis, ed. John Quincy
    Adams and Speaker Andrew Stevenson, of
    Virginia; an episode of the Twenty-
    second Congress (1832). In Massachu-
    setts Historical Society. Proceedings.
    [2d ser.] v. 39; 1906. Boston. p.
    504-553.   F61.M38, 2d ser., v. 39

580
Ford Worthington Chauncey. The recall of
    John Quincy Adams in 1808. In Massa-
    chusetts Historical Society. Proceed-
    ings. [2d ser.] v. 45; 1912. Boston.
    p. 354-373.   F61.M38, 2d ser., v. 45
        Senator Adams' support of the Jef-
    ferson administration in the Chesa-
    peake-Leopard crisis led the Federalist
    majority in the Massachusetts legisla-
    ture to select his successor six months
    earlier than the election was regular-
    ly held. Adams treated this as a form
    of recall and resigned directly.

581
Brown, Everett S. The Presidential elec-
    tion of 1824-1825. Political science
    quarterly, v. 40, Sep. 1925: 384-403.
                        H1.P8, v. 40

582
Mayo, Lawrence Shaw. Jeremy Belknap and
    J. Q. Adams, 1787. In Massachusetts
    Historical Society. Proceedings. 2d
    ser., v. 59; 1926. Boston. p. 203-
    209.   F61.M38, 2d ser., v. 59
        How the eminent scholar, after over-
    coming unexpected objections from its
    author, procured the publication of
    JQA's commencement oration in the Co-
    lumbian Magazine of Philadelphia.

583
Bobbé, Dorothie. Mr. and Mrs. John Quincy
    Adams, an adventure in patriotism. New
    York, Minton, Balch, 1930. 310 p.
                        E377.B66

584
Clark, Bennett Champ. John Quincy Adams,
    "old man eloquent." Boston, Little,
    Brown, 1932. 437 p.   E377.C63
        Bibliography: p. 419-426.

585
Rahskopf, Horace G. John Quincy Adams's
    theory and practice of public speaking.
    Archives of speech, v. 1, Sept. 1936:
    [7]-98.
                    QP306.A1A73, v. 1
        A separate copy of this issue has
    the call number E377.R2.

586
Bemis, Samuel Flagg. John Quincy Adams
    and George Washington. In Massachu-
    setts Historical Society. Proceedings.
    2d ser., v. 67; 1945. Boston. p. 365-
    384.   F61.M38, 2d ser., v. 67

587
Goodfellow, Donald M. The first Boylston
    professor of rhetoric and oratory.
    New England quarterly, v. 19, Sept.
    1946: 372-389.   F1.N62, v.19

588
Goodfellow, Donald M. "Your old friend,
    J. Q. Adams." New England quarterly,
    v. 21, June 1948: 217-231.
                    F1.N62, v. 21
        Reviews Adams' letters to Dr. Ben-
    jamin Waterhouse for over half a cen-
    tury (1785-1837).

589
Bemis, Samuel Flagg. John Quincy Adams
    and the foundations of American for-
    eign policy. New York, Knopf, 1949.
    xix, 588, xv p.   E377.B45 1949

590
Lipsky, George A. John Quincy Adams, his
    theory and ideas. Foreword by Allan
    Nevins. New York, Crowell, 1950.
    347 p.   E377.L5
        Bibliography: p. 334-339.

591
Bemis, Samuel Flagg. The scuffle in the
    rotunda: a footnote to the Presidency
    of John Quincy Adams and to the histo-
    ry of dueling. In Massachusetts His-
    torical Society. Proceedings. v. 71;
    1953-57. p. 156-166.
                    F61.M38, v. 71
        Expands a short paragraph on p. 99
    of the author's John Quincy Adams and

591

Bemis, Samuel Flagg. (Cont.)
   the Union. An opposition editor,
   Russell Jarvis, seeking to provoke the
   President's son and private secretary
   into a duel, assaulted him in the ro-
   tunda of the Capitol where he had gone
   on his father's business. Adams made
   it the subject of a message, April 15,
   1828, and the House declared the act
   censurable but did nothing to punish
   Jarvis.

592

Bemis, Samuel Flagg. John Quincy Adams
   and the Union. New York, Knopf, 1956.
   xix, 546 p.   E377.B46

593

East, Robert A. John Quincy Adams; the
   critical years: 1785-1794. New York,
   Bookman Associates [^c1962] 252 p.
                          E377.E2

594

Wiltse, Charles M. John C. Calhoun. Indianapolis, Bobbs-Merrill [1944-51]
   3 v.   E340.C15W5

595

Coit, Margaret L. John C. Calhoun, American portrait. Boston, Houghton Mifflin, 1950. 593 p.   B340.C15C63
      Bibliography: p. [573]-581.

596

Capers, Gerald M. John C. Calhoun, op-
   portunist; a reappraisal. Gainesville,
   University of Florida Press, 1960.
   275 p.   E340.C15C25

Writings

597
Jackson, Andrew. Correspondence of Andrew Jackson, edited by John Spencer Bassett. Washington, Carnegie Institution of Washington, 1926-35. 7 v. ([Carnegie Institution of Washington. Publication no. 371. Papers of the Department of Historical Research])
E382.J115

Contents.--v. 1. To April 30, 1814.--v. 2. May 1, 1814, to December 31, 1819.--v. 3. 1820-1828.--v. 4. 1829-1832.--v. 5. 1833-1838.--v. 6. 1839-1845.--v. 7. General index, by D. M. Matteson.

598
Jackson, Andrew. The statemanship of Andrew Jackson as told in his writings and speeches; edited by Francis Newton Thorpe. New York, Tandy-Thomas [c1909] 538 p.   E381.J13

599
Syrett, Harold C., ed. Andrew Jackson: his contribution to the American tradition. Indianapolis, Bobbs-Merrill [1953] 298 p.   E382.S97
(Makers of the American tradition series)

Biography

600
Eaton, John Henry. The life of Andrew Jackson, Major General in the service of the United States. Commenced by John Reid, Brevet Major, United States' Army. Completed by John Henry Eaton. Philadelphia, M. Carey. For the benefit of the children of John Reid. 1817. 425 p.   E382.E11

The somewhat enlarged edition issued at Philadelphia for the campaign of 1824 was the basis of the frequent reprintings, or thefts, of the next half-

600
Eaton, John Henry. (Cont.) century.

Will always retain interest as the work of Jackson's aide, completed by the Jackson entourage, immediately after the war which made him a national hero.

601
Walker, Alexander. Jackson and New Orleans. An authentic narrative of the memorable achievements of the American Army, under Andrew Jackson, before New Orleans, in the winter of 1814, '15. New York, J. C. Derby, 1856. 411 p.
E356.N5W2

602
Parton, James. Life of Andrew Jackson. New York, Mason Bros., 1860. 3 v.
E382.P27

The eminent biographer's last completed work was a one-volume General Jackson, written for Appleton's Great Commanders series and published in 1893, shortly after his death.

603
Sumner, William Graham. Andrew Jackson. [rev. ed.] Boston, Houghton Mifflin, 1899. 502 p. (American statesmen)
E382.S955
E176.A54, v. 17
Originally published in 1882 as Andrew Jackson as a Public Man (402 p.).

604
Brown, William Garrott. Andrew Jackson. Boston, Houghton Mifflin, 1900. 156 p. (Riverside biographical series)
E382.B87

605
Brady, Cyrus Townsend. The true Andrew Jackson. Philadelphia, Lippincott, 1906. 504 p.   E382.B8

606

Bassett, John Spencer. The life of Andrew
Jackson. New ed. New York, Macmillan,
1916. 2 v. in 1 (766 p.)
E382.B32
With minor corrections of the original edition of 1911. Reprinted in
1925, 1928, and 1931.

607

Heiskell, Samuel G. Andrew Jackson and
early Tennessee history. 2d ed.
Nashville, Ambrose Printing Co.,
1920-21. 3 v.   F436.H472
A chaotic miscellany, from which
much information can be quarried.

608

Ogg, Frederic A. The reign of Andrew
Jackson; a chronicle of the frontier
in politics. New Haven, Yale Univer-
sity Press, 1921. 249 p. (The Chron-
icles of America series, v. 20)
E173.C56, v. 20
E381.O35
"Bibliographical note": p. 237-240.
The times very skillfully set in the
framework of the career.

609

Bowers, Claude G. The party battles of
the Jackson period. Boston, Houghton
Mifflin, 1922. xix, 506 p.
E381.B79
Bibliography: p. 483-487.
A stirring narrative of the Jackson
administration, custodians for the democracy, stoutly beating off the on-
slaughts of its enemies, the forces of
aristocracy and special privilege.

610

Gammon, Samuel Rhea. The presidential
campaign of 1832. Baltimore, John
Hopkins Press, 1922. 180 p. (Johns
Hopkins University studies in histori-
cal and political science, ser. 40,
no. 1)   E383.G2
H31.J6, ser. 40, no. 1
Bibliography: p. 171-174.

611

Rowland, Eron O. (Moore). Andrew Jackson's campaign against the British,

611

Rowland, Eron O. (Moore). (Cont.)
or The Mississippi Territory in the
War of 1812, concerning the military
operations of the Americans, Creek
Indians, British, and Spanish, 1813-
1815, by Mrs. Dunbar Rowland. New
York, Macmillan, 1926. 424 p.
F341.R883
The first edition was printed in
1921, in the Publications of the Mississippi Historical Society, under the
title Mississippi Territory in the
War of 1812. The present edition is
revised and amplified.

612

Erikson, Erik McKinley. Official newspaper organs and the presidential elections of 1828, 1832 and 1836. [Nash-
ville, 1927] p. 231-247, [37]-58, 16
p.   JK524.E8 1922
Cover-title.
Thesis (Ph. D.)-Iowa University,
1922.
Reprints from the Tennessee Historical Magazine, v. 8-9.

613

James, Marquis. Andrew Jackson, the border captain. Indianapolis, Bobbs-Merrill, 1933.   E382.J26
Bibliography: p. [417]-424.

614

----- Andrew Jackson, portrait of a President. Indianapolis, Bobbs-Merrill
[c1937] 627 p.   E382.J27
Bibliography: p. [569]-578.
The two installments, which divide
at 1822, were reissued in 1938 in one
volume titled The Life of Andrew Jackson (972 p.). They have been reissued
separately as paperbacks in Grosset &
Dunlap's Universal library. To James,
Jackson "lived by valor," and governed
for the people more then of and by
them.

615

Horn, Stanley F. The Hermitage, home of
Old Hickory. Richmond, Garrett &
Massie, 1938.   E382.H79
Reissued without change by Green-

615
Horn, Stanley F. (Cont.)
berg, New York, 1950.

616
Weston, Florence. The presidential election of 1828. Washington [Ruddick
Press] 1938. 217 p.
                    JK526 1828 W4 1939
      Thesis (Ph. D.)--Catholic University
of America.
      Bibliography: p. 192-200.

617
Hammond, Bray. Jackson, [Nicholas] Biddle, and the Bank of the United States.
Journal of economic history, v. 7,
May 1947: 1-23.
      This article, which was eventually
expanded into the author's monumental
Banks and Politics in America, from
the Revolution to the Civil War
(Princeton University Press, 1957.
771 p.), traces Jackson's hostility to
the Bank of the United States to his
archaic belief that the only good mon-
ey was gold and silver, and that banks
in general were undesirable and uncon-
stitutional.

618
Lowe, Gabriel L. John H. Eaton, Jackson's campaign manager. Tennessee
historical quarterly, v. 11, June 1952:
99-147.   F431.T285, v. 11
      Eaton's activities in the presiden-
tial campaigns of 1824 and 1828 traced
through his letters in the John Coffee
and John Overton papers.

619
Ward, John William. Andrew Jackson, symbol for an age. New York, Oxford University Press, 1955. 274 p.
                    E382.W24
      Analyses the large body of contem-
porary eulogy and finds that for his
age Jackson became the embodiment of
the master concepts of nature, providence, and will.

620
Hoffman, William S. Andrew Jackson and
North Carolina politics. Chapel Hill,

620
Hoffman, William S. (Cont.)
University of North Carolina Press,
1958. 134 p. (The James Sprunt studies in history and political science,
v. 40)   F251.J28, v. 40
                    F258.J3H6
      Bibliography: p. [123]-128.

621
Caldwell, Mary French. General Jackson's
lady; a story of the life and times of
Rachel Donelson Jackson, beloved wife
of General Andrew Jackson, seventh
President of the United States. Published by the author, with the coöper-
ation of the Ladies' Hermitage Association. Nashville [Kingsport, Tenn.,
Kingsport Press] 1936. 555 p.
                    E382.1.J2C25

622
Burke, Pauline Wilcox. Emily Donelson of
Tennessee. Richmond, Va., Garrett and
Massie [1941] 2 v. illus.
                    E382.1.D6B8
      Because of the death of Mrs. Jack-
son in 1828, Mrs. Donelson, the wife
of Andrew Jackson Donelson, namesake
and ward of Andrew Jackson, was in-
vited by the President to preside over
the White House. These volumes are
filled with incidents in the social
and family life of the White House
during Jackson's administration, including the birth of the three Donelson children in the White House.

MARTIN VAN BUREN

Writings

623

Van Buren, Martin. Inquiry into the origin and course of political parties in the United States. Edited by his sons. New York, Hurd and Houghton, 1867. 436 p.   JK2261.V3

624

----- The autobiography of Martin Van Buren, edited by John C. Fitzpatrick. Washington, Govt. Print. Off., 1920. 808 p. (Annual report of the American Historical Association for the year 1918, v. 2)   E172.A60 1918, v. 2
   "The first two hundred and fifty-nine pages were edited by Mr. Worthington C. Ford."-Prefatory note.

Biography

625

Shepard, Edward M. Martin Van Buren. [Rev. ed] Boston, Houghton Mifflin, 1899. 499 p. (American statesmen)
              E387.S55
   Originally published in 1888 (404 p.).

626

Lynch, Denis Tilden. An epoch and a man, Martin Van Buren and his times. New York, Liveright, 1929. 566 p.
              E387.L98
   Bibliography: p. 547-551.

627

Whitehurst, Alto Lee. Martin Van Buren and the free soil movement. Chicago, 1935. p. 132-176.   JK2336.A7 1932
   Part of thesis (Ph. D)--University of Chicago.
   "Private edition, distributed by the University of Chicago libraries."

628

Remini, Robert V. Martin Van Buren and

628

Remini, Robert V. Martin ... (Cont.) the making of the Democratic Party. New York, Columbia University Press, 1959. 271 p.   E387.R4
   Bibliography: p. [247]-259.
   Concludes with the election of 1828.

629

Meyer, Leland W. The life and times of Colonel Richard M. Johnson of Kentucky. New York, Columbia University Press, 1932. 508 p. (Studies in history, economics and public law, no. 359)
          E346.J69M4

Writings

630

Indiana. Governor. Governors messages and letters. Messages and letters of William Henry Harrison [1801-1816], edited by Logan Esarey. Indianapolis, Indiana Historical Commission, 1922. 2 v. (Indiana historical collections, v. 7, 9)   J87.1618, v. 1-2
                    F521.I38, v. 7, 9

631

Harrison, William Henry. Remarks of General Harrison, late Envoy Extraordinary and Minister Plenipotentiary of the United States to the Republic of Colombia, on certain charges made against him by that Government. To which is added, an unofficial letter, from General Harrison to General Bolivar, on the affairs of Colombia; with notes, explanatory of his views of the present state of that country. Washington, Gales & Seaton, 1830. 69 p.
                    F2275.H32

Harrison, in the less than nine months during which he represented the United States at Bogotá, manifested such sympathy for a revolutionary faction that he was formally accused by the Colombian Government of having joined in a conspiracy to assassinate several officers of President Bolivar's administration. A few days after being superseded he addressed a letter to Bolivar exhorting him to eschew monarchy and follow the example of Washington--a letter which gained more admirers in the United States than in Colombia.

632

----- A discourse on the aborigines of the valley of the Ohio. In which the opinions of the conquest of that valley by the Iroquois, or Six Nations, in the seventeenth century, supported by Cad-

632

----- A discourse on ... (Cont.) wallader Colden ... Governor Pownal ... Dr. Franklin, the Hon. De Witt Clinton ... and Judge Haywood ... are examined and contested. To which are prefixed some remarks on the study of history. [Prepared at the request of the Historical Society of Ohio.] Cincinnati [Printed at the Cincinnati Express] 1838. 51 p. fold. map.
                    E78.04H3 1838

Biography

633

Dawson, Moses. A historical narrative of the civil and military services of Major-General William H. Harrison, and a vindication of his character and conduct as a statesman, a citizen, and a soldier. With a detail of his negotiations and wars with the Indians, until the final overthrow of the celebrated chief Tecumseh, and his brother the Prophet. Cincinnati, M. Dawson, 1824. 464 p.   E392.D27

634

Cushing, Caleb. Outlines of the life and and public services, civil and military, of William Henry Harrison. Boston, Weeks, Jordan, 1840. 71 p.
                    E392.C985

Original, finely written, and by one of the ablest Americans of the time-- these considerations will perhaps justify the inclusion of a campaign document. The historian Richard Hildreth was another penman in the Harrison ranks (The Contrast, 1840).

635

Norton, Anthony B. The great revolution of 1840. Reminiscences of the log cabin and hard cider campaign   Mount

635

Norton, Anthony B. The great ... (Cont.)
Vernon, Ohio, A. B. Norton, 1888.
376 p.   E390.N88
                JK2263 1840.N8

636

Webster, Homer J. William Henry Harrison's administration of Indiana Territory. Indianapolis, Sentinel Printing
Co., 1907. 177-297 p. (Indiana Historical Society. Publications, v. 4,
no. 3)   F521.I41, v. 4
                F526.W38

637

Goebel, Dorothy Burne. William Henry
Harrison, a political biography. Indianapolis, Historical Bureau of the
Indiana Library and Historical Dept.,
1926. 456 p. (Indiana historical collections, v. 14)   E392.G58
                   F521.L38, v. 14
   Bibliography: p. 381-422.

638

Carter, Clarence E., ed. William Henry
Harrison and the Mexican appointment,
1823-1824. Mississippi Valley historical review, v. 25, Sept. 1938: 251-
262.   F351.M69, v. 25
   Papers illustrating the pressure
which Harrison put upon President Monroe and Secretary Adams in order to
receive the appointment of first American minister to independent Mexico.

639

Cleaves, Freeman. Old Tippecanoe; William
Henry Harrison and his time. New York,
Scribner, 1939. 422 p. E392.C64
   Bibliography: p. 392-401.

640

Green, James A. William Henry Harrison,
his life and times. Richmond, Garrett
and Massie, [c1941] 536 p.
                E392.G8
   Bibliography: p. 493-529.
   Appendix I. The Harrison Literature: p. 447-483.

641

Daughters of the American Revolution.
Indiana. Francis Vigo Chapter, Vin-
cennes. Grouseland, the home of Wil-
liam Henry Harrison. [Compiled by
Benjamin F. Sager. Rev. by Mrs. W. B.
Ridgeway and Mrs. Leo Schultheis.
Vincennes.,1942] 32 p.
                F534.V7D3 1942
   First ed. published in 1928 under
title: The Harrison Mansion.

642

Gunderson, Robert Gray. The log-cabin
campaign. [Lexington] University of
Kentucky Press [1957] 292 p.
                E390.G85

643

Peckham, Howard H. Tears for Old Tippecanoe; religious interpretations of
President Harrison's death. In American Antiquarian Society, Worcester,
Mass. Proceedings. v. 69, pt. 1;
1959. Worcester. p. [17]-36.
   A look at the deluge of published
sermons occasioned by the first death
of a President in office.

Writings

644

U. S. Congress. Senate. Committee on Fi-
ance. Report [on the Bank of the Unit-
States, with Documents. Washington,
1834] 340 p. (23d Cong., 2d sess.
[Senate Document] 17) HG2529.1834.A32

Senator Tyler spent the summer and
fall of 1834 in examining the Norfolk,
Richmond, and central branches of the
Bank, and wrote and reported 48 closely printed pages (the rest being documents). No evidence was found that the
Bank had violated its charter, or that
the Government deposits were unsafe in
its hands, or that it was making a political use of its privileges.

645

Tyler, John. An address before the two
literary societies of Randolph-Macon
College, June 19, 1838. Richmond,
J. C. Walker, 1838. 18 p.   NN

646

----- An address, delivered before the
literary societies of the University of
Virginia, on the anniversary of the
declaration of independence by the
State of Virginia, June 29th, 1850.
Charlottesville, Va., J. Alexander
[1850] 24 p.   ViU

The first clause of the Constitution
of Virginia, adopted June 29, 1776,
declares that the former government
under the crown of Great Britain is
totally dissolved.

647

----- A lecture prepared at the request
of the Library Association of Petersburg, and delivered on the 4th of May,
1854. Petersburg [Va.] Banks &
Lewellen, 1854. 8 p.   HF3027.3.T9

648

----- Lecture delivered before the Mary-

648

----- Lecture delivered ... (Cont.)
land Institute for the Promotion of
the Mechanic Arts, March 20, 1855.
Subject: the prominent characters and
incidents of our history from 1812 to
1836. Published by order of the Institute. Baltimore, J. Murphy, 1855.
23 p.   E301.T98

Biography

649

Confederate States of America. Congress.
Proceedings on the announcement of the
death of Hon. John Tyler, January 20,
1862. Published by order of Congress,
by J. J. Hooper, secretary. Richmond,
Enquirer Press, 1862. 54 p.
        E397.C74 RBD

At the time of his death Tyler was
a member of the Confederate Provision-
al Congress, and had been elected to
the new Confederate House of Representatives which would convene in February.

650

Wise, Henry A. Seven decades of the Union. The humanities and materialism,
illustrated by a memoir of John Tyler,
with reminiscences of some of his great
cotemporaries. Philadelphia, Lippincott, 1872. 320 p. E301.W81

Reissued in 1881.

Governor and General Wise was asked
by the College of William and Mary to
write a memoir of its sometime rector
and chancellor, whose junior associate
he had been. The result was this
unique mixture of history, biography,
reminiscence and anecdote, in which
Tyler figures as an embodied norm by
which to measure national deviation.

651

Tyler, Lyon Gardiner. The letters and
times of the Tylers. Richmond, Whit-
tet & Shepperson, 1884-96. 3 v.
E397.T98
Vol. 3, published Williamsburg,
Va., 1896, is a supplement.
The author was President Tyler's
fourth son by his second wife, Julia
Gardiner.

652

Ewing, Thomas. Diary, August and September, 1841. American historical
review, v. 18, Oct. 1912: 97-112.
E171.A57, v. 18
As the divergence between President
Tyler and the Whig members of the cabinet whom he had inherited from Harrison revealed itself, the Secretary of
the Treasury "saw clearly that the Administration was approaching a catas-
trophe, and on [August] the 16th commenced and kept a diary for the month
preceding its dissolution."

653

Lambert, Oscar D. Presidential politics
in the United States, 1841-1844. Durham, N. C., Duke University Press,
1936. 220 p. E396.L32
Bibliography: p. 214-217.

654

Chitwood, Oliver Perry. John Tyler,
champion of the Old South. New
York, Appleton-Century [c1939] 496 p.
E397.C48
"This volume is published from a
fund contributed to the American His-
torical Association by the Carnegie
Corporation of New York."

655

Morgan, Robert J. A Whig embattled; the
Presidency under John Tyler. Lincoln,
University of Nebraska Press, 1954.
199 p. E396.M6
Bibliography: p. 191-195.

656

Wallace, Sarah A. Letters of the Pres-
identess, Julia Gardiner Tyler, 1844-
1845. Daughters of the American Rev-

656

Wallace, Sarah A. Letters of ... (Cont.)
olution magazine, v. 87, Apr. 1953:
641-646. E202.5.A12, v. 87
Letters of President Tyler's second
wife to her mother and sister, describing her eight months in the White
House.

657

Coleman, Elizabeth Tyler. Priscilla
Cooper Tyler and the American scene,
1816-1889. [University] University
of Alabama Press, 1955. 203 p.
E340.T94C6
"White House Years, 1841-1844":
p. 84-107.
Priscilla, the wife of President
Tyler's eldest son Robert, was the
daughter of an actor and had been an
actress. Since the President's first
wife was an invalid and died in September 1842, Priscilla Tyler presided
at White House functions until her
husband's departure from Washington
in March 1844.

Writings

658
Polk, James K. The diary of James K. Polk
during his Presidency, 1845 to 1849,
now first printed from the original
manuscript in the collections of the
Chicago Historical Society. Edited
and annotated by Milo Milton Quaife
with an introd. by Andrew Cunningham
McLaughlin. Chicago, McClurg, 1910.
4 v. E416.P76
F548.1.C4, v. 6-9
"This work forms volumes vi-ix of
the Chicago Historical Society's collection, a special issue of 500 copies
being printed for the purposes of that
society."

659
----- Polk; the diary of a President,
1845-1849, covering the Mexican War,
the acquisition of Oregon, and the conquest of California and the Southwest,
edited by Allan Nevins. New York,
Longmans, Green, 1952. xxxiv, 412 p.
E416.P77 1952
This selection from the 4-volume
edition was first issued, with a briefer introduction, in 1929.

660
----- Letters of James K. Polk to Cave
Johnson, 1833-1848, with introd. and
notes by St. George L. Sioussat. Ten-
nessee historical magazine, Sept. 1915,
v. 1: 209-256. F431.T28, v. 1
Johnson was, like Polk, a Tennessee
Jacksonian and served with him in the
U. S. House of Representatives. Polk
made him his Postmaster General. These
letters are nearly all marked <u>private</u>,
<u>confidential</u>, or both, and mirror
Polk's political career.

661
----- Letters of James K. Polk to Andrew
J. Donelson, 1843-1848, with introd.

661
----- Letters of ... (Cont.)
and notes by St. George L. Sioussat.
Tennessee historical magazine, Mar.
1917, v. 3: 51-73. F431.T28, v. 3
Donelson, President Jackson's nephew by marriage and his private secretary in the White House, was a figure
of consequence in the Democratic Party, and not merely because he had the
ex-President's ear.

662
----- James K. Polk and his constituents,
1831-1832. Contributed by John Spencer
Bassett. American historical review,
v. 27, Oct. 1922: 68-77.
E171.A57, v. 27
Publication of Congressman Polk's
"Memorandum book of business done for
constituents, 1st session of the 22d
Congress," an unusual kind of record.

Biography

663
Goodpasture, Albert V. The boyhood of
President Polk. Tennessee historical
magazine, v. 7, Apr. 1921: 36-50.
F431.T28, v. 7

664
McCormac, Eugene Irving. James K. Polk,
a political biography. Berkeley, University of California Press, 1922.
746 p. E417.M12
Bibliography: p. [726]-731.

665
Bassett, John Spencer, ed. The southern
plantation overseer as revealed in his
letters. Northampton, Mass., Printed
for Smith College, 1925. 280 p.
(Smith College fiftieth anniversary
publications [v. 5]) E443.B25

665
Bassett, John Spencer. (Cont.)
     Polk inherited from his father a
plantation in Fayette County, southwestern Tennessee; in 1835 he sold it
in order to acquire one in Yalobusha
County, northern Mississippi. This
publication from his papers was meant
to be a case study in plantation management, but it serves the further end
of throwing much light on Polk's private affairs. It continues after his
death until Mrs. Polk sold the proper-
ty in January 1860.

666
Moore, Powell. James K. Polk and Tennes-
     see politics, 1839-1841. In East
     Tennessee Historical Society. Publi-
     cations, no. 9, 1937: 31-52.
                    F442.1.E14, no. 9

667
Moore, Powell. James K. Polk and the
     "immortal thirteen." In East Tennes-
     see Historical Society. Publications,
     no. 11, 1939. 20-33.
                    F442.1.E14, no. 11
     The "immortal thirteen" were the
Democratic majority-of-one in the Tennessee Senate of 1841-42, whose un-
compromising party line set up the
issues on which Polk had to conduct his
unsuccessful campaign for the governorship in 1843.

668
Graebner, Norman A. James K. Polk, a
     study in Federal patronage. Mississip-
     pi Valley historical review, v. 38,
     Mar. 1952: 613-652.
                    F351.M69, v. 38

669
Sellers, Charles Grier. James K. Polk's
     political apprenticeship. In East
     Tennesee Historical Society. Publica-
     tions, no. 25, 1953: 37-53.
                    F442.1.E14, no. 25
     A more detailed treatment of Polk's
service in the Tennessee House of Representatives, 1823-25.

670
Sellers, Charles Grier. James K. Polk,
     Jacksonian, 1795-1843. Princeton,
     N. J., Princeton University Press,
     1957. 526 p.   E417.S4
     Bibliography: p. 493-509.

671
McCoy, Charles A. Polk and the Presi-
     dency. Austin, University of Texas
     Press [c1960] 238 p.
                    E417.M15

672
Nelson, Anson, and Fanny Nelson. Memo-
     rials of Sarah Childress Polk, wife
     of the eleventh President of the Unit-
     ed States. New York, A. D. F. Ran-
     dolph [1892] 284 p.   E417.N42

Writings

673

U. S. President, 1845-1849 (Polk) Messages of the President of the United States, with the correspondence, therewith communicated, between the Secretary of War and other officers of the Government, on the subject of the Mexican War. Washington, Wendell and Van Benthuysen, 1848. 1277 p. [30th Cong., 1st sess. House. Ex. doc. 60]
          E404.U59

Conveniently reprints nine earlier documents of the 29th and 30th Congresses, and includes most of General Taylor's despatches and other official correspondence during the war.

674

Taylor, Zachary. Letters of Zachary Taylor, from the battle-fields of the Mexican War; reprinted from the originals in the collection of Mr. William K. Bixby, of St. Louis, Mo. Introd. by William H. Samson. Rochester, N. Y. [Genesee Press] 1908. 194 p.
          E415.T24

Biography

675

Howard, Oliver Otis. General Taylor. New York, Appleton, 1892. 386 p. (Great commanders) E422.H85

A critical study of Taylor's military career by the well known Civil War general. Until its appearance the only lives of Taylor were the ones by routine writers published while the Mexican War was still in progress: John Frost, Joseph Reese Fry, and C. Frank Powell. Henry Montgomery's The Life of Major General Zachary Taylor, of which the 1851 edition claims to be the 20th, was continued to Taylor's death but, despite two extra chapters and some inspired hagiography, re-

675

Howard, Oliver Otis. (Cont.)
mained primarily a book on the Mexican War. The standard account of Taylor's Mexican campaigns, based on a thorough and acute analysis of the documents, is in Justin H. Smith's The War with Mexico (New York, Macmillan, 1919. 2 v.).

676

Lynch, William O. Zachary Taylor as President. Journal of Southern history, v. 4, Aug. 1938: 279-294.
          F206.J68, v. 4

Attributes Taylor's failure to exercise much influence upon the sectional crisis to John J. Crittenden's preferring the governorship of Kentucky to a cabinet post, to Taylor's refusal to substitute Robert P. Letcher, to the lack of communication between cabinet and Congress, and to Taylor's obstinate adhesion to his own compromise plan, which developed no support.

677

Dyer, Brainerd. Zachary Taylor. Baton Rouge, Louisiana State University Press, 1946. 455 p. (Southern biography series) E422.D995
"Critical essay on authorities": p. [420]-433.

678

Hamilton, Holman. Zachary Taylor. Indianapolis, Bobbs-Merrill [1941-51] 2 v. E422.H3
Contents.--[1] Soldier of the Republic.--[2] Soldier in the White House.

679

McKinley, Silas Bent, and Silas Bent. Old Rough and Ready, the life and times of Zachary Taylor. New York, Vanguard Press [1946] 329 p. E422.M15

679
McKinley, Silas Bent, and Silas Bent.
  (Cont.)
    Bibliography: p. 301-311.

MILLARD FILLMORE

Writings

680
Fillmore, Millard. Millard Fillmore papers. Edited by Frank H. Severance.
  Buffalo, Buffalo Historical Society,
  1907. 2 v. (Publications of the
  Buffalo Historical Society, v. 10-11)
        F129.B8B88, v. 10-11
    "Bibliography: some publications
  by Millard Fillmore or relating to his
  career and services": v. 2, p. 455-
  463.
    The title may mislead: when this
  publication was undertaken, it was believed that Fillmore's own papers had
  been destroyed by his son's executor
  under the terms of the latter's will.
  The Buffalo Society therefore enlisted
  Mr. Severance to undertake this compilation of his speeches, public documents, addresses, and letters in archives and manuscript repositories.
  The task was carried out with great
  thoroughness, and resulted in these
  two volumes of a total of just over
  1,000 pages. In the following year,
  1908, Fillmore's papers were redis-
  covered, largely letters received during his service as Vice President and
  President. They now fill 44 volumes
  in the Buffalo Historical Society, and
  are drawn upon in the Carman-Luthin
  articles and in Mr. Rayback's biography. Severance's first volume reprints
  Fillmore's own "Narrative of His Early
  Years" [1800-c. 1823], p. 3-15. It
  also contains a substanial biographical
  introduction, p. v-xxxvii.

681
[Fillmore, Millard] An examination of the
  question, "Is it right to require any
  religious test as a qualification to be
  a witness in a court of justice?" By
  Juridicus [pseud.] Buffalo, C. Faxon,

681
[Fillmore, Millard] An ... (Cont.)
  1832. 16 p.   NN
    Juridicus-Fillmore concluded that
  it was not only wrong, but inconsitent
  and absurd. The pamphlet, a series of
  four letters to the Buffalo Patriot
  in support of a bill which had just
  been lost in the New York Legislature,
  is reprinted in the Millard Fillmore
  Papers above, v. 1, p. 67-82.

Biography

682
Griffis, William Elliot. Millard Fill-
  more, constructive statesman, defender
  of the Constitution, President of the
  United States. Ithaca, N. Y., Andrus
  & Church [1915] 159 p.   E427.G85
    The Reverend Mr. Griffis, an early
  American specialist in Japanese cul-
  ture, took a particular interest in
  Fillmore as the President in whose ad-
  ministration Japan was "opened up."

683
Carman, Harry J., and Reinhard H. Luthin.
  The Seward-Fillmore feud and the crisis
  of 1850. The Seward-Fillmore feud and
  the disruption of the Whig Party. New
  York history, v. 24, Apr. 1943: 163-
  184; July 1943: 335-357.
              F116.N865, v. 24
    Fillmore and William H. Seward had
  been rival leaders of the New York
  Whigs since the early 1830's, and when
  the former became Vice President and
  the latter Senator they took opposite
  sides on the sectional crisis. Seward
  took a leading part in depriving Fillmore of the Whig nomination in 1852,
  but his dominance cost the party its
  Southern wing.

684
Rayback, Robert J. Millard Fillmore; biography of a President. Buffalo, Published for the Buffalo Historical Society by H. Stewart, 1959. 470 p.
(Publications of the Buffalo Historical
Society, v. 40)   E427.R3
                   F129.B8B88, v. 40
    Bibliography: p. [447]-457.

FRANKLIN PIERCE

Writings

685
Ray, Perley Orman, ed. Some papers of
Franklin Pierce, 1852-1862. American
historical review, v. 10, Oct. 1904:
110-127; Jan. 1905: 350-370.
                   E177.A57, v. 10
    28 letters, mostly to Pierce, from
Edmund Burke (of Newport, N. H.), John
W. Geary, Jefferson Davis, and others.

Biography

686
Hawthorne, Nathaniel. Life of Franklin
Pierce. Boston, Ticknor, Reed and
Fields, 1852. 144 p.
                   E432.H38
    Pierce and Hawthorne attended Bow-
doin College together and became lifelong friends, and Hawthorne owed to
Pierce most of the government jobs
which enabled him to support a family.
When the Democratic nominee asked him
to write a campaign biography, he naturally complied, and while he found the
task uncongenial, Pierce had no reason
to complain of the product. Hawthorne's appointment to the Liverpool
consulate followed the election.

687
Webster, Sidney. Franklin Pierce and his
administration. New York, Appleton
[1892] 67 p.   E432.W38
    Webster was a young New Hampshire
graduate of Harvard Law School when he
served as President Pierce's private
secretary, and had afterwards a half-

687
Webster, Sidney. Webster was ... (Cont.)
century's distinguished legal career
in New York City. This publication
reprints from the New York World a
long obituary of 1869, and a defense
of Pierce's record against statements
made in v. 5 of James Schouler's History of the United States.

688
Nichols, Roy F. Franklin Pierce, Young
Hickory of the Granite Hills. [2d ed.,
completely rev.] Philadelphia, University of Pennsylvania Press, [1958]
xvii, 625 p.   E432.N63 1958
    Bibliography: p. 577-593.
    Originally published in 1931 (615
p.).

JAMES BUCHANAN

Writings

689

Buchanan, James. The works of James Buchanan; collected and edited by John Bassett Moore. Philadelphia, Lippincott, 1908-11. 12 v. E337.8.B9

690

----- Mr. Buchanan's administration on the eve of the rebellion. New York, Appleton, 1866. 296 p. E436.B91

Biography

691

Curtis, George Ticknor. Life of James Buchanan, fifteenth President of the United States. New York, Harper, 1883. 2 v. E437.C98

692

King, Horatio. Turning on the light; a dispassionate survey of President Buchanan's administration, from 1860 to its close. Philadelphia, Lippincott, 1895. 419 p. E436.K52

King, who had been first assistant postmaster general since 1854, took charge of the department after the withdrawal of the southern cabinet members. His light is favorable to the administration's efforts to preserve peace.

693

Hensel, William U. The attitude of James Buchanan, a citizen of Lancaster County, toward the institution of slavery in the United States. Lancaster, Pa., New Era Printing Co., 1911. 20 p. E437.H51

694

Hensel, William U. The religious convictions and character of James Buchanan, fifteenth President of the United States--a citizen of Lancaster County--

694

Hensel, William U. The ... (Cont.) a member of the Presbyterian Church. Lancaster, Pa., Intelligencer Print, 1912. 34 p. E437.H52

695

Auchampaugh, Philip G. James Buchanan and his Cabinet on the eve of secession. [Lancaster, Pa.] Priv. print., 1926. 224 p. E436.A75
Bibliography: p. 202-210.

696

Sioussat, St. George L. James Buchanan, Secretary of State, March 5, 1845, to March 6, 1849. In Bemis, Samuel Flagg, ed. The American secretaries of state and their diplomacy. v. 5. New York, Knopf, 1928. p. 237-336, 391-416. E183.7.B46, v. 5

697

Klein, Philip Shriver. The story of Wheatland. Lancaster, Pa., Junior League of Lancaster, 1936. 62 p. E437.K54

On retiring as Secretary of State in 1849, Buchanan sold his house in Lancaster and bought Wheatland, a lovely country estate a mile to the west of the town, where he could take better care of his orphaned nephews and nieces. It was his home until his death in 1868, and is now a historic house open to the public.

698

Auchampaugh, Philip G. James Buchanan: a political portrait, 1856, according to his friends and enemies. [Reno? Nev., 1946] 42 p. E437.A8

699

Nichols, Roy F. James Buchanan: lessons in leadership in trying times. In

80

699
Nichols, Roy F.   James ... (Cont.)
   Dickinson College, <u>Carlisle, Pa.</u> Bul-
   wark of liberty; early years at Dickinson. [New York] F. H. Revell [1950]
   p. 165-174.   LD1663.A5
      Suggests that Buchanan was nominat-
   ed in 1856 because the party leaders
   "wanted a man who would not take ini-
   tiative, who was timid, who would take
   refuge in words, who would not inter-
   fere with their control."

700
Baylen, Joseph O.   James Buchanan's "calm
   of despotism." Pennsylvania magazine
   of history and biography, v. 77, July
   1953: 294-310.   F146.P65, v. 77
      An analysis of Buchanan's mission
   to St. Petersburg, 1832-33.

701
Klein, Philip Shriver. James Buchanan and
   Ann Coleman. Pennsylvania history,
   v. 21, Jan. 1954: 1-20.
                        F146.P597, v. 21
      A detailed account of Buchanan's
   courting of the daughter of a prosper-
   ous ironmaster of Lancaster. Her sudden death a few days after a lovers'
   quarrel in December 1819 is usually
   given as the reason for Buchanan remaining a bachelor.

702
Halstead, Murat. Trimmers, trucklers &
   temporizers; notes of Murat Halstead
   from the political conventions of 1856.
   Edited by William B. Hesseltine [and]
   Rex G. Fisher. Madison, State Historical Society of Wisconsin, 1961. 114
   p.   E435.H2

703
Klein, Philip Shriver. President James
   Buchanan, a biography. University
   Park, Pennsylvania State University
   Press [1962] xviii, 506 p.
                        E437.K53
      Bibliography: p. 473-490.
      The bibliography includes a section
   on "Historical articles" (p. 486-490)
   including many on Buchanan, especially
   in the <u>Pennsylvania Magazine of History</u>

703
Klein, Philip Shriver. (Cont.)
   <u>and Biography</u> and the <u>Journal</u> of the
   Lancaster County Historical Society.

704
Stillwell, Lucille. John Cabell Breckin-
   ridge. Caldwell, Idaho, Caxton Printers, 1936. 196 p.   E415.9.B7988
      Bibliography: p.[183]-189.

Writings

705
Lincoln, Abraham. Complete works. Edited by John G. Nicolay and John Hay. With a general introd. by Richard Watson Gilder and special articles by other eminent persons. New and enl. ed. New York, Tandy-Thomas Co. [c1905] 12 v.   E457.91 1905b
   "Memorial edition."
   "Lincoln bibliography, compiled by Daniel Fish": v. 11, p. [135]-380.
   Nicolay and Hay published their edition of the Complete Works four years after their History, in 1894. It included 1736 separate items in two volumes, and was and still is a very convenient work to consult. Tandy's enlargement added 518 more items, but his format, with its typographical inflation and other padding, ignored convenience.

706
----- Collected works. The Abraham Lincoln Association, Springfield, Illinois. Ray P. Basler, editor; Marion Dolores Pratt and Lloyd A. Dunlap, assistant editors. New Brunswick, N. J., Rutgers University Press, 1953-55. 9 v.   E457.91 1953
   Contents.--1. 1824-1848.--2. 1848-1858.--3. 1858-1860.--4. 1860-1861.--5. 1861-1862.--6. 1862-1863.--7. 1863--1864.--8. 1864-1865.--Index.

707
----- An autobiography of Abraham Lincoln, consisting of the personal portions of his letters, speeches and conversations. Compiled and annotated by Nathaniel W. Stephenson. Indianapolis, Bobbs-Merrill [1926] 501 p.
        E457.L735

708
----- The life and writings of Abraham

708
----- The life ... (Cont.)
Lincoln. Edited, and with a biographical essay, by Philip Van Doren Stern; with an introd., "Lincoln in his writings," by Allan Nevins. New York, The Modern Library [1942] xxvi, 863 p.
        E457.92 1942b

709
----- Abraham Lincoln: his speeches and writings. Edited with critical and analytical notes by Roy P. Basler. Preface by Carl Sandburg. Cleveland, World Pub. Co. [1946] xxx, 843 p.
        E457.92 1946

710
----- Abraham Lincoln, his autobiographical writings now brought together for the first time and prefaced with an introductory comment by Paul M. Angle. New Brunswick, N. J. Rutgers University Press, 1948. 62 p.
        E457.92 1948a

711
----- The Lincoln encyclopedia; the spoken and written words of A. Lincoln arranged for ready reference. Compiled and edited by Archer H. Shaw, with an introd. by David C. Mearns. New York, Macmillan, 1950. 395 p.
        E457.92 1950

712
----- The living Lincoln: the man, his mind, his times, and the war he fought, reconstructed from his own writings. Edited by Paul M. Angle and Earl Schenck Miers. New Brunswick, N. J., Rutgers University Press, 1955. 673 p.   E457.92 1955

713
----- Abraham Lincoln: selected

713

----- Abraham Lincoln: ... (Cont.)
speeches, messages, and letters. Edited, with an introd. and notes, by T.
Harry Williams. New York, Rinehart
[1957] xxi, 290 p. (Rinehart editions, 82)   E457.92 1957

714

----- The Lincoln ideals, his personality and principles as relfected in his
own words. Washington, Lincoln Sesquicentennial Commission [1959] 49 p.
          E457.2.L74

715

Howells, William Dean. Life of Abraham
Lincoln. Springfield, Ill., The Abraham Lincoln Association, 1938. xvii
p., facsim. (p. xi-xii, 17-94)
          E457.H86
     "This campaign biography corrected
by the hand of Abraham Lincoln in the
summer of 1860 is reproduced here with
careful attention to the appearance of
the original volume."
     Reproduction of a part of Samuel C.
Parks' copy of a work, with title page
reading: Lives and speeches of Abraham Lincoln and Hannibal Hamlin. Columbus, O., Follett, Foster, 1860. A
ms. note signed by Parks and dated
May 22, 1901, attests that Lincoln's
corrections were written at his request. They have been generally accepted as having high autobiographical
value. A similar facsimile with a
longer introduction (xxxii p.) was
issued at Bloomington by the Indiana
University Press in 1960.

716

Mearns, David Chambers. The Lincoln papers; the story of the collection, with
selections to July 4, 1861; introd. by
Carl Sandburg. Garden City, N. Y.,
Doubleday, 1948. 2 v. (xvii, 681 p.)
          E457.92 1948
     The selections consist chiefly of
letters and memoranda to Abraham Lincoln from the Robert Todd Lincoln Collection in the Library of Congress.

717

Lincoln, Abraham. Created equal? The
complete Lincoln-Douglas debates of
1858. Edited and with an introd. by
Paul M. Angle. [Chicago] University
of Chicago Press [1958] 421 p.
          E457.4.L77

718

----- The Illinois political campaign of
1858; a facsimile of the printer's
copy and his debates with Senator
Stephen Arnold Douglas as edited and
prepared for press by Abraham Lincoln.
[Washington] Library of Congress [1958]
212 p. (p. 25-212, facsim.)
          E457.4.L772
     At head of title: The Alfred
Whital Stern Collection of Lincoln-
iana.

719

----- In the name of the people; speeches
and writings of Lincoln and Douglas in
the Ohio campaign of 1859. Edited,
with an introd., by Harry V. Jaffa and
Robert W. Johannsen. Columbus, Published for the Ohio Historical Society
by the Ohio State University Press
[1959] 307 p.   E457.4.L773

720

----- Conversations with Lincoln. Compiled, edited, and annotated by Charles M. Segal. New York, Putnam [1961]
448 p.   E457.15.L5
     Bibliography: p. 429-437.

Biography

721

Carpenter, Francis B. Six months at the
White House with Abraham Lincoln; the
story of a picture. New York, Hurd
and Houghton, 1866. 359 p.
          E457.15.C313
     By the young painter of the Eman-
cipation Proclamation group. Frequently reissued under the less appropriate title The Inner Life of Abraham Lincoln.

722

Keckley, Elizabeth (Hobbs). **Behind the**
scenes; or, Thirty years a slave, and
four years in the White House. New
York, G. W. Carleton, 1868. 371 p.
E457.15.K26
The author, born a slave at Dinwid-
die Court House in Virginia, entered
the White House as Mrs. Lincoln's
dressmaker.

723

Lamon, Ward Hill. The life of Abraham
Lincoln; from his birth to his inauguration as President. Boston, J. R.
Osgood, 1872. 547 p. E457.L22
Much of the material came from William H. Herndon, and the actual writing was done by Chauncey F. Black.
However, there emerged the first close-
up, which retains many points of interest.

724

Welles, Gideon. Lincoln and Seward; remarks upon the memorial address of
Chas. Francis Adams, on the late William H. Seward. New York, Sheldon,
1874. 215 p. E456.W44
It may be doubted whether very many
people shared Minister Adams' delusion
that Secretary Seward was the Lincoln
administration, but, for such as did,
Secretary Welles certainly dispelled
it. Albert Mordell has lately collected Welles' magazine articles on
the war and reconstruction under the
title Selected Essays (New York, Twayne
Publishers [1959-60] 2 v.).

725

Arnold, Isaac N. The life of Abraham
Lincoln. Chicago, Jansen, McClurg,
1885. 462 p. E457.A753
By a personal friend and political
associate, it has some first-hand qualities in spite of its general air of
reticent discretion.

726

Browne, Francis F., comp. The everyday
life of Abraham Lincoln. Lincoln's
life and character portrayed by those
who knew him. New York, N. D. Thomp-

726

Browne, Francis F., comp. (Cont.)
son, 1886. 747 p. E457.B88
The revised edition of 1913 is more
of a biography, and by so much less of
a collection of first-hand materials.

727

Rice, Allen Thorndike, ed. Reminiscences
of Abraham Lincoln by distinguished
men of his time. Collected and edited
by Allen Thorndike Rice. New York,
North American Pub. Co., 1886. lxix,
656 p. E457.15.R49 1886
A "revised edition" of 1909 merely
omits a dozen contributions.

728

Herndon, William H., and Jesse William
Weik. Herndon's Lincoln; the true
story of a great life, the history and
personal recollections of Abraham Lincoln. Chicago, Belford, Clarke [c1889]
3 v. (xx, 638 p.) E457.H55

729

----- Herndon's life of Lincoln, the
history and personal recollections of
Abraham Lincoln, as originally written
by William H. Herndon and Jesse W.
Weik, with an introd. and notes by
Paul M. Angle. New York, A. & C. Boni,
1930. xlvi, 511 p. E457.H575

730

Nicolay, John G., and John Hay. Abraham
Lincoln; a history. New York, Century
Co., 1890. 10 v. E457.N653

731

Stoddard, William O. Inside the White
House in war times. New York, C. L.
Webster, 1890. 244 p. E456.S86

732

Chittenden, Lucius E. Recollections of
President Lincoln and his administra-
tion. New York, Harper, 1891. 470 p.
E457.C54

733

McClure, Alexander K. Abraham Lincoln
and men of war-times; some personal
recollections of war and politics dur-

733
McClure, Alexander K. Abraham ... (Cont.)
ing the Lincoln administration. Philadelphia, The Times Pub. Co., 1892.
462 p.   E467.M12

734
Brooks, Noah. Washington in Lincoln's
time. New York, Century Co., 1895.
328 p.   E501.B87
     An edition by Herbert Mitgang (New
York, Rinehart [1958]) adds some material on the author.

735
McCarthy, Charles H. Lincoln's plan of
reconstruction. New York, McClure,
Phillips, 1901. xxiv, 504 p.
                E456.M23

736
Nicolay, John G. A short life of Abraham Lincoln, condensed from Nicolay
and Hay's Abraham Lincoln: a history.
New York, Century Co., 1902. 578 p.
                E457.N655
     A skillful condensation of no. 730.

737
Bates, David Homer. Lincoln in the telegraph office; recollections of the
U. S. Military Telegraph Corps during
the Civil War. New York, Century Co.,
1907. 432 p.   E457.15.B32

738
DeWitt, David Miller. The assassination
of Abraham Lincoln and its expiation.
New York, Macmillan, 1909. 302 p.
                E457.5.D52

739
Abraham Lincoln, by some men who knew
him; being personal recollections of
Judge Owen T. Reeves [and four others],
with introd. by Isaac N. Phillips.
Bloomington, Ill., Pantagraph Printing
and Stationery Co. [1910] 167 p.
                E457.15.A15
     Reprinted with introduction and
notes by Paul M. Angle: Chicago, A-
mericana House Publishers, 1950.

740
Fite, Emerson D. The Presidential campaign of 1860. New York, Macmillan,
1911. 356 p.   E44.F54

741
Lamon, Ward Hill. Recollections of Abraham Lincoln, 1847-1865. Edited by
Dorothy Lamon Teillard. Washington,
The Editor, 1911. xxxvi, 337 p.
                E457.L24
     Put together by Lamon's daughter
from her father's rather fragmentary
materials.

742
Welles, Gideon. Diary of Gideon Welles,
Secretary of the Navy under Lincoln
and Johnson, with an introd. by John
T. Morse, Jr. Boston, Houghton Mifflin, 1911. 3 v.   E468.W443
     Preface signed: Edgar T. Welles.
Contents.--1. 1861-March 30, 1864.--
2. April 1, 1864-December 31, 1866.--3.
January 1, 1867-June 6, 1869.
     A new edition by Howard K. Beale
was published in 1960 by W. W. Norton
of New York. Since, however, its text
consists of a photographic reproduction of the old edition with pen-and-
ink corrections, it can be consulted
on points of detail but is quite un-
suited for continuous reading.

743
Nicolay, Helen. Personal traits of Abraham Lincoln. New York, Century Co.,
1912. 387 p.   E457.N643
     Miss Nicolay wrote the book her
father never got around to, on a subject which received no adequate presentation in his and Hay's 10-volume
chronicle.

744
Charnwood, Godfrey Rathbone Benson, 1st
baron. Abraham Lincoln. New York,
Holt, 1917. 482 p. (Makers of the
nineteenth century) E457.C47
     First edition: London, Constable,
1916. It has seldom been out of print
in America, having been reprinted by
Pocket Books in the early days of the
American paperback.

745
Tarbell, Ida M. The life of Abraham Lincoln, drawn from original sources and containing many speeches, letters and telegrams hitherto unpublished. New ed., with new matter. New York, Macmillan, 1917. 2 v. E457.T18
First edition: New York, McClure, Phillips, 1900. Latest printing in L. C., 1928.

746
Barton, William E. The soul of Abraham Lincoln. New York, G. H. Doran [1920] 407 p. E457.2.B29
"A condensed bibliography": p. 387-400.

747
Stephenson, Nathaniel W. Lincoln; an account of his personal life, especially of its springs of action as revealed and deepened by the ordeals of war. Indianapolis, Bobbs-Merrill [1922] 474 p. E457.S83
Bibliography: p. 423-429.

748
Weik, Jesse W. The real Lincoln; a portrait. Boston, Houghton Mifflin, 1922. 323 p. E457.W4
The result of 30 years of further study of Lincoln's private life and personal traits by W. H. Herndon's literary partner.

749
Dodge, Daniel Kilham. Abraham Lincoln, master of words. New York, Appleton, 1924. 178 p. E457.2.D63

750
Tarbell, Ida M. In the footsteps of the Lincolns. New York, Harper, 1924. 418 p. E457.3.T175

751
Barton, William E. The life of Abraham Lincoln. Indianapolis, Bobbs-Merrill [1925] 2 v. E457.B3

752
Clark, Allen C. Abraham Lincoln in the National Capital. Washington [W. F.

752
Clark, Allen C. Abraham ... (Cont.) Roberts]1925. 179 p. E457.C58
Reprinted from v. 27 of the Records of the Columbia Historical Society, Washington.

753
Sandburg, Carl. Abraham Lincoln, the prairie years. New York, Harcourt, Brace [1926] 2 v. E457.3.S22

754
Warren, Louis A. Lincoln's parentage & childhood; a history of the Kentucky Lincolns supported by documentary evidence. New York, Century Co., 1926. 392 p. E457.32.W283
Bibliography: p. 359-366.

755
Beveridge, Albert J. Abraham Lincoln, 1809-1858. Boston, Houghton Mifflin [1928] 2 v. E457.3.B574
Senator Beveridge had worked for over 10 years on this biography, left unfinished by his sudden death at the age of 64. It was seen through the press by Worthington Chauncey Ford.

756
Barton, William E. The lineage of Lincoln. Indianapolis, Bobbs-Merrill [c1929] 419 p. E457.32.B23
"A critical bibliography": p. 393-397.

757
Lewis, Lloyd. Myths after Lincoln. New York, Harcourt, Brace [1929] 422 p. E457.5.L67
"Sources": p. 411-414.

758
Shaw, Albert. Abraham Lincoln; profusely illustrated with contemporary cartoons, portraits and scenes. New York, Review of Reviews Corp., 1929. 2 v. E457.3.S51
Contents--v. 1. His path to the Presidency.--v. 2. The year of his election.

759
Townsend, William H. Lincoln and his
   wife's home town [Lexington, Ky.] Indianapolis, Bobbs-Merrill [c1929]
   402 p.   E457.T84

760
Barton, William E. Lincoln at Gettysburg: what he intended to say; what
   he said; what he was reported to have
   said; what he wished he had said. Indianapolis, Bobbs-Merrill [c1930]
   263 p.   E457.B315

761
Bates, Edward. Diary, 1859-66, edited by
   Howard K. Beale. Washington, U. S.
   Govt. Print. Off., 1933. xvi, 685 p.
   (American Historical Association.
   Annual report for 1930, v. 4)
                     E172.A60 1930, v. 4

762
Angle, Paul M. "Here I have lived"; a
   history of Lincoln's Springfield,
   1821-1865. Springfield, Ill., The A-
   braham Lincoln Association, 1935.
   313 p.   F529.S7A3
      Reprinted for the Association in
   1950 by the Rutgers University Press.

763
Basler, Roy P. The Lincoln legend; a
   study in changing conceptions. Boston, Houghton Mifflin, 1935. 335 p.
                     E457.B35
                     Z8505.B31
      "A classified bibliography of poet-
   ry, fiction, and drama dealing with
   Lincoln": p. 309-[327].

764
Wilson, Rufus Rockwell. Lincoln in por-
   traiture. Sixty-two portraits. New
   York, Press of the Pioneers, 1935.
   317 p.   E457.6.W55

765
Woldman, Albert A. Lawyer Lincoln. Boston, Houghton Mifflin, 1936. 347 p.
                     E472.2.W85

766
Baringer, William E. Lincoln's rise to

766
Baringer, William E. Lincoln's ...(Cont.)
   power. Boston, Little, Brown, 1937.
   373 p.   E457.3.B24

767
Hay, John. Lincoln and the Civil War in
   the diaries and letters of John Hay.
   Selected and with an introd. by Tyler
   Dennett. New York, Dodd, Mead, 1939.
   348 p.   E664.H41H42

768
Sandburg, Carl. Abraham Lincoln; the war
   years. With 414 halftones of photographs and 249 cuts of cartoons, letters, documents. New York, Harcourt,
   Brace, 1939. 4 v.   E457.4.S36

769
Bryan, George S. The great American
   myth. New York, Carrick & Evans,
   1940. 436 p.   E457.5.B88
      Stanton's response to the assasin-
   ation with a singular combination of
   secrecy, melodrama and ineptitude has
   given rise to a tangled growth of legend and conjecture, which is vigor-
   ously beaten down here.

770
Whitney, Henry Clay. Life on the cir-
   cuit with Lincoln. Introd. and notes
   by Paul M. Angle. Caldwell, Idaho,
   Caxton Printers, 1940. 530 p.
                     E457.W63
      First published in 1892.

771
Villard, Henry. Lincoln on the eve of
   '61; a journalist's story. Edited by
   Harold G. & Oswald Garrison Villard.
   New York, Knopf, 1941. 105 p.
                     E457.4.V55

772
Williams, Thomas Harry. Lincoln and the
   radicals. [Madison] University of
   Wisconsin Press [c1941] 413 p.
                     E459.W5
      Bibliography: p. 387-394.

773
Potter, David M. Lincoln and his party

773

Potter, David M. Lincoln ... (Cont.)
in the seccession crisis. New Haven,
Yale University Press, 1942. 408 p.
(Yale historical publications. Studies, 13)   E440.5.P856
     "Bibliographical note": p. [376]-
388.

774

Wilson, Rufus Rockwell, ed. Lincoln a-
mong his friends: a sheaf of intimate
memories. Assembled and annotated by
Rufus Rockwell Wilson. Caldwell, Idaho, Caxton Printers, 1942. 506 p.
               E457.15.W68

775

Carman, Harry J., and Reinhard H. Luthin.
Lincoln and the patronage. New York,
Columbia University Press, 1943. 375
p.   E456.C36
     Bibliography: p. [339]-364.

776

Pratt, Harry E. The personal finances of
Abraham Lincoln. Springfield, Ill.,
The Abraham Lincoln Association, 1943.
198 p.   E457.2.P9

777

Luthin, Reinhard H. The first Lincoln
campaign. Cambridge, Harvard University Press, 1944. 328 p.
               E440.L85
     Bibliography: p. [287]-308.

778

Meserve, Frederick Hill, and Carl Sandburg. The photographs of Abraham Lincoln. New York, Harcourt Brace [1944]
30 p., 95 plates on 48 l.
               E457.6.M569

779

Pratt, Harry E., ed. Concerning Mr. Lincoln, in which Abraham Lincoln is pic-
tured as he appeared to letter writers
of his time. Springfield, Ill., The
Abraham Lincoln Association, 1944.
145 p.   E457.15.P8

780

Baringer, William E. A house dividing;

780

Baringer, William E. A ... (Cont.)
Lincoln as President elect. Springfield, Ill., The Abraham Lincoln Association, 1945. 356 p.
               E457.4.B245
     Bibliography: p. 339-347.

781

Crenshaw, Ollinger. The slave states in
the Presidential election of 1860.
Baltimore, Johns Hopkins Press, 1945.
332 p. (The Johns Hopkins University
studies in historical and political
science, ser. 63, no. 3)
               E440.C88 1945a
               H31.J6, ser. 63, no. 3

782

Monaghan, James. Diplomat in carpet
slippers; Abraham Lincoln deals with
foreign affairs, by Jay Monaghan. Indianapolis, Bobbs-Merrill [1945]
505 p.   E469.M75
     "Sources": p. 465-482.

783

Randall, James G. Lincoln, the President. New York, Dodd, Mead, 1945-55.
4 v. (American political leaders)
               E457.R2
     Vol. 4 by J. G. Randall and Rich-
ard N. Current.
     Contents.--v. 1-2. Springfield to
to Gettysburg.--v.3. Midstream.--v.
4. Last full measure.
     The bibliographies of this work
(v. 2: 343-400; v. 4: 380-397) provide a notably full listing of articles pertaining to Lincoln in scholarly periodicals. Since we have had no
room for such articles here, the user
of this list is referred to Lincoln,
the President.

784

Ridley, Maurice R. Abraham Lincoln.
London, Blackie & Son [1945] 208 p.
(Great lives)   E457.R5
     "First published 1944. Reprinted
1945."
     Thoughtful, well-digested and sim-
ply presented, this book was abreast
of the best authorities available at

784
Ridley, Maurice R. (Cont.)
    the time of its composition and is a-
    mong the most rewarding of the brief
    lives. Written for a British audience,
    it has never been published in the U-
    nited States.

785
Wilson, Rufus Rockwell, ed. Intimate mem-
    ories of Lincoln. Assembled and anno-
    tated by Ruful Rockwell Wilson. Elmi-
    ra, N. Y., Primavera Press, 1945.
    629 p.   E457.15.W67

786
Wilson, Rufus Rockwell. Lincoln in car-
    icature; 165 poster cartoons and draw-
    ings for the press. Assembled and de-
    scribed by Rufus Rockwell Wilson. El-
    mira, N. Y., Primavera Press, 1945.
    331 p.   E457.63.W752

787
Angle, Paul M. A shelf of Lincoln books;
    a critical, selective bibliography of
    Lincolnia. New Brunswick, N. J., Rut-
    gers University Press, in association
    with The Abraham Lincoln Association
    of Springfield, Ill., 1946. xvii, 142
    p.   Z8505.A6
    A masterly elucidation, which the
    learned author has unfortunately never
    found time to bring up to date.

788
Bullard, Frederic Lauriston. Abraham Lin-
    coln & the Widow Bixby. New Brunswick,
    N. J., Rutgers University Press, 1946.
    154 p.   E457.96 1864B 1946

789
Hendrick, Burton J. Lincoln's war cabi-
    net. Boston, Little, Brown, 1946.
    482 p.   E456.H4

790
Wagenknecht, Edward C., ed. Abraham Lin-
    coln; his life, work, and character.
    An anthology of history and biography,
    fiction, poetry, drama, and belles-let-
    tres. New York, Creative Age Press,
    1947. xvii, 661 p.
                    E457.9.W2

791
Randall, James G. Lincoln and the South.
    Baton Rouge, Louisiana State Univer-
    sity Press, 1946. 161 p. (The Walter
    Lynwood Fleming lectures in southern
    history)   E457.R18

792
Angle, Paul M., ed. The Lincoln reader,
    New Brunswick, N. J., Rutgers Univer-
    sity Press, 1947. 564 p.
                    E457.A58
    Bibliography: p. [544]-547.
    Issued as a paperback: New York,
    Pocket Books [1955] (626 p.).

793
Randall, James G. Lincoln, the liberal
    statesman. New York, Dodd, Mead, 1947.
    266 p.   E457.4.R24

794
Spears, Zarel C., and Robert S. Barton.
    Berry and Lincoln, frontier merchants;
    the store that "winked out." New York,
    Stratford House, 1947. 140 p.
                    E457.35.S65

795
Thomas, Benjamin P. Portrait for poster-
    ity: Lincoln and his biographers.
    Illustrated by Romaine Proctor. New
    Brunswick, N. J., Rutgers University
    Press, 1947. xvii, 329 p.
                    E457.T43
    Bibliography: p. 311-318.

796
Cramer, John Henry. Lincoln under enemy
    fire, the complete account of his ex-
    periences during Early's attack on
    Washington. Baton Rouge, Louisiana
    State University Press [1948] 138 p.
                    E476.66.C9
    Bibliography: p. 125-130.

797
Donald, David H. Lincoln's Herndon. In-
    trod. by Carl Sandburg. New York,
    Knopf, 1948. xv, 392, xxiii p.
                    E457.4.H558
    Bibliography: p. 375-392.

798
Hesseltine, William B. Lincoln and the
war governors. New York, Knopf, 1948.
405, xxii p.   E457.4.H6 1948
    Bibliography: p. 395-405.

799
Jones, Edgar De Witt. Lincoln and the
preachers. New York, Harper [1948]
xviii, 203 p.   E457.2.J76

800
Potter, David M. The Lincoln theme and
American national historiography, an
inaugural lecture delivered before the
University of Oxford on 19 November
1947. Oxford, Clarendon Press, 1948.
24 p.   E457.P68

801
Riddle, Donald W. Lincoln runs for Con-
gress. A publication of The Abraham
Lincoln Association, Springfield, Ill.
New Brunswick, N. J., Rutgers Univer-
sity Press, 1948. 217 p.
                    E457.35.R52

802
Baringer, William E. Lincoln's Vandalia,
a pioneer portrait. Illustrated by
Romaine Proctor. New Brunswick, N. J.,
Rutgers University Press, 1949. 141 p.
                    E457.35.P225
    "A publication of The Abraham Lin-
coln Association, Springfield, Illinois."

803
Cuthbert, Norma B., ed. Lincoln and the
Baltimore plot, 1861; from Pinkerton
records and related papers. San Mari-
no, Calif., Huntington Library, 1949.
xxii, 161 p.   E457.4.C88

804
Nicolay, Helen. Lincoln's secretary, a
biography of John G. Nicolay. New
York, Longmans, Green, 1949. 363 p.
                    E467.1.N5N5

805
Sandburg, Carl. Lincoln collector; the
story of Oliver R. Barrett's great
private collection. New York, Har-

805
Sandburg, Carl. Lincoln ... (Cont.)
court, Brace, 1949. 344 p.
                    E457.65.S3

806
Wheare, Kenneth C. Abraham Lincoln and
the United States. New York, Macmillan, 1949. 286 p. (Teach yourself
history library)
                    E457.W54 1949

807
Harper, Robert S. Lincoln and the press.
New York, McGraw-Hill [1951] 418 p.
                    E457.H28
    Bibliography: p. [397]-401.

808
Randall, James G. Constitutional problems under Lincoln. Rev. ed. Urbana,
University of Illinois Press, 1951.
xxxiii, 596 p.   JK201.R3 1951
    Bibliography: p. 531-563.
    First edition: New York, Appleton,
1926.

809
Williams, Wayne C. A rail splitter for
President. [Denver] University of Den-
ver Press [1951] 242 p.
                    E457.4.W64
    Bibliography: p. 240-242.

810
Ballard, Colin R. The military genius of
Abraham Lincoln; an essay, with a pref.
by Fletcher Pratt. Cleveland, World
Pub. Co.[1952] 246 p.
                    E457.B19 1952
    First edition: London, Oxford Uni-
versity Press, 1926.

811
Bullard, Frederic Lauriston. Lincoln in
marble and bronze. New Brunswick,
N. J., Rutgers University Press [1952]
353 p. illus.   E457.6.B88
    "A publication of The Abraham Lin-
coln Association, Springfield, Illinois."

812
Bullard, Frederic Lauriston. Was "Abe"

812

Bullard, Frederic Lauriston. (Cont.)
Lincoln a gentleman? Boston, Boston
University Press, 1952. 25 p.
E457.2.B95
Dr. Bullard's paper was read to the
Boston Lincoln Group in 1944 and published soon after his death. After de-
liberating whether he told indecent
stories or ate beans with a knife, it
credits Lincoln with the essential
qualities of a gentleman.

813

Chambrun, Charles Adolphe de Pineton,
marquis de. Impressions of Lincoln
and the Civil War, a foreigner's account. Translated from the French by
Aldebert de Chambrun. New York, Random House [1952] 174 p.
E457.15.C45
The author's letters to his wife
from December 20, 1864, to June 13,
1865.
Chambrun did not reach Washington
until Feb. 22, 1865, but was received
several times by President and Mrs.
Lincoln, attended the inauguration, and
was taken to Richmond in their party.
After the assassination he prepared a
report on the trial for the French Minister of Foreign Affairs, and his com-
ments throughout are those of an in-
telligent and sympathetic observer. He
said of the President, on Feb. 27, "Nobody could be less of a parvenu."

814

Thomas, Benjamin P. Abraham Lincoln, a
biography. New York, Knopf, 1952.
xiv, 548, xii p. E457.T427 1952
Bibliography: p. [523]-548.

815

Williams, Thomas Harry. Lincoln and his
generals. New York, Knopf, 1952. 363
p. E470.W78
Bibliography: p. 355-363.

816

Woldman, Albert A. Lincoln and the Russians. Cleveland, World Pub. Co.
[1952] 311 p. E469.W6
Bibliography: p. 299-304.

817

Horner, Harlan Hoyt. Lincoln and Gree-
ley. [Urbana] University of Illinois
Press, 1953. 432 p.
E457.2.H79
Bibliography: p. 407-413.

818

Chase, Salmon P. Inside Lincoln's Cabinet; the Civil War diaries of Salmon
P. Chase. Edited by David Donald.
New York, Longmans, Green, 1954. 342
p. E415.9.C4A3

819

Hamilton, Charles Granville. Lincoln and
the Know Nothing movement. Washington,
Public Affairs Press, [1954] 24 p.
maps. (Annals of American research)
JK2341.A6H3
Bibliography: p. 21-24.
Compares election statistics of 1856
and 1860 and concludes that the essential element in Lincoln's victory was
the transfer of Know-Nothing votes to
the Republicans in the six salient
States of Illinois, Indiana, Iowa, New
York, Ohio, and Pennsylvania.

820

Moore, Guy W. The case of Mrs. Surratt:
her controversial trial and execution
for conspiracy in the Lincoln assassination. Norman, University of Oklahoma Press [c1954] 142 p.
E457.5.S985M6
Bibliography: p. 119-132.

821

Sandburg, Carl. Abraham Lincoln; the
prairie years and the war years. New
York, Harcourt, Brace [1954] 762 p.
E457.S215
"Sources and acknowledgments": p.
743-747.
A condensation of nos. 753 and 768
above.

822

Thomas, Benjamin P. Lincoln's New Salem.
Drawings by Romaine Proctor. New and
rev. ed. New York, Knopf, 1954. 166
p. E457.35.T47 1954
First published in 1934.

823
Zornow, William Frank. Lincoln & the
party divided. Norman, University of
Oklahoma Press [1954] 264 p.
E458.4.Z6
Bibliography: p. 223-247.
A study of the Presidential elec-
tion of 1864.

824
Townsend, William H. Lincoln and the
Bluegrass; slavery and civil war in
Kentucky. [Lexington] University of
Kentucky Press [1955] 392 p.
E457.T78

825
Appleman, Roy E., ed. Abraham Lincoln,
from his own words and contemporary
accounts. Rev. Washington [U. S. Govt.
Print. Off.] 1956. 55 p. ([U. S.]
National Park Service. Source book
series, no. 2)
E160.U629, no. 2 1956

826
Bruce, Robert V. Lincoln and the tools
of war. Foreword by Benjamin P. Thomas. Indianapolis, Bobbs-Merrill [1956]
368 p. E491.B7
Bibliography: p. 345-354.

827
Mitgang, Herbert, ed. Lincoln as they
saw him. Edited and narrated by Herbert Mitgang. New York, Rinehart
[1956] 519 p. E457.15.M5

828
Houser, Martin L. Lincoln's education,
and other essays. [Louis A. R. Yates,
editor] New York, Bookman Associates
[1957] 356 p. E457.2.H848
This collection omits Lincoln and
McClellan (East Peoria, Ill., Courier
Printing Co., 1946. 28 p.), a paper
which Houser (1871-1951) prepared for
the Lincoln Group of Chicago, trench-
antly rebutting the claims made by
some historians that McClellan was the
North's ablest soldier, whose failures
were the result of interference, in-
ept or malicious, on the part of Lincoln and Stanton.

829
Lorant, Stefan. Lincoln, a picture story
of his life. Rev. and enl. ed. New
York, Harper [1957] 304 p.
E457.6.L78 1957
"Contents and bibliography": p.
299-304.

830
Randall, James G. Mr. Lincoln, Edited
by Richard N. Current. New York, Dodd,
Mead, 1957. 392 p.
E457.R215
"Incorporates those parts of ...
[the four-volume study, Lincoln, the
President] which deal primarily with
Lincoln the man and with his personal
relationships."

831
Riddle, Donald W. Congressman Abraham
Lincoln. Urbana, University of Illi-
nois Press, 1957. 280 p.
E457.4.R5
Bibliography: p. [253]-266.

832
Current, Richard N. The Lincoln nobody
knows. New York, McGraw-Hill [1958]
314 p. E457.C96

833
Franklin, John Hope. Lincoln and public
morality; an address delivered at the
Chicago Historical Society on February
12, 1959. [Chicago] Chicago Historical Society, 1959. 24 p.
JA79.F66
Brief, trenchant, analysis of how
President Lincoln, by the simple cri-
terion of rejecting every act that was
against the public interest, and tol-
erating any act which was not, was
able to do favors for his friends,
bring business men into the Government,
and use the patronage to strengthen
his party and administration, without
any departure from essential honesty.

834
Graebner, Norman A., ed. The enduring
Lincoln; Lincoln sesquicentennial lec-
tures at the University of Illinois.
Urbana, University of Illinois Press,

834
Graebner, Norman A., ed. (Cont.)
1959. 129 p. E457.7.G73
Contents.--Abraham Lincoln: an im-
mortal sign, by R. P. Basler.--Abraham
Lincoln: pragmatic Democrat, by T. H.
Williams.--Abraham Lincoln: Whig in
the White House, by D. Donald.--Abra-
ham Lincoln: conservative statesman,
by N. A. Graebner.--Materials on dis-
play in the University of Illinois Library, February, 1959, selected and described by L. W. Dunlap.

835
Jaffa, Harry V. Crisis of the house di-
vided; an interpretation of the issues
in the Lincoln-Douglas debates. Garden
City, N. Y., Doubleday, 1959. 451 p.
E457.4.J32

836
Warren, Louis A. Lincoln's youth: Indi-
ana years, seven to twenty-one, 1816-
1830. New York, Appleton, Century,
Crofts [1959] xxii, 298 p.
E457.32.W284
Bibliography: p. 271-281.

837
Canby, Courtlandt, ed. Lincoln and the
Civil War; a profile and a history.
New York, G. Braziller, 1960. 416 p.
E457.C2 1960

838
Duff, John J. A. Lincoln: prarie lawyer.
New York, Rinehart [1960] 433 p.
E457.2.D8

839
Freeman, Andrew A. Abraham Lincoln goes
to New York. New York, Coward-McCann
[1960] 160 p. E438.L776

840
Halstead, Murat. Three against Lincoln;
Murat Halstead reports the caucuses of
1860. Edited with an introd, by William B. Hesseltine. Baton Rouge, Louisiana State University Press, 1960.
xxi, 321 p. E440.H22

841
Hayes, Melvin L. Mr. Lincoln runs for
President. New York, Citadel Press
[1960] 352 p. E440.H33

842
Hesseltine, William B. Lincoln's plan of
reconstruction. Tuscaloose, Ala., Confederate Pub. Co., 1960. 154 p. (Confederate centennial studies, no. 13)
E456.H43
Bibliography: p. [142]-147.

843
Luthin, Reinhard H. The real Abraham Lin-
coln; a complete one volume history of
his life and times. Englewood Cliffs,
N. J., Prentice-Hall [1960] 778 p.
E456.L8

844
McClure, Stanley W. The Lincoln Museum
and the house where Lincoln died, Washington, D. C. Rev. Washington, 1960.
42 p. illus. ([U. S.] National Park
Service. Historical handbook series,
no. 3) E457.65.M3 1960

845
Searcher, Victor. Lincoln's journey to
greatness; a factual account of the
twelve-day inaugural trip. Philadelphia, Winston [1960] 279 p.
E457.4.S4

846
U. S. Lincoln Sesquicentennial Commission.
Lincoln day by day: a chronology,
1809-1865. Earl Schench Miers, editor-
in-chief. Washington, 1960. 3 v.
E457.U66
Contents.--V. 1. 1809-48 [by] William E. Baringer.--v. 2. 1844-60 [by]
William E. Baringer.--v. 3. 1861-65
[by] C. Percy Powell. Bibliography.
Index.
Vols. 1 and 2 are built upon, and
hence largely supersede, the four original volumes of daily Lincoln chronology published by The Abraham Lincoln
Association of Springfield, Ill., 1933-
41: Lincoln, 1809-1839 and 1840-1846
by Harry E. Pratt; 1847-1853 by Benjamin P. Thomas; and 1854-1861 by Paul M.

846

U. S. Lincoln Sesquicentennial Commission.
(Cont.)
Angle (actually the first to appear).
Each had some special content which is
not reproduced in the present chronology, and they do not deserve to be forgotten.

847

Frank, John Paul. Lincoln as a lawyer.
Urbana, University of Illinois Press,
1961. 190 p.   E457.2.F78

848

Mearns, David Chambers. Largely Lincoln.
Introd. by Earl Schenck Miers. New
York, St. Martin's Press [1961] 227 p.
E457.8.M5

849

Basler, Roy P. Lincoln. New York, Grove
Press [1962] 192 p. (Evergreen profile book, 37)   E457.B34

850

Edwards, Herbert Joseph, and John Erskine
Hankins. Lincoln the writer, the development of his literary style.
[Orono] University of Maine [1962]
117 p. (University of Maine studies,
2d ser., no. 76)   E457.2.E28

851

Fehrenbacher, Don E. Prelude to greatness; Lincoln in the 1850's. Stanford, Calif., Stanford University
Press, 1962. 205 p. E457.3.F4

852

Nevins, Allan, and Irving Stone, eds.
Lincoln: a contemporary portrait.
Garden City, N. Y., Doubleday, 1962.
226 p.   E457.8.N44

853

Quarles, Benjamin. Lincoln and the Negro.
New York, Oxford University Press,
1962. 275 p.   E457.2.Q3
   Bibliography: p. 251-264.

854

Franklin, John Hope. The Emancipation
proclamation. Garden City, N. Y.,

854

Franklin, John Hope. The ... (Cont.)
Doubleday, 1963. 181 p.
E453.F8
   "Sources": p. [157]-162.

855

Hamlin, Charles Eugene. The life and
times of Hannibal Hamlin, by his grandson. Cambridge, Riverside Press, 1899.
627 p.   E415.9.H2H2

856

Helm, Katherine. The true story of Mary,
wife of Lincoln; containing the recollections of Mary Lincoln's sister
Emilie (Mrs. Ben Hardin Helm), extracts
from her wartime diary, numerous letters and other documents now first
published by her niece. New York,
Harper, 1928. 309 p. E457.25.H47

857

Morrow, Honoré (McCue) W. Mary Todd Lincoln; an appreciation of the wife of
Abraham Lincoln. New York, W. Morrow,
1928. 248 p.   E457.25.M88

858

Evans, William A. Mrs. Abraham Lincoln,
a study of her personality and her influence on Lincoln. New York, Knopf,
1932. viii, 354, xiii p.
E457.25.E94

859

Sandburg, Carl, and Paul M. Angle. Mary
Lincoln, wife and widow; part I, by
Carl Sandburg; part II, letters, docu-
ments & appendix, by Paul M. Angle.
New York, Harcourt, Brace [c1932] 357
p.   E457.25.S262

860

Randall, Ruth Painter. Mary Lincoln; bi-
ography of a marriage. Boston, Little,
Brown [c1953] 555 p. E457.25.R3
   Bibliography: p. [517]-529.

861

Randall, Ruth Painter. Lincoln's sons.
Boston, Little, Brown [1955] 373 p.
E457.25.R26

862
Randall, Ruth Painter. The courtship of
  Mr. Lincoln. Boston, Little, Brown
  [c1957] 219 p.   E457.25.R24

ANDREW JOHNSON

Writings

863
Johnson, Andrew. Speeches of Andrew John-
  son, President of the United States.
  With a biographical introd. by Frank
  Moore. Boston, Little, Brown, 1865.
  xlviii, 494 p.   E415.6.J66
        Reissued in 1866.

864
----- Trial of Andrew Johnson, President
  of the United States, before the Senate of the United States, on impeachment by the House of Representatives
  for high crimes and misdemeanors. Published by order of the Senate. Washington, Govt. Print. Off., 1868. 3 v.
                    JK595 1868.J74
        Edited by Benjamin Perley Poore.
  Reported for the Congressional Globe
  by Richard Sutton, D. F. Murphy, and
  James T. Murphy. Index by Fisher A.
  Foster.

Biography

865
Dewitt, David Miller. The impeachment
  and trial of Andrew Johnson, seventeenth President of the United States;
  a history. New York, Macmillan, 1903.
  646 p.   E667.D52

866
De Witt, David M. Vice-President Andrew
  Johnson. In Southern History Association. Papers. v. 8, Nov. 1904:
  437-442; v. 9, Jan. 1905: 1-23; Mar.:
  71-86; May: 151-159; July: 213-225.
                    F206.S73, v. 8,9
        A distinguished interpretative
  sketch which deserved something better
  than serial publication. It takes its

866
De Witt, David M. (Cont.)
  departure from the untoward circumstances of Johnson's inauguration on
  March 4, 1865.

867
Moore, William G. Notes of Colonel W. G.
  Moore, private secretary to President
  Johnson, 1866-68. Edited by St. George
  L. Sioussat. American historical re-
  view, v. 19, Oct. 1913: 98-132.
                    E171.A57, v. 19

868
Hall, Clifton R. Andrew Johnson, military governor of Tennessee, Princeton,
  Princeton University Press, 1916.
  234 p.   E351.H17

869
Winston, Robert W. Andrew Johnson, ple-
  beian and patriot. New York, Holt,
  [c1928] xvi, 549 p.
                    E667.W78
        Bibliography: p. 529-540.

870
Beale, Howard K. The critical year; a
  study of Andrew Johnson and Reconstruction. New York, Harcourt, Brace, 1930.
  454 p.   E668.B354
        Bibliography: p. 407-435.
        Reissue: New York, F. Ungar, [1958]

871
Milton, George F. The age of hate, An-
  drew Johnson and the radicals. New
  York, Coward-McCann, 1930. 787 p.
                    E667.M66

872

Stryker, Lloyd Paul. Andrew Johnson, a
    study in courage. New York, Macmillan,
    1930. xvi, 881 p.
                E667.S924
    "Authorities and abbreviations
    used": p. 838-844.

873

U. S. National Park Service. Andrew
    Johnson National Monument, [Greene-
    ville] Tennessee. [Washington, U. S.
    Govt. Print. Off., 1946] Folder ([6]
    p.)   F444.G7.U52

874

Phifer, Gregg. Andrew Johnson takes a
    trip; Andrew Johnson argues a case;
    Andrew Johnson delivers his argument;
    Andrew Johnson loses his battle. Ten-
    nessee historical quarterly, v. 11,
    1952, Mar.: 3-22; June: 148-170;
    Sept.: 212-234; Dec.: 291-328.
                F431.T285, v. 11
    A sympathetic study of Johnson's
    "swing around the circle," Aug. 28-
    Sept. 15, 1866, Johnson was using
    the only political weapon familiar
    to him, extempore oratory, to sal-
    vage the mid-term elections. It could
    only fail, from lack of party support,
    but the margin was a narrow one.

875

Roske, Ralph J. Republican newspaper
    support for the acquittal of President
    Johnson. Tennessee historical quarter-
    ly, v. 11, Sept. 1952: 263-273.
                F431.T285, v.11

876

Dorris, Jonathan Truman. Pardon and am-
    nesty under Lincoln and Johnson; the
    restoration of the Confederates to
    their rights and privileges, 1861-1898.
    Chapel Hill, University of North Caro-
    lina Press, 1953. xxi, 459 p.
                E668.D713
    Bibliography: p. 423-437.
    Since over three-quarters of this
    authoritative study is concerned with
    Johnson's policy in these matters, and
    this policy was of the greatest influ-
    ence in determining the course of Re-

876

Dorris, Jonathan Truman. (Cont.)
    construction, it is included here
    even if it is not formally biograph-
    ical.

877

Donald, David. Why they impeached An-
    drew Johnson. American heritage,
    v. 8, Dec. 1956: 21-25, 102-103.
                E171.A43, v.8
    Considers that Johnson's own va-
    garies of behavior had solidly united
    the Republican majority in Congress,
    and left them no other course if the
    victory was not to be frittered away
    and the Negro returned to a state of
    peonage.

878

Roske, Ralph J. The seven martyrs? A-
    merican historical review, v. 64,
    Jan. 1959: 323-330. E171.A57, v. 64
    Of the seven Radical Republican
    Senators who voted for President John-
    son's acquittal, none was reëlected to
    a further term, and it has usually
    been assumed that they were "hounded
    out of politics" for their independ-
    ence. Dr. Roske examines each case
    and shows that other factors were cer-
    tainly or probably responsible: one
    was dead, one invalided, several re-
    placed by Democrats, etc.

879

Hyman, Harold M. Johnson, Stanton and
    Grant; a reconsideration of the Army's
    role in the events leading to impeach-
    ment. American historical review, v.
    66, Oct. 1960: 85-100.
                E171.A57, v. 66
    Shows that the state governments
    set up under presidential Reconstruc-
    tion used the courts to bring ruinous
    suits against Army officers executing
    the Reconstruction statutes, and that
    Grant and Stanton, failing to get pro-
    tection from President or Supreme
    Court, necessarily turned to Congress.

880

Lomask, Milton. Andrew Johnson: Pres-
    ident on trial. New York, Farrar,

880
Lomask, Milton. Andrew ... (Cont.)
   Straus [1960] 376 p.   E666.L84

881
McKitrick, Eric L. Andrew Johnson and
   Reconstruction. [Chicago] University
   of Chicago Press [1960] 533 p.
      "Selected bibliography, with notes":
   p. 511-521.

ULYSSES S. GRANT

Writings

882
Grant, Ulysses S. Personal memoirs of
   U. S. Grant. New York, C. L. Webster,
   1885-86. 2 v.   E672.G76
      An early appreciation from an un-
   expected quarter was Matthew Arnold's
   General Grant, an Estimate (Boston,
   Cupples, Upham, 1887. 66 p.). The
   essay had been published earlier in
   the year in Murray's Magazine (London).

883
Grant, Ulysses S. Personal memoirs. ed-
   ited with notes and an introd. by
   E[verette] B. Long. Cleveland, World
   Pub. Co. [1952] 608 p.   E672.G7617

884
Cramer, Michael J. Ulysses S. Grant; conversations and unpublished letters.
   New York, Eaton & Mains, 1897. 207 p.
                        E672.C89
      Cramer married Grant's youngest sis-
   ter in 1863, and, as U. S. Minister to
   Denmark, in July 1878 was host to General and Mrs. Grant in Copenhagen.

885
Grant, Ulysses S. General Grant's letters
   to a friend [Elihu B. Washburne],
   1861-1880. With introd, and notes by
   James Grant Wilson. 132 p. New York,
   T. Y. Crowell, 1897.   E672.G762

886
Grant, Ulysses S. Letters of Ulysses S.
   Grant to his father and his youngest

886
Grant, Ulysses S. Letters ... (Cont.)
   sister, 1857-78, edited by his nephew,
   Jesse Grant Cramer. New York, Putnam,
   1912. 182 p.   E672.G764

Biography

887
Young, John Russell. Around the world
   with General Grant: a narrative of
   the visit of General U. S. Grant, ex-
   President of the United States, to
   various countries in Europe, Asia, and
   Africa, in 1877, 1878, and 1879. New
   York, American News Co., 1879. 2 v.
                        G440.G7Y7

888
Church, William Conant. Ulysses S. Grant
   and the period of national preservation and reconstruction. New York,
   Putnam, 1897. 473 p. (Heroes of the
   nations)   E672.C56

889
Porter, Horace. Campaigning with Grant.
   New York, Century Co., 1897. 546 p.
                        E672.P84
      Reissue with introduction and notes
   by Wayne C. Temple: Bloomington, Indiana University Press, 1961. 558 p.
      Reminiscences of the campaign of
   1864-65 by a colonel on Grant's staff.

890
Garland, Hamlin. Ulysses S. Grant; his

890
Garland, Hamlin. Ulysses ... (Cont.)
    life and character. New York, Mac-
    millan, 1898. xix, 524 p.
                    E672.C23
        Reissued in 1920

891
Eaton, John. Grant, Lincoln and the
    freedmen; reminiscences of the Civil
    War with special reference to the work
    for the contrabands and freedmen of
    the Mississippi Valley. By John Eaton
    in collaboration with Ethel Osgood Ma-
    son. New York, Longmans, Green, 1907.
    xxxviii, 331 p.   E453.E14
        Eaton, chaplain of a regiment of
    Ohio volunteers, was put by General
    Grant in charge of the problems aris-
    ing from uprooted Negroes in the De-
    partment of the Tennessee from Novem-
    ber 1862. He traces his connexion with
    Grant through the latter's last ill-
    ness.

892
Shrady, George F. General Grant's last
    days, by one of his consulting sur-
    geoans; with a short biographical
    sketch of Dr. Shrady. New York, Priv.
    print. [De Vinne Press] 1908. 74 p.
                    E672.S56

893
Stevens, Walter B. Grant in St. Louis;
    from letters in the manuscript collec-
    tion of William K. Bixby. [St. Louis]
    Franklin Club of St. Louis, 1916.
    172 p.   E672.S84

894
Coolidge, Louis A. Ulysses S. Grant.
    Boston, Houghton Mifflin, 1917. 596
    p.   E672.C74
        Reissued in 1922.
        Unusual among Grant biographies in
    that it devotes the greater part of
    its text to Grant's political career
    after Appomattox.

895
Grant, Jesse R. In the days of my father,
    General Grant. New York, Harper, 1925.
    329 p.   E672.G765

896
Woodward, William E. Meet General Grant.
    New York, H. Liveright, 1928. 512 p.
                    E672.W87
        Bibliography: p. 503-506.
        Reissued in 1946.

897
Fuller, John F. C. The generalship of
    Ulysses S. Grant. New York, Dodd,
    Mead, 1929. 452 p. E672.F96

898
Conger, Arthur L. The rise of U. S.
    Grant. New York, Century Co. [1931]
    390 p.   E672.C734
        "A short bibliography": p. 379-382.

899
Coleman, Charles H. The election of 1868;
    the Democratic effort to regain con-
    trol. New York, Columbia University
    Press, 1933. 407 p. (Studies in his-
    tory, economics and public law, no.
    392)   H31.C7, no. 392
                    E670.C73
        Bibliography: p. 385-396.

900
Fuller, John F. C. Grant and Lee, a
    study in personality and generalship.
    London, Eyre and Spottiswoode, 1933.
    323 p.   E468.F96
        Reissue: Bloomington, Indiana Uni-
    versity Press, 1957.

901
Hesseltine, William B. Ulysses S. Grant,
    politician. New York, Dodd, Mead,
    1935. 480 p. (American political
    leaders)   E672.H46
        Bibliography: p. 453-460.
        Reissue: New York, F. Ungar [1957].

902
Ratner, Sidney. Was the Supreme Court
    packed by President Grant? Political
    science quarterly, v. 50, Sept. 1935:
    343-358.   H1.P8, v. 50
        Yes, in the sense that on Feb. 7,
    1870, Grant nominated two justices who
    would probably reassert the constitu-
    tionality of the Legal Tender Act of
    1862. No, in the sense that Grant

902
Ratner, Sidney. Was the ... (Cont.)
    consulted them on the matter or ap-
    pointed unqualified men pliable to his
    will.

903
Green, Horace. General Grant's last
    stand; a biography. New York, Scrib-
    ner, 1936. 334 p.   E672.G79

904
Nevins, Allan. Hamilton Fish; the inner
    history of the Grant administration.
    New York, Dodd, Mead, 1936. xxi,
    932 p.   E664.F52N42
        Reissue: New York, F. Ungar [1957].
    2 v.

905
Brooks, William E. Grant of Appomattox,
    a study of the man. Indianapolis,
    Bobbs-Merrill [1942] 347 p.
                          E672.B872
        Bibliography: p. 315-336.

906
Lewis, Lloyd. Captain Sam Grant. Boston,
    Little, Brown, 1950. 512 p.
                          E672.L48 1950
        Bibliography: p. [473]-484.

907
Macartney, Clarence E. Grant and his
    generals. New York, McBride Co.
    [1953] 352 p.   E467.M114

908
Catton, Bruce. U. S. Grant and the Amer-
    ican military tradition. Boston, Lit-
    tle, Brown [1954] 201 p. (The Library
    of American biography) E672.C3 1954
        "A note on the sources": p. [191]-
    193.

909
Cadwallader, Sylvanus. Three years with
    Grant, as recalled by war correspondent
    Sylvanus Cadwallader. Edited, and with
    an introd. and notes, by Benjamin P.
    Thomas. New York, Knopf, 1955. xiv,
    353, viii p.   E470.C14

910
Miers, Earl Schenck. The web of victory;
    Grant at Vicksburg. New York, Knopf,
    1955. xiv, 320, xii p.
                          E475.27.M64
        Bibliography: p. 303-306.

911
Catton, Bruce. Grant moves south. With
    maps by Samuel H. Bryant. Boston,
    Little, Brown [1960] 564 p.
                          E672.C293
        A continuation of Lloyd Lewis' Cap-
    tain Sam Grant (no. 906).
        Bibliography: p. [539]-547.

912
Nason, Elias. The life and public serv-
    ices of Henry Wilson, late Vice-Presi-
    dent of the United States. Boston,
    B. B. Russell, 1876. 452 p.
                          E415.9.W6N2

913
Hollister, Ovando J. Life of Schuyler
    Colfax. Chicago, Funk & Wagnalls,
    1887. 535 p.   E415.9.C68H7 1887

914
Smith, Willard H. Schuyler Colfax; the
    changing fortunes of a political idol.
    Indianapolis, Indiana Historical Bu-
    reau, 1952. 475 p. (Indiana histor-
    ical collections, v. 33)
                     E415.9.C68S5
                     F521.I 38, v. 33

915
Ross, Ishbel. The general's wife; the
    life of Mrs. Ulysses S. Grant. New
    York, Dodd, Mead, 1959. 372 p.
                          E672.R77

Writings

916
Hayes, Rutherford B. Diary and letters
of Rutherford Birchard Hayes, nineteenth President of the United States.
Edited by Charles Richard Williams.
[Columbus] Ohio State Archaeological
and Historical Society, 1922-26. 5 v.
E682.H45
Contents.--v. 1, 1834-1860.--v. 2.
1861-1865.--v. 3. 1865-1881.--v. 4.
1881-1893.--v. 5. 1891-1892.

917
Hayes, Rutherford B. The Hayes-Bryan correspondence, edited by E. W. Winkler.
Southwestern historical quarterly,
v. 25-30, 1921-26. F381.T45, v. 25-30
In 20 installments, beginning in
v. 25, Oct. 1921: 98-120, and appear-
ing in each successive issue through
v. 30, July 1926: 68-74.
This remarkable correspondence between Hayes and his Texan friend at
Kenyon College, Guy Bryan, begins in
Jan. 1843, is interrupted only during
the Civil War, and concludes in the
last year of Hayes' life, 1892.

918
[Smyth, William Henry] Conversations with
Hayes: a biographer's notes. Edited
by Curtis W. Garrison. Mississippi
Valley historical review, Dec. 1938,
v. 25: 369-380. F351.M69, v. 25
Interviews, 1879-1887, selected from
the materials left by Smyth, manager
of the Chicago office of the Associated
Press, to his son-in-law, C. R. Williams, when the latter inherited the
task of the "authorized" biography of
Hayes.

919
Parker, Wyman W. President Hayes's graduation speeches. Ohio State archaeological and historical quarterly, v.

919
Parker, Wyman W. President ... (Cont.)
63, Apr. 1954: 134-145.
F486.051, v. 63
Texts, from recently identified
manuscripts in the Hayes Memorial Library, of the oration (p. 138-143) and
the valedictory (p. 143-146) which
Hayes delivered at the graduation of
his eight-man class from Kenyon College, Aug. 3, 1842. Tradition has it
that Hayes greatly distinguished himself on this occasion.

920
Hayes, Rutherford B. Teach the freeman;
the correspondence of Rutherford B.
Hayes and the Slater Fund for Negro
Education, 1881-1887. Edited by Louis
D. Rubin. [Baton Rouge] Louisiana
State University Press [1959] 2 v.
LC2707.J6

Biography

921
Howells, William Dean. Sketch of the
life and character of Rutherford B.
Hayes. New York, Hurd and Houghton,
1876. 195, 31 p. E682.H85
The author's second exercise in
campaign biography, the first having
been 16 years earlier (no. 715)

922
Williams, Charles Richard. The life of
Rutherford Birchard Hayes, nineteenth
President of the United States. Bos-
ton, Houghton Mifflin Co., 1914. 2 v.
E682.W7

923
Burgess, John W. The administration of
President Hayes; the Larwill lectures,
1915, delivered at Kenyon College. New
York, Scribner, 1916. 154 p. E681.B95

924

Shores, Venila Lovina. The Hayes-Conkling
controversy, 1877-1879. Northampton,
Mass., Department of History of Smith
College [1919] (Smith College studies
in history, v. 4, no. 4) p. 215-279.
E681.S56

Hayes sought to replace Senator
Roscoe Conkling's machine lieutenants
in the top jobs of the New York Cus-
tomhouse with reform men, but encoun-
tered a determined resistance from the
Republican stalwarts.

925

[Keeler, Lucy Elliot] Illustrated catalogue, the Spiegel Grove State Park,
the Hayes Memorial Library and Museum,
and the Hayes homestead, Fremont, Ohio.
Columbus, Ohio State Archaeological and
Historical Society, 1926. 104 p.
F499.F9K32

926

Haworth, Paul L. The Hayes-Tilden election. Indianapolis, Bobbs-Merrill
[c1927] 365 p. JK526.1876.H42

927

Eckenrode, Hamilton J. Rutherford B.
Hayes, statesman of reunion, by H. J.
Eckenrode assisted by Pocahontas Wilson
Wight. New York, Dodd, Mead, 1930.
363 p. (American political leaders)
E682.E19
Bibliography: p. 345-349.

928

Garrison, Curtis W. A President's library. Ohio State archaeological and
historical quarterly, v. 48, Apr. 1939:
127-133. F486.051, v. 48

Hayes left a library, now the prop-
erty of the State of Ohio, of some
8,000 volumes, several thousand pamphlets, several newspaper files, over
100 volumes of clippings, and the Hayes
Papers. His enthusiasm was Emerson,
and he had good collections of Americana and Middle-Western Americana. His
later acquisitions were largely the
social and economic discussion of the
1870's and 80's, with prison reform a
specialty.

929

Garrison, Curtis W. President Hayes:
the opponent of prohibition. North-
west Ohio quarterly, v. 16, July-Oct.
1944: 164-177. F497.A15N6, v. 16

Hayes took an occasional drink before he became President, but, in full
agreement with his wife, banished alcohol from the White House as an example to an intemperate nation. But
he consistently opposed statutory prohibition, which could only add to the
evils of drink "the crimes of law-
breaking, of perjury, of hypocrisy, of
meanness."

930

Marchman, Watt P. The Hayes Memorial.
Columbus, Ohio State Archaeological
and Historical Society, 1950. 38 p.
F499.F9M3

931

Parker, Wyman W. The college reading of
a President. Library quarterly, v. 21,
Apr. 1951: 107-112. Z671.L713, v. 21

Hayes, unable to afford Yale, was a
student at Kenyon College from 1838-42,
during which time he was a member of
the Philomathesian Society and borrowed
145 books from its library. The author
has identified the titles "by matching
the numbers charged against Hayes with
the accession record in use at the
time," and finds them rich in politics,
history, fiction, poetry and rhetoric.

932

Van Sickle, C. E., and James T. May. The
birthplace of President Hayes; a study
in oral tradition. Ohio State archaeological and historical quarterly, v.
61, Apr. 1952: 167-172.
F486.051, v. 61

Using deed books of Delaware County,
the authors throw doubt upon the tra-
ditional site in Delaware, Ohio, in
1952 a filling station distinguished
by a D. A. R. marker, in favor of Lot
61, then occupied by the William Street
Methodist Church.

933

Barnard, Harry. Rutherford B. Hayes, and

933
Barnard, Harry. Rutherford ... (Cont.)
  his America. Indianapolis, Bobbs-Merrill [1954] 606 p.   E682.B3
     "Selected bibliography": p. 571-588.

934
Scott, George T. Illinois' testimonial
  to Mrs. Rutherford B. Hayes. [Spring-
  field, Ill., 1953] 21 p.
                      E682.S3
     "Reprinted, with appendix added,
from Journal of the Illinois State Historical Society, spring, 1953."
     The story of six morocco-bound man-
uscript volumes on parchment, containing the tributes of Illinois abstain-
ers, presented to Mrs. Hayes in 1881
because of her stand against alcohol
in the White House. They are now in
the Hayes Memorial Library at Fremont,
Ohio. The appendix is devoted to brief
excerpts from the testimonials.

JAMES A. GARFIELD

Writings

935
Garfield, James A. Works. Edited by
  Burke A. Hinsdale. Boston, J. R. Osgood, 1882-83. 2 v.   E661.G23
     Garfield's "works' were practically
all intended for oral delivery, and
his friend's thorough compilation includes 99 separate pieces, of which
two-thirds were delivered in the House
of Representatives. The few that were
not addresses were contributed to the
Atlantic Monthly, the North American
Review, and Johnson's New Universal
Cyclopaedia. A considerable number of
the addresses, in Congress and out,
originally appeared as separates.

936
----- Ought the Negro to be disfran-
  chised? Ought he to have been en-
  franchised? North American review,
  v. 128, Mar. 1879: 244-250.
                      AP2.N7, v. 128
     In a symposium of eight notables,
Garfield returns an emphatic No to the

936
----- Ought the Negro ... (Cont.)
  first, and an emphatic Yes to the second question. This item was not collected by Hinsdale in The Works.

937
----- My campaign in East Kentucky.
  North American review, v. 143, Dec.
  1886: 525-535.   AP2.N7, v. 143
     A narrative of the Middle Creek cam-
paign (Dec. 1861--March 1862) which,
according to "Edmund Kirke" (James R.
Gilmore), was written in the third person by Garfield himself for use in
Kirke's 1880 biography.

937a
----- My public life, by President Garfield. North American review, v. 144,
  May 1887: 451-461.   AP2.N7, v. 144
     On Garfield's nomination, Harper and
Brothers commissioned James R. Gilmore,
whose pen name was Edmund Kirke, to
write a biography. After he had been

937a
----- My public life, ... (Cont.)
shown what was already in proof, Garfield dictated this summary of his career in Congress to a stenographer.

938
----- Garfield-Hinsdale letters; correspondence between James Abram Garfield
and Burke Aaron Hinsdale. Edited by
Mary L. Hinsdale. Ann Arbor, University of Michigan Press, 1949. 556 p.
E687.G232
This noteworthy correspondence between Garfield and his successor as
President of Hiram College extends from
1857 to 1881.

Biography

939
Guiteau, Charles J., defendant. Report
of the proceedings in the case of the
United States vs. Charles J. Guiteau,
tried in the Supreme Court of the District of Columbia, holding a criminal
term, and beginning November 14, 1881.
In three parts. H. H. Alexander and
Edward D. Easton, official stenogra-
phers. Washington, Govt. Print. Off.,
1882. 3 v.   Law

940
Hinsdale, Burke A. President Garfield
and education; Hiram College memorial.
Boston, J. R. Osgood, 1882. 433 p.
E687.H67
Includes a sketch by Hinsdale of
Garfield's relation to Hiram College
and to education in general; the 8
addresses at the college memorial service on Sept. 25, 1881; an introduction
to Garfield's educational addresses;
and 12 of the latter, a few of which
do not appear in Hinsdale's edition of
The Works of J. A. Garfield. A similar
publication 50 years later, Garfield
of Hiram, edited by Harold E. Davis
(Hiram, Ohio, Hiram Historical Society, 1931. 68 p.), adds little, but
does contain an interesting section
of extracts from the Garfield literature, mostly eulogistic.

941
Fuller, Corydon E. Reminiscences of
James A. Garfield, with notes preliminary and collateral. Cincinnati,
Standard Pub. Co., 1887. 441 p.
E687.F96
The author became a friend of Garfield at the opening term of Hiram College in 1851, and remained in fairly
close touch with him down to Garfield's
entering the Union Army. If he suc-
ceeds in telling more about Corydon E.
Fuller than most people need to know,
he also prints a long series of letters
from Garfield to him.

942
Connery, Thomas B. Secret history of the
Garfield-Conkling tragedy. Cosmopolitan, v. 23, June 1897: 145-162.
AP2.C8, v. 23
The author, who in 1880-81 was managing editor of the New York Herald
in the absence of the younger J. G.
Bennett, was called in as a press ally
when Senator Conkling began his on-
slaught on the Garfield administration,
and heard much of the preceding negotiations.

943
Barker, Wharton. The secret history of
Garfield's nomination. Pearson's magazine, v. 35, May 1916: 435-443.
AP2.P35, v. 35
The author, an influential Philadelphia financier, was one of the earliest to propose Garfield's nomination
as a way out of the cutthroat warfare
between the Grant, Blaine, and John
Sherman factions.

944
Smith, Theodore Clarke. The life and letters of James Abram Garfield. New
Haven, Yale University Press, 1925.
2 v.   E687.S66
Contents.--v. 1. 1831-1877.--v. 2.
1877-1882.

945
Caldwell, Robert Granville. James A.
Garfield, party chieftain. New York,
Dodd, Mead, 1931. 383 p. (American

945
Caldwell, Robert Granville. (Cont.)
  political leaders)   E687.C25

946
Wasson, Woodrow W. James A. Garfield:
  his religion and education; a study in
  the religious and educational thought
  and activity of an American statesman.
  Nashville, Tennesee Book Co., 1952.
  155 p.   E687.W3
    A documented and objective study of
  Garfield's affiliation with The Disci-
  ples of Christ, and of the influence of
  this connexion in his life.

947
Clancy, Herbert J. The Presidential election of 1880. Chicago, Loyola University Press, 1958. 294 p. (Jesuit
  studies; contributions to the arts and
  sciences by members of the Society of
  Jesus)   E685.C5
    Bibliography: p. 269-278.

CHESTER A. ARTHUR

Biography

948
Chandler, William E. President Chester A.
  Arthur. Address, at Fairfield, Vermont, on August 19, 1903; on the occasion of the completion by the State of
  Vermont of a monument and tablet to
  mark the birthplace of President Chester A. Arthur. Concord, N. H., Rum-
  ford Print. Co., 1903. 46 p.
                    E692.C45
    The speaker had been Arthur's Sec-
  retary of the Navy and shared with him
  the initial steps in creating a modern
  navy.

949
Howe, George Frederick. Chester A. Arthur; a quarter-century of machine
  politics. New York, Dodd, Mead, 1934.
  307 p. (American political leaders)
                    E692.H67
    "Select bibliography": p. 292-295.
    Reissued by F. Ungar, New York
  [1957]

950
Shelley, Fred. The Chester A. Arthur
  Papers. In U. S. Library of Congress. Quarterly journal of current
  acquisitions, v. 16, May 1959: 115-
  122.   Z663.A3, v. 16
    A definitive statement on the de-
  struction by President Arthur of the
  bulk of his papers, and on the rem-
  nants that have been salvaged. For
  the latter, see also: U. S. Library
  of Congress. Manuscript Division.
  Index to the Chester A. Arthur papers
  (Washington, 1961 [i. e. 1962] ix,
  13 p. Its Presidents' papers index
  series).

Writings

951

Cleveland, Grover. Writings and speeches.
Selected and edited, with an introd.,
by George F. Parker. New York, Cassell
[^c1892] xxvii, 571 p. E696.C61

952

----- Addresses, state papers and letters. Edited by Albert Ellery Bergh.
New York, Sundial Classics Co., 1909.
499 p. E696.C613

953

----- Letters of Grover Cleveland, 1850-
1908. Selected and edited by Allan
Nevins. Boston, Houghton Mifflin,
1933. xix, 640 p. E697.C63

954

Cleveland, Grover. Public papers of
Grover Cleveland, Governor. 1883
[-1884] Albany, Argus Co., 1883-84.
2 v. in 1. J87.N717 1883-84

955

Dumont, Neill, comp. The President's pension vetoes. Comprising the reports
of Congress, the vetoes of President
Cleveland, the bills vetoed in pension
cases pending before the first session
of the 49th Congress. Washington
[^c1886] 352 p. UB373.D89

956

Cleveland, Grover. The self-made man in
American life. New York, Crowell
[^c1897] 32 p. JK2271.C63
An address delivered at Princeton
University on its 151st anniversary.

957

----- Presidential problems. New York,
Century Co., 1904. 281 p.
JK246.C68
Contents.--The independence of the
executive.--The government in the Chi-

957

----- Presidential problems. ... (Cont.)
cago strike of 1894.--The bond issues.--The Venezuelan boundary affair.
Most of these pieces originated as
addresses at Princeton University.

958

----- Fishing and shooting sketches.
New York, Outing Pub. Co., 1906.
209 p. SH441.C5

959

----- Good citizenship. Philadelphia,
H. Altemus Co., [1908] 78 p.
JK1763.C6
Contents.--Introduction.--Good cit-
izenship.--Patriotism and holiday ob-
servance.

Biography

960

Parker, George F. Recollections of
Grover Cleveland. New York, Century
Co., 1909. 427 p. E697.P25
By a zealous political supporter of
Cleveland, who incorporates much dis-
cussion of his career by the ex-Presi-
dent himself.

961

Williams, Jesse Lynch. Mr. Cleveland, a
personal impression. New York, Dodd,
Mead, 1909. 74 p. E697.W73
The author, a writer of fiction and
plays, was a Princeton neighbor of
Cleveland's after 1900.

962

Gilder, Richard Watson. Grover Cleveland:
a record of friendship. New York,
Century Co., 1910. 270 p.
E697.C46
The author, the well-known editor
of The Century, made President Cleve-

962
Gilder, Richard Watson. (Cont.)
land's acquaintance when he was pro-
moting an international copyright law.

963
Keen, William W. The surgical operations
on President Cleveland in 1893. Phil-
adelphia, G. W. Jacobs [°1917] 52 p.
E697.K20
Reprinted from the Saturday Evening
Post, Sept. 22, 1917, and subsequently
included with six other papers of the
author in a volume with the same title
(Philadelphia, Lippincott, 1928).

964
Thomas, Harrison Cook. The return of the
Democratic Party to power in 1884.
New York, Columbia University, 1919.
261 p. (Studies in history, economics
and public law, v. 89, no. 2)
E695.T452
H31.C7, v. 89, no. 2

965
McElroy, Robert McN. Grover Cleveland,
the man and the statesman. An authorized biography. New York, Harper,
1923. 2 v. E697.M142

966
Armitage, Charles H. Grover Cleveland as
Buffalo knew him. [Buffalo] Buffalo
Evening News, 1926. 278 p.
E697.A73

967
Lynch, Denis Tilden. Grover Cleveland, a
man four-square. New York, H. Liveright [1932] 581 p.
E697.L96

968
Nevins, Allan. Grover Cleveland; a study
in courage. New York, Dodd, Mead,
1932. 832 p. (American political
leaders) E697.N466
Bibliography: p. 767-772.

969
Robertson, Pearl Louise. Grover Cleveland
as a political leader. [Chicago]
1939. p. 35-83, 282-288.

969
Robertson, Pearl Louise. (Cont.)
E697.R64
Part of thesis (Ph. D.)--University
of Chicago, 1937.

970
Dulebohn, George Roscoe. Principles of
foreign policy under the Cleveland ad-
ministrations. Philadelphia, 1941.
102 p. E696.D8 1941
Thesis (Ph. D.)--University of
Pennsylvania, 1940.
Bibliography: p. 99-102.

971
Knoles, George Harmon. The presidential
campaign and election of 1892. Stanford University, Calif., Stanford University Press, 1942. 268 p. (Stanford University publications. History,
economics, and political science.
v. 5, no. 1) E705.K57
A536.L54, v. 5, no. 1
Bibliography: p. 248-252.

972
Merrill, Horace Samuel. Bourbon leader:
Grover Cleveland and the Democratic
Party. Boston, Little, Brown [1957]
224 p. (The Library of American biog-
raphy) E697.M4

973
Wilson, William L. The Cabinet diary of
William L. Wilson, 1896-1897. Edited
by Festus P. Summers. With an introd.
by Newton D. Baker. Chapel Hill, University of North Carolina Press [1957]
276 p. E706.W5
Wilson became Postmaster General on
Mar. 3, 1895, but the diary does not
begin until Jan. 1, 1896.

974
LaFeber, Walter. The background of Cleveland's Venezuelan policy: a reinter-
pretation. American historical review,
v. 66, July 1961: 947-967.
E171.A57, v. 66
Rejects the views which attribute
the invocation of the Monroe Doctrine
to domestic political attacks, to Secretary Olney's bellicose temper, or to

974
LaFeber, Walter. The ... (Cont.)
a resurgence of Manifest Destiny;
Cleveland and Olney acted because they
considered that the strategic and economic interests of the United States
were endangered by European encroach-
ments.

975
Holcombe, John W., and Hubert M. Skinner.
Life and public services of Thomas A.
Hendricks, with selected speeches and
writings. Indianapolis, Carlon and
Hollenback, 1886. 637 p.
E664.H49H7
"Selected speeches and writings":
p. 415-637.

976
Stevenson, Adlai E., 1835-1914. Something of men I have known, with some
papers of a general nature, political,
historical, and retrospective. Chicago, McClurg, 1909. 442 p.
E661.S84

Writings

977

Harrison, Benjamin. Speeches of Benjamin Harrison, twenty-third President of the United States; a complete collection of his public addresses from February, 1888, to February, 1892. Compiled by Charles Hedges. New York, United States Book Co. [c1892] 580 p.
E660.H29

978

----- Public papers and addresses of Benjamin Harrison, twenty-third President of the United States. March 4, 1889, to March 4, 1893. Washington, Govt. Print. Off., 1893. 302 p.
E701.H3

979

----- This country of ours. New York, Scribner, 1897. xxiv, 360 p.
JK251.H322

Much of it originally appeared as a series of articles in the Ladies Home Journal, 1896-97.

980

----- Views of an ex-President; being his addresses and writings on subjects of public interest since the close of his administration as President of the United States, compiled by Mary Lord Harrison. Indianapolis, Bowen-Merrill Co. [1901] 532 p. E660.H31

981

----- The correspondence between Benjamin Harrison and James G. Blaine, 1882-1893. Collected and edited by Albert T. Volwiler. Philadelphia, American Philosophical Society, 1940. 314 p. (Memoirs of the American Philosophical Society, v. 14, 1940)
E702.H36
Q11.P612, v. 14

Biography

982

Lockridge, Ross F., Jr. The Harrisons. In U. S. Benjamin Harrison Memorial Commission. Benjamin Harrison memorial ... Report of the Commission. [Washington] U. S. Govt. Print. Off., 1941. ([U. S.] 77th Cong., 1st sess. House. Document 154) p. 19-210.
E702.U5

983

Dozer, Donald M. Benjamin Harrison and the Presidential campaign of 1892. American historical review, v. 54, Oct. 1948: 49-77.
E171.A57, v. 54

984

De Santis, Vincent P. Benjamin Harrison and the Republican Party in the South, 1889-1893. Indiana magazine of history, v. 51, Dec. 1955: 279-302.
F521.I51, v. 51

Harrison "worked feverishly throughout his presidency to rejuvenate southern Republicanism" and might have succeeded if the Senate had not defeated the Force Bill of 1890.

985

Sievers, Harry J. Benjamin Harrison. New York, University Publishers [c1959-60. v. 1, 2d ed., rev., 1960] 2 v. E702.S55

To be completed in 3 v.
Bibliography: v. 1, p. 321-331; v. 2, p. 433-448.
First edition of v. 1: Chicago, Regnery, 1952.
Contents.--[v. 1] Hoosier warrior; through the Civil War years, 1833-1865.--[v. 2] Hoosier statesman; from the Civil War to the White House, 1865-1888.

986

Foster, Harriet N. (McIntyre). Mrs. Ben-
    jamin Harrison, the first President-
    General of the National Society of the
    Daughters of the American Revolution.
    [Indianapolis?] 1908.   27 p.
                    E702.Z6
        This was the first Mrs. Harrison,
    born Caroline Lavinia Scott, who died
    in 1892.

987

McElroy, Robert M. Levi Parsons Morton,
    banker, diplomat and statesman. New
    York, 1930. xvii, 340 p.
                    E664.M85M14

Writings

988
McKinley, William. Speeches and address-
es of William McKinley, from his elec-
tion to Congress to the present time.
New York, Appleton, 1893. 664 p.
E660.M145

989
----- The tariff in the days of Henry
Clay, and since. An exhaustive re-
view of our tariff legislation from
1812 to 1896. New York, Henry Clay
Pub. Co., 1896. 256 p.
HF1753.M15
Also published as v. 7 of <u>Works of
Henry Clay</u>, edited by Calvin Colton
(New York, Henry Clay Pub. Co., 1897.
7 v.).

990
----- Speeches and addresses of William
McKinley, from March 1, 1897 to May 30,
1900. New York, Doubleday and McClure,
1900. 388 p. E660.M17

991
----- A Civil War diary of William McKinley. Edited by H. Wayne Morgan. Ohio
historical quarterly, v. 69, July 1960:
272-290. F486.051, v. 69
Covers June 15-Nov. 3, 1861, when
the 23d Ohio Volunteers were at first
at Camp Chase near Columbus, and after
Aug. 15 maneuvering with McClellan's
forces in the difficult mountain country of West Virginia.

Biography

992
Olcott, Charles S. The life of William
McKinley. Boston, Houghton Mifflin,
1916. 2 v. E711.6.043

993
Kuhns, William T. Memories of old Canton

993
Kuhns, William T. Memories ... (Cont.)
and my personal recollections of William McKinley. [Canton, Ohio] Priv.
published [^{c}1937] 64 p.
F499.C2K8

994
Dawes, Charles Gates. A journal of the
McKinley years. Edited, and with a
foreword, by Bascom N. Timmons. Chicago, Lakeside Press, 1950. xxiv,
458 p. E711.D3
Dawes, a young Chicago utilities
man, took the leading part in swinging
Illinois' votes for McKinley's nomination, and became Mark Hanna's lieuten-
ant in the election of 1896. He
served as Comptroller of the Currency
from the beginning of 1898 until
McKinley's assassination. The extracts
continue, after Dawes' return to business, into 1908.

995
Bristow, Joseph L. Fraud and politics at
the turn of the century; McKinley and
his administration as seen by his
principal patronage dispenser and in-
vestigator. Edited by Joseph Q. Bristow and Frank B. Bristow. With a foreword by Charles G. Dawes. New York,
Exposition Press [1952] 126 p.
E711.B75
The author was fourth Assistant Postmaster General, 1897-1905, and subsequently a Senator from Kansas.

996
Whicher, George F., <u>ed</u>. William Jennings
Bryan and the campaign of 1896. Boston, Heath [1953] 109 p. (Problems
in American civilization; readings selected by the Dept. of American Studies, Amherst College) E664.B87W6
Bibliography: p. 107-109.

997
Spielman, William Carl. William McKinley, stalwart Republican; a biographical study. New York, Exposition Press [1954] 215 p.   E711.6.S73
   Bibliography: p. 207-210.

998
Fine, Sidney. Anarchism and the assassination of McKinley. American historical review, v. 60, July 1955: 777-799.   E171.A57, v. 60
   Although Leon Czolgosz was an isolated and unbalanced man, his deed aroused a wide-spread terror of anarchism in the country, led to the persecution of anarchist individuals and groups, and produced a wave of anti-anarchism bills, which became law in three States.

999
Leech, Margaret. In the days of McKinley. New York, Harper [1959] 686 p.   E711.6.L4

1000
Fite, Gilbert C. Republican strategy and the farm vote in the Presidential election of 1896. American historical review, v. 65, July 1960: 787-806.   E171.A57, v. 65
   The Domocrats attributed low prices of farm products to the demonetizing of silver; the Republican press worked hard to put the blame on increased production and increased competition in the foreign market. A sudden increase in the foreign demand for wheat in October sent the price up, and may well have gained many farmers' votes for McKinley.

1001
Morgan, H. Wayne. Governor McKinley's misfortune: the Walker-McKinley fund of 1893. Ohio historical quarterly, v. 69, Apr. 1960: 103-120.   F486.051, v. 69
   McKinley in February 1893 suddenly found himself responsible for an indebtedness of $130,000 through the failure of a friend, the Youngstown businessman Robert Walker, whose notes

1001
Morgan, H. Wayne. Governor ... (Cont.) he had endorsed. The sum was raised, not merely by wealthy Republicans, but by the Republican rank and file, and did not in the least damage McKinley's political prospects.

1002
Magie, David. Life of Garret Augustus Hobart, twenty-fourth Vice-President of the United States. New York, Putnam, 1910. 300 p.   E664.H73M1

1003
Hobart, Jennie (Tuttle) Second lady. New York, Priv. Print. [Mount Vernon, N. Y., W. E. Rudge] 1933. 36 p.
   E711.H69
   "The material included in the main portion of this book appeared under the title 'Second lady' in the issue for June 29, 1929, of 'The Saturday Evening Post'."   AP2.S2
   The author, the wife of Vice President Garret A. Hobart, frequently acted as the President's hostess at White House functions. Mrs. McKinley's poor health prevented her from assuming the full responsibilities of a First Lady.

THEODORE ROOSEVELT

Writings

1004

Roosevelt, Theodore. Works. National
ed. [New York, Scribner, 1926] 20 v.
E660.R842

"Prepared under the auspices of the
Roosevelt Memorial Association: Herman Hagedorn, editor."

Vols. 1-19 each have, as introduction, a short study of Roosevelt by
various authors.

Bibliographies.

Gebbie and Co. of Philadelphia
brough out a leather-bound "Uniform
edition" of The Complete Writings of
Theodore Roosevelt in 1902-3, 22 v.
The Review of Reviews Co. issued an
inexpensive "Statesman edition" in
1904, 14 v. Scribner issued its "Memorial edition," of which this is a
less expensive counterpart, in 1923-26,
24 v. (J. B. Bishop's life, no. 1058
below, was included).

1005

----- Letters. Selected and edited by
Elting E. Morison; John M. Blum, associate editor. Cambridge, Harvard University Press, 1951-54. 8 v.
E757.R7958

Contents.--v. 1-2. The years of
preparation, 1868-1900.--v. 3-4. The
Square Deal, 1901-1905.--v. 5-6. The
Big Stick, 1905-1909.--v. 7-8. The
days of Armageddon, 1909-1919.

1006

----- Theodore Roosevelt cyclopedia.
Edited by Albert Bushnell Hart and
Herbert Ronald Ferleger. New York
City, Roosevelt Memorial Association,
1941. 674 p. E757.R82

1007

----- The hunting and exploring adven-
tures of Theodore Roosevelt. Told in
his own words and edited by Donald Day.

1007

----- The hunting ... (Cont.)
Introd. by Elting E. Morison. New
York, Dial Press, 1955. 431 p.
SK33.R63

1008

----- Theodore Roosevelt's America; selections from the writings of the Oys-
ter Bay naturalist. Edited by Farida
A. Wiley. New York, Devin-Adair, 1955.
418 p. SK33.R72

1009

----- The free citizen; a summons to
service of the democratic ideal. Selections from his writings and stories from his record edited by Hermann
Hagedorn. New York, Macmillan, 1956.
238 p. JK1763.R67

1010

----- The Theodore Roosevelt treasury;
a self-portrait from his writings.
Compiled and with an introd. by Hermann Hagedorn. New York, Putnam [1957]
342 p. E660.R885

1011

----- Hunting trips of a ranchman;
sketches of sport on the northern cat-
tle plains. New York, Putnam, 1885.
318 p. SK45.R6
Frequently reissued.

1012

----- Life of Thomas Hart Benton. Bos-
ton, Houghton Mifflin, 1887. 372 p.
(American statesmen)
E176.A53, v. 23
Reissued several times.

1013

----- Gouverneur Morris. Boston, Houghton Mifflin, 1888. 370 p. (American
statesmen)

1013
----- Gouverneur ... (Cont.)
                E176.A53, v. 8
                E302.6.M7R7
        Several reissues.

1014
----- Ranch life and the hunting-trail.
        Illustrated by Frederic Remington.
        New York, Century Co.[1888] 186 p.
                F595.R778

1015
----- The naval war of 1812; or, The his-
        tory of the United States Navy during
        the last war with Great Britain; to
        which is appended an account of the
        Battle of New Orleans. 4th ed. New
        York, 1889. xxxviii, 549 p.
                E360.R86 1889
        First published 1882 (xviii, 498 p.).

1016
----- The winning of the West [1769-1807]
        New York, Putnam, 1889-1896. 4 v.
                F351.R79

1017
----- The wilderness hunter; an account
        of the big game of the United States
        and its chase with horse, hound, and
        rifle. New York, Putnam [c1893] xvi,
        472 p.   SK45.R75 1893

1018
----- New York. New ed. with post-
        script, 1890-1895. New York, Longmans,
        Green, 1895. xvii, 232 p. (Historic
        towns)   F128.3.R79
        First edition, 1891.

1019
Lodge, Henry Cabot, and Theodore Roose-
        velt. Hero tales from American history.
        New York, Century Co., 1895. 335 p.
                E178.3.L82

1020
Roosevelt, Theodore. American ideals and
        other essays, social and political.
        New York, Putnam, 1897. 354 p.
                H35.R7
        15 essays, most of which originally
        appeared as magazine articles; fre-

1020
Roosevelt, Theodore. American ... (Cont.)
        quently reissued.

1021
----- The Rough Riders. New York, Scrib-
        ner, 1899. 298 p. E725.7.R78

1022
New York (State) Governor, 1899-1901.
        Public papers of Theodore Roosevelt,
        Governor, 1899 [-1900]. Albany, Bran-
        dow Print. Co., 1899-1900. 2 v.
                J87.N717 1899-1900

1023
Roosevelt, Theodore. Oliver Cromwell.
        New York, Scribner, 1900. 260 p.
                DA426.R78

1024
----- The strenuous life; essays and
        addresses. New York, Century Co.,
        1900. 225 p.   H35.R78 1900

1025
----- The naval operations of the war
        between Great Britain and the United
        States, 1812-1815. Boston, Little,
        Brown, 1901. 290 p. E360.R84
        A reprint of chapter 41, of v. 6 of
        Sir W. L. Clowes' The Royal Navy, a
        History (Boston and London, 1897-1903).

1026
----- Presidential addresses and state
        papers. New York, Collier [1905?]
        4 v.   E660.R77

1027
----- Good hunting; in pursuit of big
        game in the West. New York, Harper,
        1907. 106 p.   SK33.R6
        Seven articles which appeared in
        Harpers Round Table, 1896-97.

1028
----- Outdoor pastimes of an American
        hunter. New and enl. ed. New York,
        Scribner, 1908. 420 p.
                SK45.R748
        First edition, 1905 (369 p.).

1029

----- African and European addresses.
With an introd. presenting a description of the conditions under which the
addresses were given during Mr. Roosevelt's journey in 1910 from Khartum
through Europe to New York, by Lawrence
F. Abbott. New York, Putnam, 1910.
xli, 249 p.   JA38.R7

1030

----- African game trails, an account of
the African wanderings of an American
hunter-naturalist. New York, Scribner, 1910. xv, [61], 529 p.
                SK252.A3
     Frequently reissued.

1031

----- The new nationalism. New York,
The Outlook Co., 1910. xxi, 268 p.
                JK271.R7

1032

----- Realizable ideals (the Earl lectures.) San Francisco, Whittaker &
Ray-Wiggin Co., 1912. 154 p.
                HN64.R765
     "Delivered under the auspices of
Pacific Theological Seminary ... in
the spring of 1911."

1033

----- History as literature, and other
essays. New York, Scribner, 1913.
310 p.   PS2734.R5H5 1913

1034

----- Theodore Roosevelt, an autobiography. New York, Macmillan, 1913.
647 p.   E757.R79
     Frequently reissued.

1035

----- Life-histories of African game
animals, by Theodore Roosevelt and
Edmund Heller. With illustrations
from photographs, and from drawings
by Philip R. Goodwin; and with forty
faunal maps. New York, Scribner, 1914.
2 v.   QL731.R7

1036

----- Through the Brazilian wilderness.

1036

----- Through the ... (Cont.)
With illustrations from photographs
by Kermit Roosevelt and other members
of the expedition. New York, Scribner,
1914. 383 p.   F2515.R78

1037

----- America and the World War. New
York, Scribner, 1915. 277 p.
                D615.R6

1038

----- A book-lover's holidays in the
open. New York, Scribner, 1916.
373 p.   PS2734.R5B6 1916

1039

----- Fear God and take your own part.
New York, Doran [1916] 414 p.
                UA23.R7

1040

----- The foes of our own household.
New York, Doran, [1917] 347 p.
                D619.R64

1041

----- National strength and international duty. Princeton, Princeton University Press, 1917. 103 p. (Stafford
Little lectures for 1917)
                D619.R67

1042

----- The great adventure; present-day
studies in American nationalism. New
York, Scribner, 1918. 204 p.
                D619.R65

1043

----- Theodore Roosevelt's letters to
his children. Edited by Joseph Bucklin Bishop. New York, Scribner, 1919.
240 p.   E757.R8

1044

----- Letters from Theodore Roosevelt to
Anna Roosevelt Cowles, 1870-1918. New
York, Scribner, 1924. 323 p.
                E757.R796

1045

----- Selections from the correspondence

1045

----- Selections from ... (Cont.) of Theodore Roosevelt and Henry Cabot Lodge, 1884-1918. New York, Scribner, 1925. 2 v.   E757.R799

1046

----- Theodore Roosevelt's diaries of boyhood and youth. New York, Scribner, 1928. 365 p.   E757.R7956

1047

----- Letters to Kermit from Theodore Roosevelt, 1902-1908. Edited with an introd. and pref. by Will[iam H.] Irwin. New York, Scribner, 1946. 296 p.   E757.R785

1048

----- Letters of Theodore Roosevelt, Civil Service Commissioner, 1889-1895. [Washington] U. S. Civil Service Commission, 1958. 52 p. JK691.R62
    42 letters, about half of which do not appear in E. E. Morison's great compilation (no. 1005), and including several which Roosevelt signed along with one or both of the other commissioners. Forthright and fascinating, they exhibit first-rate abilities and a firm determination to maintain and expand the merit system.

Biography

1049

Leupp, Francis E.   The man Roosevelt, a portrait sketch.   New York, Appleton, 1904. 341 p.   E757.L65
    By a journalist who had observed Roosevelt carefully during his earlier years in politics.

1050

Riis, Jacob A.   Theodore Roosevelt, the citizen. New York, The Outlook Co., 1904. 471 p.   E757.R57

1051

Burroughs, John.   Camping and tramping with Roosevelt.   Boston, Houghton Mifflin, 1907. 110 p.
                    E757.B97

1052

Hale, William Bayard.   A week in the White House with Theodore Roosevelt; a study of the President at the nation's business.   New York, Putnam, 1908. 153 p.
                    E757.H17

1053

Donovan, Michael J.   The Roosevelt that I know; ten years of boxing with the President--and other memories of famous fighting men, by Mike Donovan. New York, B. W. Dodge, 1909. 234 p.
                    GV1131.D7

1054

Shaw, Albert.   A cartoon history of Roosevelt's career, illustrated by 630 contemporary cartoons.   New York, Review of Reviews Co. [^{c}1910] 253 p.
                    E757.S53

1055

Abbott, Lawrence F.   Impressions of Theodore Roosevelt.   Garden City, N. Y., Doubleday, Page, 1919. xvii, 315 p.
                    E757.A13

1056

Sewall, William Wingate.   Bill Sewall's story of T. R.   New York, Harper [1919] 115 p.   E757.S5
    Roosevelt found the author a guide in the Maine wilderness and transferred him to a ranch in the Dakotas.

1057

Thayer, William R.   Theodore Roosevelt, an intimate biography.   Boston, Houghton Mifflin, 1919. 474 p.
                    E757.T372

1058

Bishop, Joseph Bucklin.   Theodore Roosevelt and his time shown in his own letters.   New York, Scribner, 1920. 2 v.   E757.B625

1059

Gilman, Bradley.   Roosevelt, the happy warrior. Boston, Little, Brown, 1921. 376 p.   E757.G5

1060

Hagedorn, Hermann.   Roosevelt in the Bad

1060
Hagedorn, Hermann. Roosevelt ... (Cont.)
Lands. Boston, Houghton Mifflin, 1921.
491 p. (Publications of the Roosevelt
Memorial Association, v. 1)
E757.H142

1061
Howland, Harold J. Theodore Roosevelt and
his times; a chronicle of the Progressive movement. New Haven, Yale University Press, 1921. 289 p. (The Chronicles of America series, v. 47)
E173.G56, v. 47
E757.H862

1062
Robinson, Corinne Roosevelt. My brother,
Theodore Roosevelt. New York, Scrib-
ner, 1921. 365 p. E757.R65

1063
Reisner, Christian F. Roosevelt's religion. New York, Abingdon Press [c1922]
385 p. E757.R36
Thoroughly documented with extracts
from memoirs and Roosevelt's writings.

1064
Butt, Archibald W. The letters of Archie
Butt, personal aide to President Roose-
velt. Edited, with a biographical
sketch of the author, by Lawrence F.
Abbott. Garden City, N. Y., Doubleday,
Page, 1925. 395 p. E748.B94B942

1065
David, Oscar King. Released for publication; some inside political history of
Theodore Roosevelt and his times, 1898-
1918. Boston, Houghton Mifflin, 1925.
461 p. E757.D25
Reminiscences of a Washington correspondent who served as secretary of the
Progressive National Committee in 1912.

1066
Dennett, Tyler. Roosevelt and the Russo-
Japanese War; a critical study of A-
merican policy in Eastern Asis in
1902-5, based primarily upon the private papers of Theodore Roosevelt.
Garden City, N. Y., Doubleday, Page,
1925. 357 p. E756.D32

1066
Dennett, Tyler. Roosevelt and ... (Cont.)
Reissue: Gloucester, Mass., P.
Smith, 1959.

1067
Foulke, William Dudley. Roosevelt and the
spoilsmen. New York, National Civil
Service Reform League [c1925] 107 p.
E757.F76
A sketch of Roosevelt's outstanding
services to the cause of civil service
reform, by the Indiana reformer whom
he appointed to the U. S. Civil Service Commission.

1068
Moore, Joseph Hampton. Roosevelt and the
Old Guard. Philadelphia, Macrae Smith
[c1925] 300 p. E756.M83
By a Pennsylvania Republican who
subsequently became Mayor of Philadelphia.

1069
Lang, Lincoln A. Ranching with Roosevelt, by a companion rancher. Philadelphia, Lippincott, 1926. 369 p.
F655.L26

1070
Hill, Howard C. Roosevelt and the Car-
ibbean. Chicago, University of Chicago Press [1927] 232 p.
E756.H65

1071
Wood, Frederick S. Roosevelt as we knew
him; the personal recollections of one
hundred and fifty of his friends and
associates. Philadelphia, Winston
[1927] 485 p. E757.W86

1072
Looker, Earle. The White House gang.
New York, F. H. Revell [c1929] 244 p.
E757.3.L6
"Theodore Roosevelt started the ad-
venturous rollicking, joyous career of
the White House Gang by sending his
youngest son, Quentin, to the Force
Public School on Massachusetts Ave-
nue": p. 13.

1073
Einstein, Lewis. Roosevelt, his mind in
action. Boston, Houghton Mifflin,
1930. 259 p.   E757.E35

1074
Wister, Owen. Roosevelt, the story of a
friendship, 1880-1919. New York, Macmillan, 1930. 372 p.
E357.W8

1075
McCaleb, Walter Flavius. Theodore Roosevelt. New York, A. & C. Boni, 1931.
383 p.   E757.M125

1076
Pringle, Henry F. Theodore Roosevelt,
a biography. New York, Harcourt, Brace
[C1931] 627 p.   E757.P96
    Bibliography: p. 607-612.
    Several times reissued, most recent-
ly in paperback form as Harcourt
Brace's Harvest book no. 15.

1077
Bailey, Thomas A. Theodore Roosevelt and
the Japanese-American crises; an account of the international complica-
tions arising from the race problem on
the Pacific Coast. Stanford University,
Calif., Stanford University Press
[C1934] 353 p.   E183.8.J3B17

1078
Partridge, Bellamy. An imperial saga; the
Roosevelt family in America. New York,
Hillman-Curl, 1936. 325 p.
E757.3.P36

1079
Hagedorn, Hermann. The bugle that woke
America; the saga of Theodore Roose-
velt's last battle for his country.
New York, John Day [C1940] 223 p.
E757.H1415

1080
Hurwitz, Howard Lawrence. Theodore Roosevelt and labor in New York State, 1880-
1900. New York, Columbia University
Press, 1943. 316 p. (Studies in history, economics and public law, no.
500)

1080
Hurwitz, Howard Lawrence ... (Cont.)
            HD8083.N7H8 1943
            H31.C7, no. 500
    Bibliography: p. 299-309.

1081
O'Gara, Gordon Carpenter. Theodore Roosevelt and the rise of the modern Navy.
Princeton, Princeton University Press
[1943] 138 p.   E182.O34
    Bibliography: p. 127-133.

1082
Mowry, George E. Theodore Roosevelt and
the Progressive movement. Madison,
University of Wisconsin Press, 1946.
405 p.   E757.M9
    "Manuscripts and works cited": p.
385-393.

1083
Hagedorn, Hermann. A guide to Sagamore
Hill: the place, the people, the life,
the meaning. New York, Theodore Roose-
velt Association [1953] 74 p.
E757.H1417

1084
Blum, John Morton. The Republican Roose-
velt. Cambridge, Harvard University
Press, 1954. 170 p.
E757.B65

1085
Hagedorn, Hermann. The Roosevelt family
of Sagamore Hill. New York, Macmillan,
1954. 435 p.   E757.3.H3

1086
Beale, Howard K. Theodore Roosevelt and
the rise of America to world power.
Baltimore, Johns Hopkins Press, 1956.
600 p. (The Albert Shaw lectures on
diplomatic history, 1953)
            E757.B4
    Includes bibliography.

1087
Cutright, Paul Russell. Theodore Roosevelt, the naturalist. New York, Harper [1956] 297 p.
            QH31.R72C8
    Bibliography: p. 283-287.

1088

Zwierlein, Frederick J. Theodore Roosevelt and Catholics, 1882-1919. St.
Louis, V. T. Suren; for sale by Art
Print Shop, Rochester, N. Y., 1956.
xiii, 392 p.   E757.Z8

1089

Brooks, Chester L., and Ray H. Mattison.
Theodore Roosevelt and the Dakota Bad-
lands. Washington, National Park Service, 1958. 60 p.   E757.B86

1090

Cuba. Comisión Organizadora del Centenario del Nacimiento de Teodoro Roosevelt. Teodoro Roosevelt, homenaje en
el centenario de su natalicio. Habana,
1958. 159 p.   E757.C92
     Contents.--Theodore Roosevelt en sus
relaciones con Cuba, por R. Guerra.--
Theodore Roosevelt, por E. S. Santo-
venia.--Esbozo, por N. Carbonell.--Ras-
gos de Teodoro Roosevelt, por P. F.
Lavin.--Ofrenda: al ocurrir la muerte
de Teodoro Roosevelt, el 6 de enero de
1919, por M. Sanguilly et al.--Frases
de Teodoro Roosevelt.

1091

Putnam, Carleton. Theodore Roosevelt, a
biography. v. 1. The formative years,
1858-1886. New York, Scribner, 1958.
          E757.P968, v. 1
     Bibliography: p. 609-616.

1092

Wagenknecht, Edward C. The seven worlds
of Theodore Roosevelt. New York, Longmans, Green, 1958. xvii, 325 p.
          E757.W14
     Bibliography: p. 301-317.

1093

Lorant, Stefan. The life and times of
Theodore Roosevelt. Garden City, N. Y.,
Doubleday [1959] 640 p.
          E757.L85

1094

Peirce, Clyde R. The Roosevelt Panama
libel cases. New York, Greenwich Book
Publishers [1959] 150 p.
          E756.P4

1094

Peirce, Clyde R. The Roosevelt ... (Cont.)
     During the election of 1908 the New
York World, followed by the Indianapolis News, implied that part of the
$40,000,000 paid in the Panama settle-
ment had gone to an American syndicate.
This study follows the unsuccessful
suits for libel brought by an infu-
riated Roosevelt, with special attention to press opinion.

1095

Harbaugh, William Henry. Power and re-
sponsibility; the life and times of
Theodore Roosevelt. New York, Farrar,
Straus and Cudahy [1961] 568 p.
          E757.H28
     Bibliography: p. 523-549.

1096

Smith, William Henry. The life and
speeches of Hon. Charles Warren Fairbanks, Republican candidate for Vice-
President. Indianapolis, W. B. Bur-
ford, 1904. 252 p.
          E664.F16S6

1097

Longworth, Alice (Roosevelt). Crowded
hours; reminiscences. New York, Scribner, 1933. 355 p.
          E748.L87L8

WILLIAM HOWARD TAFT

Writings

1098

Taft, William Howard. Four aspects of civic duty. New York, Scribner, 1906. 111 p. (Yale lectures on the responsibilities of citizenship)
JK424.T2

    Reissue: New Haven, Yale University Press, 1911.

1099

----- Present day problems; a collection of [15] addresses delivered on various occasions. New York, Dodd, Mead, 1908. 355 p.   JK246.T2
    E761.T16

1100

U. S. War Dept. Special report of William H. Taft, Secretary of War, to the President, on the Philippines. Washington, Govt. Print. Off., 1908. 177 p. (60th Cong., 1st sess. Senate. Document 200)   DS685.A85 1908

1101

Taft, William Howard. Political issues and outlooks; speeches delivered between August, 1908, and February, 1909. New York, Doubleday, Page, 1909. 299 p.   E660. T11

1102

U. S. President, 1909-1913. Presidential addresses and state papers of William Howard Taft. v. 1. From March 4, 1909, to March 4, 1910. New York, Doubleday, Page, 1910. 612 p.
    E761.U61
    No more published.

1103

Taft, William Howard. Addresses of President Taft on arbitration. Washington, 1911. 66 p. JX1963.T2 1911 a

1104

----- Popular government; its essence,

1104

----- Popular ... (Cont.) its permanence and its perils. New Haven, Yale University Press, 1913. 283 p.   JF223.T3

1105

----- The anti-trust act and the Supreme Court. New York, Harper, 1914. 132 p.   HD2778.T14

1106

----- The United States and peace. New York, Scribner, 1914. 182 p.
    JX1961.U6T3
    "Four chapters ... delivered last winter as lectures under the auspices of the [New York Peace] Society. They were also published as contributions to the Independent."--Foreword.

1107

----- Ethics in service; addresses delivered in the Page lecture series, 1914, before the senior class of the Sheffield Scientific School, Yale University. New Haven, Yale University Press, 1915. 101 p.
    JK271.T3

1108

----- Our chief magistrate and his powers. New York, Columbia University Press, 1916. 165 p. (Columbia University lectures ... George Blumenthal Foundation, 1915) JK516.T34
    Reissues: 1925, 1938.

1109

----- The presidency, its duties, its powers, its opportunities and its limitations; three lectures. New York, Scribner, 1916. 145 p. (University of Virginia, Barbour-Page Foundation)
    JK516.T35

1110

Taft, William Howard, and William Jennings Bryan. World peace; a written debate between William Howard Taft and William Jennings Bryan. New York, Doran [c1917] 156 p.

JX1975.T3

1111

----- Taft papers on League of Nations. Edited by Theodore Marburg and Horace E. Flack. New York, Macmillan, 1920. xx, 340 p.   JX1975.T28

1112

----- Representative government in the United States; being the opening lecture of the James Stokes lectureship on politics, at New York University. New York, New York University Press, 1921. 49 p.   JK271.T35

1113

----- Liberty under law, an interpretation of the principles of our constitutional government. New Haven, Published for the University of Rochester by the Yale University Press, 1922. 51 p. (The Cutler lecture for 1921)

JK273.T27

Biography

1114

Butt, Archibald W. Taft and Roosevelt; the intimate letters of Archie Butt. Garden City, N. Y., Doubleday, Doran, 1930. 2 v.   E748.B94B943

115

Ragan, Allen E. Chief Justice Taft. Columbus, Ohio, Ohio State Archaeological and Historical Society, 1938. 139 p. ([Ohio State Archaeological and Historical Society] Ohio historical collection, v. 8) E762.R25

F486.0526, v. 8

Law

"Index of cases": p. 129-130.
Bibliography: p. 123-128.

1116

Pringle, Henry F. The life and times of William Howard Taft; a biography.

1116

Pringle, Henry F. The life ... (Cont.) New York, Farrar & Rinehart, [c1939] 2 v. (1106 p.)   E762.P75

1117

Hicks, Frederick C. William Howard Taft, Yale professor of law & New Haven citizen; an academic interlude in the life of the twenty-seventh President of the United States and the tenth Chief Justice of the Supreme Court. New Haven, Yale University Press, 1945. 158 p. (Yale Law Library publications, no. 10)

E762.H5

1118

Barker, Charles Edwin. With President Taft in the White House; memories of William Howard Taft. Chicago, A. Kroch, 1947. 73 p.

E762.B3

By his physical culture director.

1119

Taft, Helen (Herron). Recollections of full years. New York, Dodd, Mead, 1914. 395 p.   E762.1.T12

Published serially in the Delineator (New York) v. 84-85, May-Nov. 1914.

TT500.D3, v. 84, 85

WOODROW WILSON

Writings

1120
Wilson, Woodrow. Public papers. Authorized ed. Edited by Ray Stannard Baker
and William E. Dodd. New York, Harper
[^c1925-27] 6 v. in 3.
E660.W722
Bibliography edited by H. S. Leach:
[v. 2] p. 475-506; [v. 4] p. 437-483;
[v. 6] p. 543-636.
Contents.--[v. 1-2] College and
state; educational, literary and political papers (1875-1913).--[v. 3-4]
The new democracy; Presidential messages, addresses, and other papers
(1913-1917).--[v. 5-6] War and peace;
Presidential messages, addresses, and
public papers (1917-1924).
Also issued in 6 v.

1121
Wilson, Woodrow. Wit and wisdom of Woodrow Wilson; extracts from the public
speeches of the leader and interpreter
of American democracy, with master-
pieces of eloquence. Compiled and
classified by Richard Linthicum. Garden City, N. Y., Doubleday, Page, 1916.
220 p. E660.W74

1122
----- The wisdom of Woodrow Wilson; being
selections from his thoughts and com-
ments on political, social and moral
questions. Comp. and with an introd.
by Charles J. Herold. New York, Bren-
tano's, 1919. xx, 196 p.
E660.W73

1123
----- Woodrow Wilson's case for the League of Nations. Compiled with his approval by Hamilton Foley. Princeton,
Princeton University Press, 1923. 271
p. D642.W45 1923
"A compilation of President Wilson's
official and detailed explanation of

1123
----- Woodrow Wilson's ... (Cont.)
the League of Nations covenant and of
the Treaty of Versailles, made to the
Foreign Relations Committee of the
Senate, and to the people of the United States, when the treaty was before
the Senate in 1919."--Foreword.

1124
----- Wilson's ideals. Edited by Saul
K. Padover. Washington, American
Council on Public Affairs [1943] 151
p. E660.W728

1125
----- Woodrow Wilson, selections for today. Edited by Arthur Bernon Tourtel-
lot. New York, Duell, Sloan and Pearce
[1945] 258 p. E742.W685
Bibliography: p. 251-254.

1126
----- Woodrow Wilson's own story. Selected and edited by Donald Day. Boston, Little, Brown [1952] 371 p.
E767.W833

1127
----- The politics of Woodrow Wilson,
selections from his speeches and writings. Edited, with an introd., by
August Heckscher. New York, Harper
[1956] xxiv, 389 p.
E767.W832

1128
----- The Wilson reader. Selected and
edited by Frances Farmer. New York,
Oceana Publications, 1956. 286 p.
(Docket series, v. 4)
E742.5.W5

1129
----- Congressional government; a study
in American politics. Boston, Houghton

1129

----- Congressional ... (Cont.)
Mifflin, 1885.   333 p.
                         JK1061.W73
      12th ed.: 1896. 344 p.

1130

----- Division and reunion, 1829-1889.
New York, Longmans, Green, 1893. xix,
326 p. (Epochs of American history
[v. 3])   E178.E63, v. 3

1131

----- An old master, and other political
essays. New York, Scribner, 1893.
181 p.   JF111.W74
      Contents.--An old master.--The study
of politics.--Political sovereignty.--Character of democracy in the
United States.--Government under the
Constitution.

1132

----- George Washington. Illustrated by
Howard Pyle. New York, Harper,
[c1896] 333 p.   E312.W75
      Also entered above under George
Washington (no. 264)

1133

----- Mere literature, and other essays.
Boston, Houghton, Mifflin, 1896.
247 p.   PS3339.W3M4 1896
      Contents.--Mere literature.--The
author himself.--On an author's choice
of company.--A literary politician
[Walter Bagehot]--The interpreter of
English liberty [Edmund Burke]--The
truth of the matter.--A calendar of
great Americans.--The course of American history.

1134

----- The state; elements of historical
and practical politics. Rev. ed.
Boston, Heath, 1898.   xxxv, 656 p.
                         JC11.W76
      1st ed., 1889 (xxxvi, 686 p.).

1135

----- When a man comes to himself. New
York, Harper [c1901] 37 p.
                    BJ1581.W76 1901
      Reprinted from The Century Magazine,

1135

----- When a man comes ... (Cont.)
v. 62, June 1901: 268-273.

1136

----- A history of the American people.
New York, Harper, 1902. 5 v.
                         E178.W76
      Contents.--1. The swarming of the
English.--2. Colonies and nations.--3.
The founding of the Government.--4.
Critical changes and Civil War.--Re-
union and nationalization.
      A Documentary edition in 10 v., in
which by the addition of original
sources each of the above volumes became two, was issued in 1918(E178.W78).

1137

----- Constitutional government in the
United States. New York, Columbia
University Press, 1908. 236 p. (Co-
lumbia University lectures. George
Blumenthal Foundation. 1907)
                         JK246.W82
      Reissued in 1927 and, as Columbia
paperback 15, in 1961.

1138

----- The new freedom; a call for the
emancipation of the generous energies
of a people. New York, Doubleday,
Page, 1913. 294 p.   JK271.W6
      Compiled by William Bayard Hale
from the stenographic reports of Wilson's campaign speeches. For a def-
initive treatment of the same material, see the edition by J. W. Davidson, no. 1144 below.

1139

----- John Wesley's place in history.
New York, Abingdon Press [1915]
48 p.   BX8495.W563
      "An address delivered at Wesleyan
University on the occasion of the
Wesleyan bicentennial."

1140

----- Robert E. Lee, an interpretation.
Chapel Hill, University of North Carolina Press, 1924. 42 p.
                      E467.1.L4W75

1141
Turnbull, Laura Shearer. Woodrow Wilson,
a selected bibliography of his published writings, addresses and public
papers. Princeton, Princeton University Press, 1948. 173 p.
Z8976.9.T8

1142
Wilson, Woodrow. Leaders of men. Edited,
with introd. and notes, by T. H. Vail
Motter. Princeton, Princeton Univer-
sity Press, 1952. 70 p.
HM141.W53
"The manuscript from which this e-
dition is now first published dates
from 1890 and is in the Woodrow Wilson
Collection at the Library of Congress."

1143
----- The study of public administration.
Introd. by Ralph Purcell. Washington,
Public Affairs Press [1955] 23 p.
JF1351.W53
"Originally appeared under the title
'Study of Administration' in the June
1887 issue of the Political Science
Quarterly."

1144
----- A crossroads of freedom, the 1912
campaign speeches. Edited by John
Wells Davidson; with a pref. by Charles
Seymour. New Haven, Published for the
Woodrow Wilson Foundation [by] Yale
University Press, 1956. xviii, 570 p.
E765.W5
"Source notes": p. 527-545.

1145
----- The priceless gift; the love let-
ters of Woodrow Wilson and Ellen Axson
Wilson. Edited by Eleanor Wilson
McAdoo. With a foreword by Raymond B.
Fosdick. New York, McGraw-Hill [1962]
324 p. E767.W838

Biography

1146
Bryan, William Jennings. A tale of two
conventions. New York, Fund & Wagnalls, 1912. xviii, 307 p.
JK2263 1912.B7

1147
Hale, William Bayard. Woodrow Wilson;
the story of his life. Garden City,
N. Y., Doubleday, Page, 1912. 233 p.
E664.W74H16

1148
----- The story of a style. New York,
B. W. Huebsch, 1920. 303 p.
PS3339.W3Z7 1920
An unusual sort of book which close-
ly analyzes Wilson's writings and
speeches and finds in them an increas-
ing predominance of sound over fact.

1149
Dodd, William E. Woodrow Wilson and his
work. 4th ed., rev. Garden City,
N. Y., Doubleday, Page, 1921. 454 p.
E767.D635
Originally published in 1920 (369
p.).
Reissue: New York, P. Smith, 1932.

1150
Lansing, Robert. The peace negotiations;
a personal narrative. Boston, Houghton Mifflin, 1921. 328 p.
D644.L3

1151
McCombs, William F. Making Woodrow Wilson President. Edited by Louis Jay
Lang. New York, Fairview Pub. Co.,
1921. 309 p. E766.M14

1152
Miller, David Hunter. Some legal aspects
of the visit of President Wilson to
Paris. Harvard law review, v. 36,
Nov. 1921: 51-78. Law

1153
Seymour, Charles. Woodrow Wilson and the
World War. New Haven, Yale University
Press, 1921. 382 p. (The Chronicles
of America series, v. 48)
E173.C56, v. 48
E766.S62
"Bibliographical note": p. 361-365.

1154
Tumulty, Joseph P. Woodrow Wilson as I
know him. Garden City, N. Y., Double-

1154
Tumulty, Joseph P. Woodrow ... (Cont.)
  day, Page, 1921. 553 p.
      E767.T9

1155
Baker, Ray Stannard. Woodrow Wilson and
  world settlement, written from his unpublished and personal material. Garden City, N. Y., Doubleday, Page, 1922.
  3 v.   D644.B27
      Reissue: Gloucester, Mass., P.
  Smith, 1960.

1156
Annin, Robert Edwards. Woodrow Wilson; a
  character study. New York, Dodd, Mead,
  1924. 404 p.   E767.A55

1157
Kerney, James. The political education
  of Woodrow Wilson. New York, Century
  Co. [1924] xxi, 503 p.
      E766.K38

1158
Lawrence, David. The true story of Woodrow Wilson. New York, Doran [1924]
  368 p.   E767.L43

1159
Redfield, William C. With Congress and
  Cabinet. Garden City, N. Y., Doubleday, Page, 1924. 307 p.
      JK424.R4
      By the first Secretary of Commerce
  (1913-19).

1160
White, William Allen. Woodrow Wilson,
  the man, his times and his task. Boston, Houghton Mifflin, 1924. 527 p.
      E767.W58

1161
House, Edward M. The intimate papers
  [1912-19] of Colonel House arranged
  as a narrative by Charles Seymour.
  Boston, Houghton Mifflin, 1926-28.
  4 v.   E766.H85

1162
Houston, David F. Eight years with Wilson's Cabinet, 1913 to 1920; with a

1162
Houston, David F. Eight years ... (Cont.)
  personal estimate of the President.
  Garden City, N. Y., Doubleday, Page,
  1926. 2 v.   E766.H86
      By the Secretary of Agriculture.

1163
Baker, Ray Stannard. Woodrow Wilson; life
  and letters. New York, Scribner, 1927-
  39. 8 v.   E767.B16
      Contents.--[1] Youth, 1856-1890.--
  [2] Princeton, 1890-1910.--3. Governor, 1910-1913.--4. President, 1913-
  1914.--5. Neutrality, 1914-1915.--6.
  Facing war, 1915-1917.--7. War leader,
  1917-1918.--8. Armistice, Mar. 1-Nov.
  11, 1918.
      The Potomac edition, issued in 1946,
  is in 7 v., v. 1 and 2 of the original
  issue being combined.

1164
Viereck, George Sylvester. The strangest
  friendship in history; Woodrow Wilson
  and Colonel House. New York, Liveright
  [c1932] 375 p.   E767.V35

1165
Daniel, Marjorie L. Woodrow Wilson--his-
  torian. Mississippi Valley historical
  review, v. 21, Dec. 1934: 361-374.
      F351.M69, v. 21

1166
Lansing, Robert. War memoirs of Robert
  Lansing, Secretary of State. Indian-
  apolis, Bobbs-Merrill [c1935] 383 p.
      D619.L347

1167
McAdoo, Eleanor R. Wilson. The Woodrow
  Wilsons. In collaboration with Margaret Y. Gaffey. New York, Macmillan,
  1937. 301 p.   E767.3.M22

1168
Notter, Harley. The origins of the foreign policy of Woodrow Wilson. Baltimore, Johns Hopkins Press, 1937.
  695 p.   E767.N67
      "Selected bibliography: p. 655-664.

1169
Sears, Louis Martin. Woodrow Wilson.
In The Marcus W. Jernegan essays in
American historiography, edited by
William T. Hutchinson. Chicago, Uni-
versity of Chicago Press [1937]
p. 102-121.   E175.5.M37

1170
Loth, David G. Woodrow Wilson, the fifteenth point. Philadelphia, Lippincott [c1941] 365 p.
E767.L85

1171
Diamond, William. The economic thought
of Woodrow Wilson. Baltimore, Johns
Hopkins Press, 1943. 210 p. (Johns
Hopkins University studies in histor-
ical and political science, ser. 61,
no. 4)   H31.J6, ser. 61, no.4
E767.D5

1172
Daniels, Josephus. The Wilson era; years
of peace, 1910-1917. Chapel Hill, U-
niversity of North Carolina Press,
1944. xvi, 615 p.   E766.D3

1173
Daniels, Winthrop M. Recollections of
Woodrow Wilson. New Haven, Priv.
print. [Printing-Office of the Yale
University Press] 1944. 59 p.
E767.D2 1944
By a professor of economics who
was Wilson's colleague at Princeton,
1892-1910.

1174
Elliot, Margaret R. (Axson). My Aunt
Louisa and Woodrow Wilson. Chapel
Hill, University of North Carolina
Press [1944] 302 p.
E767.3.E4
An account of the author's life
spent in the homes of her aunt and
brother-in-law.

1175
Johnson, Gerald W. Woodrow Wilson, the
unforgettable figure who has returned
to haunt us. With the collaboration
of the editors of Look magazine.

1175
Johnson, Gerald W. Woodrow ... (Cont.)
New York, Harper [1944] 293 p.
E767.J7
A Look picture book.

1176
Bell, Herbert C. F. Woodrow Wilson and
the people. Garden City, N. Y.,
Doubleday, Doran, 1945. 392 p.
E767.B44
"Getting to know Wilson in a well
equipped library": p. 381-384.

1177
Daniels, Josephus. The Wilson era; years
of war and after, 1917-1923. Chapel
Hill, University of North Carolina
Press, 1946. xviii, 654 p.
E766.D33

1178
Myers, William Starr, ed. Woodrow Wilson, some Princeton memories [by]
George McLean Harper, Robert K. Root,
Edward S. Corwin [and others] Princeton, Princeton University Press, 1946.
91 p.   E767.M8

1179
Bailey, Thomas A. Wilson and the peace-
makers; combining Woodrow Wilson and
the lost peace and Woodrow Wilson and
the great betrayal. New York, Macmillan, 1947 [c1944, 1945] 2 v. in 1.
D643.A7B32
"Bibliographical notes': v. [1],
p. 326-370; v. [2], p. 370-416.

1180
Link, Arthur S. Wilson. Princeton,
Princeton University Press, 1947-60.
3 v.   E767.L65
Contents.--[1] The road to the
White House.--[2] The new freedom.--
[3] The struggle for neutrality,1914-
1915.
Bibliography: v. [1] p. [529]-543;
v. [2] p. [473]-488; v. [3] p. [695]-
711.

1181
Hugh-Jones, Edward M. Woodrow Wilson and
American liberalism. New York, Mac-

1181
Hugh-Jones, Edward M. Woodrow ... (Cont.)
   millan, 1949. 295 p. (Teach yourself
   history library)   E767.H86 1949

1182
Blum, John Morton. Joe Tumulty and the
   Wilson era. Boston, Houghton Mifflin,
   1951. 337 p.   E748.T84B6

1183
Fifield, Russell H. Woodrow Wilson and
   the Far East; the diplomacy of the
   Shantung question. New York, Crowell
   [1952] 383 p.   DS793.S4F5
      Bibliography: p. 369-376.

1184
Taylor, James Henry. Woodrow Wilson in
   church, his membership in the congre-
   gation of the Central Presbyterian
   Church, Washington, D. C., 1913-1924.
   Charleston, S. C. [1952] 44 p.
               E767.T3

1185
Gerson, Louis L. Woodrow Wilson and the
   rebirth of Poland, 1914-1920; a study
   in the influence on American policy of
   minority groups of foreign origin.
   New Haven, Yale University Press, 1953.
   166 p. (Yale historical publications.
   Miscellany 58)   D651.P7G4
      "Bibliographical essay": p. 140-
   145.

1186
Daniels, Jonathan. The end of innocence.
   Philadelphia, Lippincott [1954] 351 p.
               E766.D26
      "[An] attempt to tell what I learn-
   ed of democracy from seeing in action
   my father [Josephus Daniels] Woodrow
   Wilson, and FDR."--p. 19.

1187
Link, Arthur S. Woodrow Wilson and the
   Progressive era, 1910-1917. New York,
   Harper [c1954] xvii, 331 p. (The
   New American nation series)
               E766.L5
      "Essay on sources": p. 283-313.

1188
Buehrig, Edward H. Woodrow Wilson and
   the balance of power. Bloomington,
   Indiana University Press, 1955. 325 p.
               E766.B95

1189
Alsop, Em Bowles, ed. The greatness of
   Woodrow Wilson, 1856-1956. Introd. by
   Dwight D. Eisenhower. New York, Rine-
   hart [1956] 268 p. E767.A45

1190
Blum, John Morton. Woodrow Wilson and
   the politics of morality. Boston,
   Little, Brown [1956] 215 p. (The
   Library of American biography)
               E767.B64

1191
Garraty, John A. Woodrow Wilson; a great
   life in brief. New York, Knopf, 1956.
   206 p. Series   E767.G26

1192
George, Alexander L., and Juliette L.
   George. Woodrow Wilson and Colonel
   House; a personality study. New York,
   J. Day [1956] 362 p.   E767.G4

1193
Seymour, Charles. Woodrow Wilson in per-
   spective. Stamford, Conn., Overbrook
   Press [1956] 21 p.   E767.S45

1194
Buehrig, Edward H., ed. Wilson's foreign
   policy in perspective. Bloomington,
   Indiana University Press, 1957.
   176 p.   E766.B92

1195
Curry, Roy Watson. Woodrow Wilson and
   Far Eastern policy, 1913-1921. New
   York, Bookman Associates [c1957]
   411 p. (Bookman monograph series)
               DS518.8.C8
      Bibliography: p. 381-396.

1196
Link, Arthur S. Wilson the diplomatist;
   a look at his major foreign policies.
   Baltimore, Johns Hopkins Press, 1957.
   165 p. (The Albert Shaw lectures on

1196
Link, Arthur S.   Wilson the ... (Cont.)
diplomatic history, 1956)
E767.L66

1197
Link, Arthur S.   Woodrow Wilson and the
world of today; essays by Arthur S.
Link, William L. Langer [and] Eric F.
Goldman.   Edited by Arthur P. Dudden.
Philadelphia, University of Pennsylva-
nia Press [1957] 96 p.
E767.L67

1198
McKinley, Silan Bent.   Woodrow Wilson, a
biography.   New York, Praeger [1957]
284 p.   E767.M14

1199
Hoover, Herbert.   The ordeal of Woodrow
Wilson.   New York, McGraw-Hill [1958]
318 p.   E767.H78
   Bibliography: p. 305-307.
   Also entered under President Hoo-
ver's writings below (no. 1261)

1200
Latham, Earl, _ed_.   The philosophy and policies of Woodrow Wilson.   Edited for
the American Political Science Association.   [Chicago] University of Chicago Press [1958] 266 p.   E767.L3

1201
Martin, Laurence W.   Peace without victory; Woodrow Wilson and the British
liberals.   New Haven, Yale University
Press, 1958.   230 p.   (Yale historical
publications.   Miscellany 70)
D570.1.M36
   "Bibliographical essay": p. 213-
219.

1202
Walworth, Arthur Clarence.   Woodrow Wilson.   New York, Longmans Green, 1958.
2 v.   E767.W34
   Contents.--[1] American prophet.--
[2] World prophet.

1203
Link, Arthur S.   President Wilson and his
English critics; an inaugural lecture

1203
Link, Arthur S.   President ... (Cont.)
delivered before the University of
Oxford on 13 May 1959. Oxford, Clarendon Press, 1959.   21 p.
E767.1.L5
   Argues that the distorted images of
Wilson's character and purposes which
British statesmen formed during 1914-
20 led them to reject the great possi-
bility of an Anglo-American entente in
making a lasting peace and a new international order.

1204
Craig, Hardin.   Woodrow Wilson at Prince-
ton.   Norman, University of Oklahoma
Press [1960] 175 p.
LD4605 1902.C7

1205
Grayson, Cary T.   Woodrow Wilson, an intimate memoir.   New York, Holt, Rinehart and Winston [1960] 143 p.
E767.G85

1206
Scheiber, Harry N.   The Wilson administration and civil liberties, 1917-1921.
Ithaca, N. Y., Cornell University Press
[1960] 69 p.   (Cornell studies in
American history, literature, and folk-
lore, no. 6)   E173.C7, no. 6

1207
Kelly, Frank K.   The fight for the White
House; the story of 1912.   New York,
Crowell [1961] 308 p.   E765.K4

1208
Quirk, Robert E.   An affair of honor;
Woodrow Wilson and the occupation of
Veracruz.   [Lexington] Published for
the Mississippi Valley Historical As-
sociation [by] University of Kentucky
Press [1962] 184 p.   F1234.Q62
   "Essay on sources": p. 173-178.

1209
Marshall, Thomas R.   Recollections of
Thomas R. Marshall, Vice-President and
Hoosier philosopher; a Hoosier salad.
Indianapolis, Bobbs-Merrill [c1935]
397 p.   E664.M365M36

1210

Thomas, Charles M. Thomas Riley Marshall,
Hoosier statesman. Oxford, Ohio, Mis-
sissippi Valley Press, 1939. 296 p.
E748.M36T5
Bibliography: p. 269-281.

1211

Wilson, Edith Bolling Galt. My memoir.
Indianapolis, Bobbs-Merrill [c1939]
386 p.   E767.3.W55

1212

Hatch, Alden. Edith Bolling Wilson,
First Lady extraordinary. New York,
Dodd, Mead, 1961. 285 p.
E767.3.W57

WARREN G. HARDING

Writings

1213

Harding, Warren G. Rededicating America;
life and recent speeches of Warren G.
Harding, by Frederick E. Schortemeier.
With foreword by Will H. Hays. Indian-
apolis, Bobbs-Merrill [c1920] 256 p.
E786.H25

1214

----- Our common country; mutual good
will in America. With foreword by the
editor, Frederick E. Schortemeier.
Indianapolis, Bobbs-Merrill [c1921]
302 p.   E169.H26

1215

----- Speeches and addresses of Warren
G. Harding, President of the United
States, delivered during the course of
his tour from Washington, D. C., to
Alaska and return to San Francisco,
June 20 to August 2, 1923. Reported
and compiled by James W. Murphy, offi-
cial reporter, U. S. Senate. [Wash-
ington, 1923] 395 p.
E785.H3

Biography

1216

Chapple, Joseph Mitchell. Life and times
of Warren G. Harding, our after-war
President, by Joe Mitchell Chapple.
Boston, Chapple Pub. Co., 1924.
386 p.   E786.C45

1217

Slosson, Preston W. Warren G. Harding:
a revised estimate. Current history,
v. 33, Nov. 1930: 174-179.
D410.C8, v. 33
Harding had striking intellectual
limitations and "a positive relish for
bad company," but was himself a fund-
amentally honorable man and honest
politician, who put party expediency
and party harmony first among political ends, and was a peacemaker in a
time of widespread and embittered political rancors.

1218

Daugherty, Harry M., and Thomas Dixon.
The inside story of the Harding trag-
edy. New York, Churchill Co., 1932.
E786.D28
By Harding's Attorney General and a
literary collaborator.

1219

Adams, Samuel Hopkins. Incredible era;
the life and times of Warren Gamaliel
Harding. Boston, Houghton Mifflin,
1939. 456 p.   E786.A34

1220

Harris, Ray Baker. Background and youth
of the seventh Ohio President. Ohio
State archaeological and historical
quarterly, v. 52, July 1943: 260-275.
E486.051, v. 52

1221

----- Warren G. Harding, an account of his nomination for the Presidency by the Republican Convention of 1920. Washington, 1957.   27 p.
E783.H3H3

A chapter from a biography of Harding which circumstances forced the author to abandon. It combats the notion that Harding's nomination was dictated by a "Senatorial oligarchy," "a meeting of a handful of men in a smoke-filled room" (the Harvey-Brandegee room at the Hotel Blackstone, Chicago, on the night of June 11-12, 1920).

1222

Bagby, Wesley M. The road to normalcy; the Presidential campaign and election of 1920. Baltimore, Johns Hopkins Press, 1962. 206 p. (The Johns Hopkins University studies in historical and political science, ser. 80, no. 1)
H31.J6, ser. 80, no. 1
JK526 1920.B2

1223

Noggle, Burl. Teapot Dome: oil and politics in the 1920's. [Baton Rouge] Louisiana State University Press [1962] 234 p.   E785.N6

Traces the origin of the principal scandal of the Harding administration, its background in the conservation movement, and the means whereby the Republican Party overcame "what appeared to be, in the spring of 1924, an insurmountable handicap."

CALVIN COOLIDGE

Writings

1224

Coolidge, Calvin. Calvin Coolidge, his ideals of citizenship as revealed through his speeches and writings, by Edward Elwell Whiting. Boston, W. A. Wilde, 1924. 391 p.
E792.C64

1225

----- The mind of the President, as revealed by himself in his own words; President Coolidge's views on public questions, selected and arranged by subjects, and edited by C[ampbell] Bascom Slemp with an introd. and notes. Garden City, N. Y., Doubleday, Page, 1926. 357 p.   E791.U55

1226

Coolidge, Calvin. Have faith in Massachusetts; a collection of speeches and messages. Boston, Houghton Mifflin,

1226

Coolidge, Calvin. Have faith ... (Cont.) 1919. 224 p.   F70.C77

1227

----- The price of freedom; speeches and addresses. New York, Scribner, 1924. 420 p.   E660.C725

1228

----- America's need for education, and other educational addresses. Boston, Houghton Mifflin [c1925] 86 p. (Riverside educational monographs)
LA201.C6

1229

----- Foundations of the Republic; speeches and addresses. New York, Scribner, 1926. 463 p.
E742.U53

1230

----- The autobiography of Calvin Coolidge. New York, Cosmopolitan Book Corp., 1929. 246 p.
E792.C6

Biography

1231

Rogers, Cameron. The legend of Calvin Coolidge. Garden City, N. Y., Doubleday, Doran, 1928. 179 p.
E792.R72

A deft assembling of material largely anecdotal.

1232

Bradford, Gamaliel. The genius of the average: Calvin Coolidge. Atlantic monthly, v. 145, Jan. 1930: 1-13.
AP2.A8, v. 145

"...The essence and the explanation of Calvin Coolidge is the rooted, dominating habit of unceasing, unquestioning, orderly, systematic labor."

1233

Slosson, Preston W. Calvin Coolidge: his place in history. Current history, v. 33, Oct. 1930: 1-6.
D410.C8, v. 33

If untried by crises, Coolidge was at least "the most successful politician of his time," and if part of this was owing to the times, "some part also was the just meed of a cool, steady brain that was rarely inspired but rarely fell into serious error."

1234

White, William Allen. A Puritan in Babylon, the story of Calvin Coolidge. New York, Macmillan, 1938. xvi, 460 p.
E792.W577

1235

Fuess, Claude M. Calvin Coolidge, the man from Vermont. Boston, Little, Brown, 1940. 522 p.
E792.F85
Bibliography: p. [501]-504.

1236

MacKay, Kenneth Campbell. The progres-

1236

MacKay, Kenneth Campbell. (Cont.) sive movement of 1924. New York, Columbia University Press, 1947. 298 p. (Studies in history, economics and public law, no. 527)
E795.M3 1947
H31.C7, no. 527
Bibliography: p. 279-291.

1237

Fuess, Claude M. Calvin Coolidge--twenty years after. In American Antiquarian Society, Worcester, Mass. Proceedings, v. 63, 1954. p. 351-369.
E173.A35, v. 63

1238

Bates, James Leonard. The Teapot Dome scandal and the election of 1924. American historical review, v. 60, Jan. 1955: 303-322. E171.A57, v. 60

1239

Lathem, Edward Connery, ed. Meet Calvin Coolidge; the man behind the myth. Brattleboro, Vt., Stephen Greene Press, 1960. 223 p. E792.L3

An anthology of 34 pieces by Mrs. Coolidge, friends, acquaintances, and contemporaries.

1240

Orton, Vrest. Calvin Coolidge's unique Vermont inauguration; the facts winnowed from the chaff: the authentic account of the swearing in of Calvin Coolidge as 30th President of the United States by his father at the Coolidge homestead, Plymouth Notch, Vermont in 1923. Rutland, Vt., Tuttle Pub. Co. [1960] 93 p.
E792.O7

Reproduces some remarkable photographs and otherwise contains more of interest on Coolidge's Vermont background than the title indicates.

1241

Dawes, Charles G. Notes as Vice President, 1928-1929. Boston, Little, Brown, 1935. 329 p.
E748.D22D22

1242

Timmons, Bascom N. Portrait of an American: Charles G. Dawes. New York, Holt [1953] 344 p.   E748.D22T55

1243

Ross, Ishbel. Grace Coolidge and her era; the story of a President's wife. New York, Dodd, Mead, 1962. 370 p.   E792.1.C6R6

HERBERT HOOVER

Writings

1244

Hoover, Herbert. Principles of mining; valuation, organization and administration; copper, gold, lead, silver, tin and zinc. New York, Hill Pub. Co., 1909. 199 p. incl. illus., tables, diagrs.   TN145.H7

1245

Agricola, Georg, 1494-1555. Georgius Agricola De re metallica, tr. from the 1st Latin ed. of 1556, with biographical introd., annotations and appendices upon the development of mining methods, metallurgical processes, geology, mineralogy and mining law, from the earliest times to the 16th century, by Herbert Clark Hoover and Lou Henry Hoover. London, Mining magazine, 1912. xxxi, 640 p.   TN617.A4

1246

Hoover, Herbert. American individualism. Garden City, N. Y., Doubleday, Page, 1922. 72 p.   HM136.H6

1247

----- The new day; campaign speeches of Herbert Hoover, 1928. Stanford University, Calif., Stanford University Press [c1928] 230 p.   E796.H78

1248

----- Campaign Speeches of 1932, by President Hoover [and] ex-President Coolidge. Garden City, N. Y., Doubleday, Doran, 1933. 329 p.   E805.H66

1249

----- Hoover after dinner; addresses de-

1249

----- Hoover after dinner; ... (Cont.) livered before the Gridiron Club of Washington, D. C., with other informal speeches; with an introd. by Theodore G. Joslin. New York, Scribner, 1933. 144 p.   E742.H77

1250

----- The challenge to liberty. New York, Scribner, 1934. 212 p.   JC599.U5H6

1251

----- The state papers and other public writings [1929-33] Collected and edited by William Starr Myers. Garden City, N. Y., Doubleday, Doran, 1934. 2 v.   E801.H66

1252

----- Addresses upon the American road, 1933-1938. New York, Scribner, 1938. 390 p.   E743.H65

1253

----- Further addresses upon the American road, 1938-1940. New York, Scribner, 1940. 265 p.   E743.H678

1254

----- America's first crusade. New York, Scribner, 1943. 81 p.   D643.A7H7

1255

----- The problems of lasting peace, by Herbert Hoover and Hugh Gibson. Garden City, New York, Doubleday, Doran, 1943. 303 p.   JX1953.H73 1943
    "First printing, May 25, 1942 ...

1255

----- The problems of ... (Cont.)
Tenth printing (revised edition), January 15, 1943."

1256

----- Addresses upon the American road;
World War II, 1941-1945. New York,
Van Nostrand, 1946. 442 p.
D743.9.H68

1257

----- Addresses upon the American road,
1945-1948. New York, Van Nostrand,
1949. 319 p. E744.H65 1949

1258

----- Addresses upon the American road,
1948-1950. Stanford, Stanford University Press, 1951. 221 p. E813.H6

1259

----- Memoirs. New York, Macmillan,
1951-52. 3 v. E802.H7
Contents.--v. 1. Years of adventure, 1874-1920.--[v. 2] The Cabinet
and the Presidency, 1920-1933.--[v. 3]
The Great Depression, 1929-1941.

1260

----- Addresses upon the American road,
1950-1955. Stanford, Calif., Stanford
University Press, 1955. 365 p.
E743.H653 1955

1261

----- The ordeal of Woodrow Wilson. New
York, McGraw-Hill [1958] xiii, 318 p.
E767.H78
Bibliography: p. 305-307.
Also entered under President Wilson
above (no. 1199)

1262

----- An American epic. Chicago, H.
Regnery Co., 1959-61. 3 v. D637.H6
Bibliography: v. 2, p. 469-473.
Contents.--v. 1. Introduction. The
relief of Belgium and northern France,
1914-1930.--v. 2. Famine in forty-
five nations. Organization behind the
Front, 1914-1923.--v. 3. Famine in
forty-five nations. The battle on the
front line, 1914-1923.

1263

----- Addresses upon the American road,
1955-1960. Caldwell, Idaho, Caxton
Printers, 1961. 415 p. E742.5.H6

Biography

1264

Irwin, William H. Herbert Hoover, a
reminiscent biography, by Will Irwin.
New York, Century Co. [1928] 315 p.
E664.H7817

1265

Peel, Roy V., and Thomas C. Donnelly.
The 1928 campaign, an analysis. New
York, R. R. Smith, 1931. 183 p.
JK526 1928.P42
"Select bibliography": p. 177-183.

1266

Surface, Frank M., and Raymond L. Bland.
American food in the World War and reconstruction period; operations of the
organizations under the direction of
Herbert Hoover, 1914 to 1924. Stanford University, Calif., Stanford University Press, 1931. xxiii, 1033 p.
D637.S8

1267

Corey, Herbert. The truth about Hoover.
Boston, Houghton Mifflin, 1932.
318 p. E802.C85

1268

Emerson, Edwin. Hoover and his times;
looking back through the years. Illustrated with contemporary cartoons.
Garden City, N. Y., Garden City Pub.
Co., 1932. xvi, 632 p. E801.E75

1269

Joslin, Theodore G. Hoover off the record. Garden City, N. Y., Doubleday,
Doran, 1934. 367 p. E801.J65
By Hoover's press secretary, 1931-
33.

1270

Myers, William Starr, and Walter H. Newton. The Hoover administration; a
documented narrative. New York, Scribner, 1936. 553 p. E801.M94

1271
Wilbur, Ray Lyman, and Arthur Mastick Hyde. The Hoover policies. New York, Scribner, 1937. 667 p. E801.W55

1272
Myers, William Starr. The foreign policies of Herbert Hoover, 1929-1933. New York, Scribner, 1940. 259 p. E801.M93

1273
Hinshaw, David. Herbert Hoover, American Quaker. New York, Farrar, Straus [1950] xx, 469 p. E802.H65

1274
Willis, Edward Frederick. Herbert Hoover and the Russian prisoners of World War I; a study in diplomacy and relief, 1918-1919. Stanford, Stanford University Press [1951] 67 p. D627.G3W5

1275
De Conde, Alexander. Herbert Hoover's Latin-American policy. Stanford, Stanford University Press [1951] 154 p. (Stanford books in world politics) F1418.D38
    Bibliography: p. 129-144.

1276
Moore, Edmund Arthur. A Catholic runs for President; the campaign of 1928. New York, Ronald Press Co. [1956] 220 p. E796.M6

1277
Wolfe, Harold. Herbert Hoover: public servant and leader of the loyal opposition, a study of his life and career. New York, Exposition Press [1956] 507 p. E802.W74

1278
Lyons, Eugene. The Herbert Hoover story. Washington, Human Events, 1959. 358 p. E802.L85 1959
    First published in 1948 under title: Our unknown ex-President, a portrait of Herbert Hoover (340 p.) The present edition adds a chapter 21, "Postscript - 1959."

1279
McGee, Doroth Horton. Herbert Hoover; engineer, humanitarian, statesman. New York, Dodd, Mead, 1959. 307 p. E802.M2

1280
Warren, Harris G. Herbert Hoover and the great depression. New York, Oxford University Press, 1959. 372 p. E801.W28

1281
Guerrant, Edward O. Herbert Hoover: Franklin Roosevelt; comparisons and contrasts. Cleveland, H. Allen [1960?] 114 p. (Men and issues in American history) E747.G8

1282
Lochner, Louis P. Herbert Hoover and Germany. New York, Macmillan, 1960. 244 p. E802.L63

1283
Brandes, Joseph. Herbert Hoover and economic diplomacy; Department of Commerce policy, 1921-1928. Pittsburgh, University of Pittsburgh Press, 1962. 237 p. HF73.U5B7
    Bibliography: p. 221-229.

1284
Silva, Ruth C. Rum, religion, and votes: 1928 re-examined. University Park, Pennsylvania State University Press, 1962. 76 p. JK526 1928.S5

1285
Seitz, Don C. From Kaw teepee to Capitol; the life story of Charles Curtis, Indian, who has risen to high estate. New York, F. A. Stokes, 1928. 223 p. E664.C978S4

1286
Ewy, Marvin. Charles Curtis of Kansas, Vice President of the United States. Emporia, Graduate Division of the Kansas State Teachers College, 1961. 58 p. (The Emporia State research studies, v. 10, no. 2) E748.C982E9

FRANKLIN D. ROOSEVELT

Writings

1287

Roosevelt, Franklin D. The public papers and addresses of Franklin D. Roosevelt, with a special introd. and explanatory notes by President Roosevelt. [Compiled by Samuel I. Rosenman] New York, Random House, 1938-[50] 13 v.
E806.R749

Vols. 6-9 published by Macmillan; vols. 10-13 by Harper.

Contents.--v. 1. The genesis of the New Deal, 1928-1932.--v. The year of crisis, 1933.--v.3. The advance of recovery and reform, 1934.--v. 4. The Court disapproves, 1935.--v. 5. The people approve, 1936.--[v. 6] The Constitution prevails, 1937.--[v. 7] The continuing struggle for liberalism, 1938.--[v. 8] War-and neutrality, 1939.--[v. 9] War--and aid to democracies, 1940.--[v. 10] The call to battle stations, 1941.--[v. 11] Humanity on the defensive, 1942.--[v. 12] The tide turns, 1943.--[v. 13] Victory and the threshold of peace, 1944-45.

1288

----- F. D. R.: his personal letters. Foreword by Eleanor Roosevel
by Elliott Roosevelt. New York, Duell, Sloan & Pearce, 1947-50. 4 v.
E807.R649

1289

----- Nothing to fear; the selected addresses of Franklin Delano Roosevelt, 1932-1945. Edited, with an introd. and historical notes, by B. D. Zevin. Foreword by Harry L. Hopkins [Boston] Houghton Mifflin, 1946. xxi, 470 p.
E806.R7445

1290

----- As FDR said; a treasury of his speeches, conversations and writings, by Frank Kingdon. New York, Duell,

1290

----- As FDR said; ... (Cont.) Sloan and Pearce [1950] 256 p.
E807.R648

1291

----- The wit and wisdom of Franklin D. Roosevelt. Edited, with an introd., by Maxwell Meyersohn, with the collaboration of Adele Archer. Boston, Beacon Press, 1950. 154 p. (The Beacon Press wit and wisdom series)
E806.R79

1292

----- Franklin D. Roosevelt's own story, told in his own words from his private and public papers as selected by Donald Day. Boston, Little, Brown, 1951. 461 p. E807.R6485

1293

----- The Roosevelt reader; selected speeches, messages, press conferences, and letters of Franklin D. Roosevelt. Edited and with an introd. by Basil Rauch. New York, Rinehart, 1957. 391 p. E742.5.R65

1294

----- The happy warrior, Alfred E. Smith; a study of a public servant. Boston, Houghton Mifflin, 1928. 40 p.
E748.S63R7

1295

Roosevelt, Franklin D., ed. Records of the town of Hyde Park, Dutchess County, edited for the Dutchess County Historical Society. Hyde Park, New York, 1928. 340 p. (Collections of the Dutchess County Historical Society, v. 3) F127.D8D92, v. 3

Contents.--Records of the town meetings.--Church records.

1296

----- Government--not politics. New
York, Cavici-Friede [c1932] 107 p.
JK271.R54

1297

----- Looking forward. New York, John
Day [1933] 279 p.   E743.R66

1298

----- On our way. New York, John Day
[c1934] 300 p.   E806.R745

1299

New York (State) Governor, 1929-1932.
Public papers of Franklin D. Roosevelt,
forty-eighth Governor of the State of
New York, second term, 1932. Albany,
J. B. Lyon, 1939. 712 p.
J87.N717 1932

1300

Roosevelt, Franklin D., ed. Records of
Crum Elbow precinct, Dutchess County,
N. Y., 1738-1761, together with records
of Charlotte precinct, 1762-1785, records of Clinton precinct, 1786-1788,
and records of the town of Clinton,
1789-1799. [Poughkeepsie, New York]
1940. 196 p. (Collections of the
Dutchess County Historical Society,
v. 7)   F127.D8D92, v. 7
F129.C96R6

1301

----- F.D.R., columnist; the uncollected
columns of Franklin D. Roosevelt.
Foreword by Eleanor Roosevelt. Edited
by Donald Scott Carmichael. Chicago,
Pellegrine & Cudahy [1947] 180 p.
E742.5.R57

A collection of the newspaper col-
umns written for the Macon (Georgia)
Daily Telegraph in 1925 and for the
Beacon (New York) Standard in 1928.

1302

----- Wartime correspondence between
President Roosevelt and Pope Pius XII,
with an introd. & explanatory notes by
Myron C. Taylor, personal representa-
tive of the President of the United
States of America to His Holiness Pope
Pius XII. New York, Macmillan, 1947.

1302

----- Wartime correspondence ... (Cont.)
127 p.   D753.R69

1303

----- Roosevelt and Daniels, a friendship in politics. Edited with an
introd. by Carroll Kilpatrick. Chapel
Hill, University of North Carolina
Press [1952] xvi, 226 p.   E807.R655

1304

----- Franklin D. Roosevelt & conservation, 1911-1945. Compiled and edited
by Edgar B. Nixon. Hyde Park, N. Y.,
General Services Administration, National Archives and Records Service,
Franklin D. Roosevelt Library, 1957.
2 v.   HC103.7.R59

Biography

1305

Guilfoyle, James H. On the trail of the
forgotten man; a journal of the Roosevelt presidential campaign. Boston,
Peabody Master Printers, 1933. 222 p.
E805.G85

Concerned largely with the part
played in the campaign by James M.
Curley, mayor of Boston.

1306

Lindley, Ernest K. The Roosevelt revolution, first phase. New York, Viking
Press, 1933. 328 p.   E806.L56

1307

Roosevelt, Sara Delano. My boy Franklin,
as told by Mrs. James Roosevelt to
Isabelle Leighton and Gabrielle For-
bush. New York, R. Long & R. R. Smith,
1933. 115 p.   E807.R66

1308

Peel, Roy V. and Thomas C. Donnelly. The
1932 campaign, an analysis. New York,
Farrar & Rinehart [c1935] 242 p.
E805.P44

1309

Lindley, Ernest K. Half way with Roosevelt. Rev. ed. [New York] Viking
Press, 1937. 449 p.   E806.L543

1310
Farley, James A. Behind the ballots; the personal history of a politician. New York, Harcourt, Brace, 1938. 392 p.
E748.F24F3

1311
Moley, Raymond. After seven years. New York, Harper, 1939. 446 p.
E806.M67

1312
Jackson, Robert H. The struggle for judicial supremacy, a study of a crisis in American power politics. New York, Knopf, 1941. xx, 361 p. JK1541.J27
"Table of cases": p. [355]-361.

1313
Koenig, Louis William. The Presidency and the crisis; powers of the Office from the invasion of Poland to Pearl Harbor. New York, King's Crown Press, 1944. 166 p.
E806.K6 1944a

1314
Rauch, Basil. The history of the New Deal, 1933-1938. New York, Creative Age Press, 1944. 368 p. E806.R3

1315
McIntire, Ross T. White house physician. In collaboration with George Creel. New York, Putnam [1946] 244 p.
E807.M2

1316
Perkins, Frances. The Roosevelt I knew. New York, Viking Press, 1946. 408 p.
E807.P4

1317
Roosevelt, Elliott. As he saw it. With a foreword by Eleanor Roosevelt. New York, Duell, Sloan and Pearce [1946] xviii, 270 p. E807.R64

1318
Reilly, Michael F. Reilly of the White House. By Michael F. Reilly, as told to William J. Slocum. New York, Simon and Schuster, 1947. 248 p.
E807.R43

1319
Robinson, Edgar Eugene. They voted for Roosevelt; the presidential vote, 1932-1944. Stanford University, Calif., Stanford University Press [1947] 207 p.
JK1967.R6
"General note on sources": p. 186-207.

1320
Beard, Charles A. President Roosevelt and the coming of the war, 1941; a study in appearances and realities. New York, Yale University Press, 1948. 614 p. E806.B434
Sequel to the author's American Foreign Policy in the Making, 1932-1940.

1321
Farley, James A. Jim Farley's story; the Roosevelt years. New York, Whittlesey House [1948] 388 p. E806.F255

1322
Hull, Cordell. Memoirs. New York, Macmillan, 1948. 2 v. (1804 p.)
E748.H93A3
Prepared with the assistance of Andrew Berding.

1323
Nesbitt, Victoria Henrietta. White House diary, by Henrietta Nesbitt, F.D.R.'s housekeeper. Garden City, N. Y., Doubleday, 1948. 314 p. F204.W5N4

1324
Shawen, Lena Belle. A President's hobby. New York, H. L. Lindquist, ©1949. 48 p. HE6207.R66S5
Roosevelt as a stamp collector.

1325
Stettinius, Edward R. Roosevelt and the Russians; the Yalta Conference. Edited by Walter Johnson. Garden City, N. Y., Doubleday, 1949. xvi, 367 p.
D734.C7S8

1326
Tully, Grace G. F.D.R., my boss. With a foreword by William O. Douglas. New York, Scribner, 1949. 391 p.

1326
Tully, Grace G. F.D.R., my ... (Cont.)
E807.T78

1327
Gunther, John. Roosevelt in retrospect,
a profile in history. New York, Harper [1950] 410 p. E807.G85
Bibliography: p. 381-385.

1328
Leahy, William D. I was there; the personal story of the Chief of Staff to
Presidents Roosevelt and Truman, based
on his notes and diaries made at the
time. With a foreword by President
Truman. New York, Whittlesey House
[1950] 527 p.   D769.L4
"Much of this narrative is based on
my daily sessions with Roosevelt, and
subsequently with Truman, on military
affairs and foreign policy. Most of
these talks took place in the Oval
Study of the White House, where so
much history has been made"--The Author: p. 2.

1329
Lorant, Stefan. FDR; a pictorial biography. New York, Simon and Schuster,
1950. 159 p.   E807.L78

1330
Rauch, Basil. Roosevelt: from Munich to
Pearl Harbor; a study in the creation
of a foreign policy. New York, Crea-
tive Age Press, 1950. 527 p.
E807.R3 1950
"Reference notes": p. [497]-514.

1331
Sherwood, Robert E. Roosevelt and Hop-
kins, an intimate history. Rev. ed.
New York, Harper [1950] xix, 1002 p.
E807.S45 1950
First published in 1948.

1332
Rosenau, James N., ed. The Roosevelt
treasury. Garden City, N. Y., Doubleday, 1951. xvi, 461 p. E807.R687
Bibliography: p. 451-461.

1333
Evjen, Henry O. The Willkie campaign; an
unfortunate chapter in Republican
leadership. Journal of politics, v.
14, May 1952: 241-256.   JA1.J6, v. 14

1334
Freidel, Frank B. Franklin D. Roosevelt.
Boston, Little, Brown 1952-56.
3 v.   E807.F74
Contents.--1. The apprenticeship.--
2. The ordeal.--3. The triumph.
To be completed in 6 v.

1335
Gosnell, Harold F. Champion campaigner:
Franklin D. Roosevelt. New York, Mac-
millan, 1952. 235 p. E807.G68

1336
Rosenman, Samuel I. Working with Roosevelt. New York, Harper [1952]
560 p.   E807.R73

1337
Ickes, Harold L. The secret diary of
Harold L. Ickes. New York, Simon and
Schuster, 1953-54. 3 v. E806.I2
Contents.--[v. 1] The first thou-
sand days, 1933-1936.--v. 2. The in-
side struggle, 1936-1939.--v. 3. The
lowering clouds, 1939-1941.

1338
Walker, Turnley. Roosevelt and the Warm
Springs story. New York, A. A. Wyn
[1953] 311 p.   E807.W3

1339
Bellush, Bernard. Franklin D. Roosevelt
as Governor of New York. New York,
Columbia University Press, 1955
[c1952] 338 p. (Columbia studies in
the social sciences, no. 585)
E807.B4
H31.C7, no. 585

1340
Crownover, A. Blair. Franklin D. Roosevelt and the primary campaigns of the
1938 congressional election. [Prince-
ton] 1955. 177 p. E806.C8
Thesis (A. B.)--Princeton University.

1341

Robinson, Edgar Eugene. The Roosevelt
leadership, 1933-1945. Philadelphia,
Lippincott [^c1955] 491 p.
E806.R722

1342

Burns, James MacGregor. Roosevelt: the
lion and the fox. New York, Harcourt,
Brace [1956] 553 p.   E807.B835

1343

Flynn, John T. The Roosevelt myth. Rev.
ed. New York, Devin-Adair, 1956.
465 p.   E807.F59 1956
    John T. Flynn (b. 1882) was in 1933
a liberal journalist specializing in
financial questions. His dissatisfac-
tion with some of President Roosevelt's
measures in the financial field eventually turned into a radical antipathy
to the man and all his works, express-
ed in Country Squire in the White
House (New York, Doubleday, Doran,
1940. 131 p.), in the first edition
of the present work (1948. 438 p.),
and in this enlarged edition, which is
in effect a compendium of anti-Roose-
velt interpretation, opinion, and
rumor.

1344

Fusfeld, Daniel R. The economic thought
of Franklin D. Roosevelt and the origins of the New Deal. New York, Columbia University Press, 1956, ^c1954.
337 p. (Columbia studies in the so-
cial sciences, no. 586)
            H31.C7, no. 586
    Bibliography: p. [305]-320.

1345

Perkins, Dexter. The new age of Franklin Roosevelt, 1932-45. [Chicago]
University of Chicago Press, 1957.
193 p. (The Chicago history of American civilization)   E806.P465
    "Suggested reading": p. 176-181.

1346

Schlesinger, Arthur M., Jr. The age of
Roosevelt. Boston, Houghton Mifflin,
1957-1960. 3 v.   E806.S34
    Contents.--[1] The crisis of the

1346

Schlesinger, Arthus M., Jr. (Cont.)
old order, 1919-1933.--[2] The coming
of the New Deal.--[3] The politics of
upheaval.

1347

Tugwell, Rexford G. The democratic Roosevelt; a biography of Franklin D. Roosevelt. Garden City, N. Y., Doubleday,
1957. 712 p.   E807.T76
    Bibliography: p. 683-686.

1348

Greer, Thomas H. What Roosevelt thought;
the social and political ideas of
Franklin D. Roosevelt. [East Lansing]
Michigan State University Press, 1958.
244 p.   E807.G7
    "Bibliographical note": p. 229-234.

1349

Hassett, William D. Off the record with
F.D.R., 1942-1945. With an introd. by
Jonathan Daniels. New Brunswick,
N. J., Rutgers University Press, 1958.
366 p.   E807.H34

1350

Crocker, George N. Roosevelt's road to
Russia. Chicago, H. Regnery, 1959.
312 p.   E744.C845

1351

Einaudi, Mario. The Roosevelt revolution. New York, Harcourt, Brace
[1959] 372 p.   E806.E5

1352

Range, Willard. Franklin D. Roosevelt's
world order. Athens, University of
Georgia Press [1959] 219 p.
                E806.R26

1353

Roosevelt, James, and Sidney Shalett.
Affectionately, F.D.R.; a son's story
of a lonely man. New York, Harcourt,
Brace [1959] 394 p.   E807.R657

1354

Bellush, Bernard. An interpretation of
Franklin D. Roosevelt. In Sheehan,
Donald H., and Harold C. Syrett, eds.

138

1354
Bellush, Bernard. An ... (Cont.)
  Essays in American historiography;
  papers presented in honor of Allan
  Nevins. New York, Columbia Univer-
  sity Press, 1960. p. 287-309.
                    E175.S48

1355
Gould, Jean. A good fight: the story
  of F.D.R.'s conquest of polio. New
  York, Dodd, Mead, 1960. 308 p.
                    E807.G67

1356
Harrity, Richard, and Ralph G. Martin.
  The human side of F.D.R. New York,
  Duell, Sloan and Pearce [c1960]
  1 v. (chiefly illus.) E807.H33

1357
Woods, John A. Roosevelt and modern
  America. New York, Macmillan [1960,
  c1959] 192 p. (Teach yourself history library)   E807.W68

1358
Asbell, Bernard. When F.D.R. died. New
  York, Holt, Rinehart and Winston
  [1961] 211 p.   E807.A85

1359
Halasz, Nicholas. Roosevelt through
  foreign eyes. Princeton, N. J., Van
  Nostrand [1961] 340 p. E807.H3

1360
Rollins, Alfred Brooks. Roosevelt and
  Howe. New York, Knopf, 1962. 479 p.
                    E807.R627

1361
Roosevelt, Eleanor R. This is my story.
  New York, Harper, 1937. 365 p.
                    E807.1.R44

1362
----- My days. New York, Dodge Pub. Co.
  [1938] 254 p.   E807.1.R42

1363
James, Marquis. Mr. Garner of Texas.
  Indianapolis, Bobbs-Merrill [c1939]
  158 p.   E748.G23J3

1364
Black, Ruby A. Eleanor Roosevelt, a
  biography. New York, Duell, Sloan
  and Pearce [c1940] 331 p.
                    E807.1.R48

1365
Macdonald, Dwight. Henry Wallace, the
  man and the myth. New York, Vanguard
  Press [1948] 187 p. E748.W23M3

1366
Timmons, Bascom N. Garner of Texas, a
  personal history. New York, Harper
  [1948] 294 p.   E748.G23T5

1367
Knapp, Sally E. Eleanor Roosevelt, a
  biography. New York, Crowell Co.
  [1949] 185 p.   E807.1.R57

1368
Roosevelt, Eleanor R. This I remember.
  New York, Harper [1949] 387 p.
                    E807.1.R428

1369
Stiles, Lela. The man behind Roosevelt;
  the story of Louis McHenry Howe.
  Cleveland, World Pub. Co. [1954]
  311 p.   E748.H787S8
     A life of the journalist who was
  Roosevelt's chief political aide from
  1912 until his death early in 1936.

1370
Harrity, Richard, and Ralph G. Martin.
  Eleanor Roosevelt: her life in pic-
  tures. New York, Duell, Sloan and
  Pearce [1958] 212 p. E807.1.R53

1371
Roosevelt, Eleanor R. On my own. New
  York, Harper [1958] 241 p.
                    E807.1.R424

1372
Steinberg, Alfred. Mrs. R, the life of
  Eleanor Roosevelt. New York, Put-
  nam [1958] 384 p.   E807.1.R59
     Bibliography: p. 373-375.

1373
Johnson, Donald Bruce. The Republican

1373
Johnson, Donald Bruce. The ... (Cont.)
  Party and Wendell Wilkie. Urbana,
  University of Illinois Press, 1960.
  354 p.   E748.W7J6 1960a
    Bibliography: p. 327-336.

1374
Roosevelt, Eleanor R. Autobiography.
  New York, Harper, 1961. 454 p.
                  E807.1.R35
    "Both an abbreviated and an aug-
  mented edition" of This Is My Story,
  This I Remember, and On My Own.

HARRY S. TRUMAN

Writings

1375
Truman, Harry S. The Truman program;
  addresses and messages. Introd. by
  Francis J. Myers; edited by M. B.
  Schnapper. Washington, Public Affairs
  Press [1949] 261 p. E813.T69

1376
----- Mr. President; the first publication from the personal diaries, private letters, papers, and revealing
  interviews of Harry S. Truman, thirty-
  second President of the United States
  of America. By William Hillman. Pictures by Alfred Wagg. New York, Farrar, Straus and Young [1952] 253 p.
                  E814.T7

1377
----- Memoirs. Garden City, N. Y.,
  Doubleday, 1955-56. 2 v. E814.T75
    Contents.--v. 1. Year of deci-
  sions.--v. 2. Years of trial and
  hope.

1378
----- The Truman administration, its
  principles and practice. Edited by
  Louis W. Koenig. New York, New York
  University Press, 1956. 394 p.
                  E813.T68

1379
----- Freedom and equality, addresses.
  David S. Horton, editor. Columbia,
  University of Missouri Press [1960]
                  JC599.U5T7

1380
----- Mr. Citizen. [New York] Geiss
  Associates; distributed by Random
  House [1960] 315 p. E814.A33

1381
----- Truman speakes. [Lectures and
  discussions held at Columbia University on April 27, 28, and 29, 1959]
  New York, Columbia University Press,
  1960. 133 p. JK516.T7

Biography

1382
McNaughton, Frank, and Walter Hehmeyer.
  Harry Truman, President. New York,
  Whittlesey House [1948] 294 p.
                  E814.M27
1383
Ernst, Morris L., and David Loth.
  The people know best; the ballots vs.
  the polls. [Washington] Public Af-
  fairs Press [1949] 169 p.
                  E815.E7
    A critical review of the techniques
  used by the many columnists, commenta-

1383
Ernst, Morris L., and David Loth. (Cont.)
tors and pollsters who predicted a
landslide for Thomas E. Dewey in 1948.
The authors warn the voting public to
"beware of prophets."

1384
Daniels, Jonathan. The man of Independence. Philadelphia, Lippincott
[1950] 384 p.   E814.D3
    Bibliography: p. 371-373.

1385
Forrestal, James. The Forrestal diaries.
Edited by Walter Millis with the col-
laboration of E. S. Duffield. New
York, Viking Press, 1951. xxiv, 581 p.
                    E813.F6

1386
Hersey, John. Profiles. Mr. President.
New Yorker, v. 27, Apr. 7, 1951: 42+;
Apr. 14: 38+; Apr. 21: 36+; Apr. 28:
36+; May 5: 36+.
                    AP2.N6763, v.27
    "In general, it can be said that
Hersey's series is the most enlighten-
ing single source as yet available on
Truman as President and on the daily
tasks of being President in our time.
It is superb reporting."--R. E. Neu-
stadt in no. 64 above, p. 213.

1387
Rovere, Richard H., and Arthur M. Schlesinger, Jr. The general and the President, and the future of American foreign policy. [New York] Farrar, Straus
and Young [1951] 336 p.   E745.M3R6

1388
Michigan. University. Survey Research
Center. The people elect a President,
by Angus Campbell and Robert L. Kahn,
with the editorial assistance of Sylvia
Eberhart. Ann Arbor, Survey Research
Center, Institute for Social Research,
University of Michigan, 1952. 73 p.
(Its Publication no. 9)
                    JK526 1952.M5

1389
Abels, Jules. The Truman scandals. Chi-

1389
Abels, Jules. The Truman ... (Cont.)
cago, H. Regnery, 1956. 329 p.
                    E813.A2

1390
----- Out of the jaws of victory. New
York, Holt [1959] 336 p.   E815.A2

1391
Spanier, John W. The Truman-MacArthur
controversy and the Korean War. Cambridge, Mass., Belknap Press, 1959.
311 p.   DS919.S62
    Bibliography: p. 298-306.

1392
Schmidt, Karl M. Henry A. Wallace, quix-
otic crusade 1948. [Syracuse] Syracuse University Press, 1960. 362 p.
(Men and movements series)   E815.S35

1393
Steinberg, Alfred. The man from Missouri;
the life and times of Harry S. Truman.
New York, Putnam [1962] 447 p.
                    E814.S74

1394
Barkley, Alben W. That reminds me. Garden City, N. Y., Doubleday, 1954.
288 p.   E748.B318A3
    Autobiography.

1395
Truman, Margaret. Souvenir, Margaret
Truman's own story; by Margaret Truman,
with Margaret Cousins. New York, Mc-
Graw-Hill [1956] 365 p.   E814.1.T7
    The greater part of the book (p. 91-
331) is concerned with the years dur-
ing which the Trumans were in the White
House or Blair House; the later chap-
ters are increasingly taken up with
Miss Truman's concert tours.

DWIGHT D. EISENHOWER

Writings

1396

Eisenhower, Dwight D. Eisenhower speaks:
Dwight D. Eisenhower in his messages
and speeches. Selected and edited by
Rudolph L. Treuenfels. New York, Far-
rar, Straus, 1948. xix, 299 p.
E836.E3A4

1397

----- What Eisenhower thinks. Edited
and interpreted by Allan Taylor. [New
rev. ed.] New York, Crowell [1953]
185 p.   E836.A58 1953
First published in 1952.

1398

----- Peace with justice; selected ad-
dresses. With a foreword by Grayson
Kirk. New York, Columbia University
Press, 1961. 273 p.   E835.E42

1399

----- Crusade in Europe. Garden City,
New York, Doubleday, 1948.   559 p.
D743.E35 1948

Biography

1400

Butcher, Harry C. My three years with
Eisenhower; the personal diary of Captain Harry C. Butcher, USNR, naval
aide to General Eisenhower, 1942 to
1945. New York, Simon and Schuster,
1946. xvii, 911 p.   D811.B86

1401

McKeogh, Michael J., and Richard Lock-
ridge. Sgt. Mickey and General Ike.
New York, Putnam [1946] 185 p.
D811.M24

1402

Summersby, Kathleen M. Eisenhower was
my boss, by Kay Summersby. Edited

1402

Summersby, Kathleen M. (Cont.)
by Michael Kearns. New York, Prentice-
Hall [1948] 302 p.   E745.E35S8

1403

American Academy of Political and Social
Science, Philadelphia. Meaning of the
1952 presidential election. Edited by
James C. Charlesworth. Philadelphia,
1952. 252 p. (Its Annals, v. 283)
E816.A53
H1.A4, v. 283

1404

Davis, Kenneth S. Soldier of democracy;
a biography of Dwight Eisenhower.
[New ed.] Garden City, N. Y., Doubleday, 1952. 577 p.   E745.E35D3 1952
First published in 1945 (566 p.).

1405

Gunther, John. Eisenhower, the man and
the symbol. New York, Harper [1952]
180 p.   E745.E35G8

1406

Hatch, Alden. General Ike, a biography
of Dwight D. Eisenhower. Rev. and
enl. ed. New York, Holt [1952]
320 p.   E745.E35H3 1952
First published in 1944 (288 p.).

1407

Blumberg, Nathan B. One-party press?
Coverage of the 1952 presidential campaign in 35 daily newspapers. Lincoln, University of Nebraska Press
[1954] 91 p.   E816.B55

1408

Campbell, Angu, Gerald Gurin, and Warren E. Miller. The voter decides.
Evanston, Ill., Row, Peterson [1954]
242 p.   JK526 1952.C3
Based on a survey of the 1952 elec-

1408
Campbell, Angus, Gerald Gurin, and War-
    ren E. Miller. (Cont.)
    tion conducted by the Survey Research
    Center at the University of Michigan.

1409
David, Paul T., Malcolm Moos, and Ralph M.
    Goldman. Presidential nominating pol-
    itics in 1952. Baltimore, Johns Hop-
    kins Press [1954] 5 v.   JK521.D35
        "Report of the cooperative research
    project on convention delegations pre-
    pared under the auspices of the Amer-
    ican Political Science Association with
    the cooperation of the Brookings Insti-
    tution."
        Contents.--v. 1. The national sto-
    ry.--v. 2. The Northeast.--v. 3. The
    South.--v. 4. The Middle West.--v. 5.
    The West.

1410
De Grazia, Alfred. The western public,
    1952 and beyond. Stanford, Calif.,
    Stanford University Press [1954]
    226 p.   E816.D4

1411
Taylor, Robert L. A week inside the
    White House. Collier's, v. 133, Feb. 19,
    1954: 23-27; Mar. 5, 1954: 30-37.
                    AP2.C65, v. 133
        A veteran journalist, given virtual-
    ly free access to the working quarters
    of the White House, describes the Pres-
    ident's daily routine on the job and
    his regular recreations.

1412
Smith, A. Merriman. Meet Mister Eisen-
    hower. New York, Harper [1955]
    308 p.   E836.S55

1413
Donovan, Robert J. Eisenhower: the in-
    side story. New York, Harper [1956]
    xviii, 423 p.   E835.D6

1414
Janowitz, Morris, and Dwaine Marvick.
    Competitive pressure and democratic
    consent; an interpretation of the 1952
    presidential election. Ann Arbor, Bur-

1414
Janowitz, Morris. Competitive ... (Cont.)
    eau of Government, Institute of Public
    Administration, University of Michigan,
    1956. 122 p. (Michigan governmental
    studies, no. 32)   JK526 1952.J3

1415
Pusey, Merlo J. Eisenhower, the Presi-
    dent. New York, Macmillan, 1956.
    300 p.   E835.P8

1416
Rovere, Richard H. The Eisenhower years;
    affairs of state. New York, Farrar,
    Straus and Cudahy [1956] 390 p.
                          E835.R6

1417
Smith, Walter Bedell. Eisenhower's six
    great decisions: Europe, 1944-1945.
    New York, Longmans, Green, 1956.
    237 p.   D756.S55

1418
Snyder, Marty. My friend Ike, by Marty
    Snyder with Glenn D. Kittler. New
    York, F. Fell, 1956. 237 p.
                          E836.S58

1418a
Thomson, Charles A. H. Television and
    presidential politics; the experience
    in 1952 and the problems ahead.
    Washington, Brookings Institution,
    1956. 173 p.   JK524.T45

1419
Scoble, Harry M. Press and politics, 1956.
    Boston, 1957. 113 p. (Boston Univer-
    sity studies in political science,
    no. 3)   PN4867.S35

1420
Childs, Marquis W. Eisenhower: captive
    hero; a critical study of the general
    and the President. New York, Harcourt,
    Brace [1958] 310 p.   E836.C5

1421
Thomson, Charles A. H., and Frances M.
    Shattuck. The 1956 Presidential cam-
    paign. Washington, Brookings Institu-
    tion [1960] 382 p.   E839.T48

1422

Adams, Sherman. Firsthand report; the
story of the Eisenhower administration. New York, Harper [1961]
481 p.   E835.A3

1423

Smith, A. Merriman. A President's odyssey. New York, Harper [1961] 272 p.
E825.S55

1424

Benson, Ezra Taft. Cross fire, the eight
years with Eisenhower. Garden City,
N. Y., Doubleday, 1962. 627 p.
E835.B43

1425

Eulau, Heinz. Class and party in the
Eisenhower years; class roles and per-
spectives in the 1952 and 1956 elections. [New York] Free Press of Glen-
coe [1962] 162 p.   E816.E78

1426

Harris, Seymour E. The economics of the
political parties, with special attention to Presidents Eisenhower and Kennedy. New York, Macmillan, 1962.
382 p.   HC106.5.H319

1427

Rutgers University, New Brunswick, N. J.
Eagleton Institute of Politics. Inside politics: the national conventions, 1960, edited by Paul Tillett.
Dobbs Ferry, N. Y., Oceana Publications, 1962. 281 p. (America's politics series, no. 2)   E840.R8

1427a

Hughes, Emmet John. The ordeal of power;
a political memoir of the Eisenhower
years. New York, Atheneum, 1963.
372 p.   E835.H8 1963
    Recollections and reflections of a
Presidential speech-writer, who was
allowed to sit in on a number of Cabinet meetings.

1428

Brandon, Dorothy B. Mamie Doud Eisenhower; a portrait of a First Lady.
New York, Scribner, 1954. 307 p.

1428

Brandon, Dorothy B. Mamie ... (Cont.)
E837.B7

1429

Hatch, Alden. Red carpet for Mamie. New
York, Holt [1954] 277 p.   E837.E4H3

1430

De Toledano, Ralph. Nixon. Rev. and expanded ed. New York, Duell, Sloan and
Pearce [1960] 250 p.   E748.N5D4 1960
    First edition: New York, Holt
[1956].

1431

Mazo, Earl. Richard Nixon, a political
and personal portrait. Rev. to include
new material. New York, Avon Book Division, Hearst Corp. [1960] 270 p.
(Avon T-416)   E748.N5M3 1960
    First edition: New York, Harper
[1959].

1432

Nixon, Richard M. Six crises. Garden
City, N. Y., Doubleday, 1962. 460 p.
E748.N5A3

JOHN F. KENNEDY

Writings

1433

Kennedy, John F. Why England slept. New York. W. Funk, 1940. xx, 252 p.
DA578.K4
Reissued in 1961, and published as a paperback in 1962 (Doubleday Dolphin books, C379).

1434

-----, ed. As we remember Joe. Cambridge, Priv. print., University Press, 1945. 60 p.   InU
A collection of tributes to John F. Kennedy's eldest brother, Lt. Joseph P. Kennedy Jr., killed in World War II. The edition was limited to 150 copies for distribution to relatives and friends.

1435

----- Profiles in courage. New York, Harper [c1956] 266 p.
E176.K4

1436

----- A nation of immigrants. [New York, Anti-Defamation League of B'nai B'rith, 1959?] 40 p. (The One nation library)
JV6453.K4

1437

----- The strategy of peace. Edited by Allan Nevins. New York, Harper, 1960. 233 p.   E835.K48
Speeches and statements on U. S. foreign policy.

1438

----- To turn the tide; a selection from President Kennedy's public statements from his election through the 1961 adjournment of Congress, setting forth the goals of his first legislative year. Edited by John W. Gardner. Introd. by President Kennedy. New York, Harper, 1962. 235 p.   E841.K43

Biography

1439

Burns, James MacGregor. John Kennedy; a political profile. New York, Harcourt, Brace & World [1961] xxiii, 309 p.
E842.B8 1961
"Bibliographical note': p. 283-284. First published in 1960.

1440

David, Paul T., ed. The Presidential election and transition, 1960-1961; Brookings lectures and additional papers [by] Paul T. David [and others] Washington, Brookings Institution [1961] 353 p.   E840.D38

1441

Donovan, Robert J. PT109, John F. Kennedy in World War II. New York, McGraw-Hill [1961] 247 p.   E842.D6

1442

Lowe, Jacques. Portrait: the emergence of John F. Kennedy. New York, McGraw-Hill [1961] 223 p.   E842.L65
The majority of these handsomely reproduced photographs were taken by Mr. Lowe, and the running commentary is also by him.

1443

Markmann, Charles Lam, and Mark Sherwin. John F. Kennedy: a sense of purpose. New York, St. Martin's Press [1961] 346 p.   E841.M3

1444

Michener, James A. Report of the county chairman. New York, Randon House [1961] 310 p.   E840.M5

1445

Tanzer, Lester, ed. The Kennedy circle. Washington, Luce [1961] 315 p. E841.T3

1446

White, Theodore H. The making of the
   President, 1960. New York, Atheneum
   Publishers, 1961. 400 p. E840.W5

1447

Fuller, Helen. Year of trial; Kennedy's
   crucial decisions. New York, Harcourt, Brace [1962] 307 p. E841.F8

1448

Kraus, Sidney, ed. The great debates:
   background, perspective, effects.
   [Bloomington] Indiana University Press
   [1962] 439 p. E840.K7
     Includes the text of the 4 tele-
   vised debates between Kennedy and Richard M. Nixon in the 1960 campaign.

1449

Manchester, William R. Portrait of a
   President: John F. Kennedy in profile. Boston, Little, Brown [1962]
   238 p. E842.M3

1450

Tregaskis, Richard W. John F. Kennedy:
   war hero. [New York, Dell Pub. Co.,
   1962] 223 p. (A Dell book, F194)
               E842.T7 1962a
     An expanded ed. of John F. Kennedy
   and PT-109.

1451

Dinneen, Joseph F. The Kennedy family.
   Boston, Little, Brown [1960, ^c1959]
   238 p. E747.D5

1452

Thayer, Mary Van Rensselaer. Jacqueline
   Bouvier Kennedy. Garden City, N. Y.,
   Doubleday, 1961. 127 p. illus.
               E843.K4T5

1453

Wolff, Perry S. A tour of the White
   House with Mrs. John F. Kennedy. Garden City, N. Y., Doubleday, 1962.
   258 p. F204.W5W73
    Based on the television program,
   with additional information and illustrations.

SUBJECT INDEXES

ELECTIONS

FIRST LADIES (and White House hostesses).

VICE PRESIDENTS

INDEX OF AUTHORS, EDITORS, TITLE ENTRIES, etc.

Betts, Edwin Morris, 415, 420, 458
Beveridge, Albert J., 755
Bible, N. T., Gospels, 404
Biddle, Alexander, 355
Binkley, Wilfred E., 51, 72
Bishop, Joseph Bucklin, 1043, 1058
Bixby, William K., 408, 674
Black, Chauncey F., 723
Black, Ruby A., 1364
Blaine, James G., 981
Blanchard, Robert, 109
Bland, Raymond L., 1266
Blum, John M., 1005, 1084, 1182, 1190
Blumberg, Nathan B., 1407
Bobbé, Dorothie De Bear, 376, 583
Bolles, Blair, 54
Bolton, Charles Knowles, 79
Bond, Beverly W., 531
Boorstin, Daniel J., 478
Booth, Edward Townsend, 135
Borden, Morton, 157
Boston Athenaeum, 240
Boutell, Lewis Henry, 429
Bowen, Clarence Winthrop, 261
Bowers, Claude G., 126, 144, 439, 452,
    470, 609
Boyd, Julian P., 383, 471
Boyden, William L., 121
Boykin, Edward C., 230
Bradford, Gamaliel, 1232
Brady, Cyrus Townsend, 605
Brandes, Joseph, 1283
Brandon, Dorothy B., 1428
Brant, Irving, 515
Bristow, Joseph L., 995
Brooke, Walter Edwin, 245
Brooks, Chester L., 1089
Brooks, Noah, 734
Brooks, William E., 905
Brown, Everett S., 27, 581
Brown, Stuart Gerry, 527
Brown, William Burlie, 55
Brown, William Garrott, 604
Brown, Wilson, 204
Browne, Charles A., 463
Browne, Francis F., 726
Brownlow, Louis, 26
Bruce, David K. E., 163
Bruce, Robert V., 826
Bryan, George S., 769
Bryan, Guy, 917
Bryan, William Alfred, 328
Bryan, William Jennings, 1110, 1146

Buehrig, Edward H., 1188, 1194
Bullard, Frederic Lauriston, 788, 811,
    812
Bullock, Helen C. Duprey, 459, 472
Burgess, John W., 923
Burke, Pauline Wilcox, 622
Burnham, Walter Dean, 98
Burns, Edward McNall, 514
Burns, James MacGregor, 1342, 1439
Burroughs, John, 1051
Butcher, Harry C., 1400
Butcher, Walter, 99
Butler, Benjamin F., 2
Butt, Archibald W., 1064, 1114
Butterfield, Consul W., 236, 237
Butterfield, Lyman H., 342, 367, 371, 383

C

Cabell, Joseph C., 423
Cabell, Nathaniel F., 423
Cadwallader, Sylvanus, 909
Caldwell, Lynton K., 468
Caldwell, Mary French, 621
Caldwell, Robert Granville, 945
Callender, James Thomson, 431
Campbell, Angus, 1388, 1408
Canby, Courtlandt, 837
Capers, Gerald M., 596
Cappon, Lester J., 358
Carman, Harry J., 683, 775
Carmichael, Donald Scott, 1301
Carpenter, Francis B., 721
Carrington, Henry B., 266
Carter, Clarence E., 638
Catton, Bruce, 908, 911
Chamberlain, Lawrence H., 22
Chambrun, Charles, Marquis de, 813
Chandler, William E., 948
Chapple, Joseph Mitchell, 1216
Charlesworth, James C., 1403
Charnwood, Godfrey R. B., 1st Baron, 744
Chase, Salmon P., 818
Childs, Marquis W., 1420
Chinard, Gilbert, 318, 365, 409, 410, 412,
    413, 440, 445, 449, 456, 462
Chittenden, Cecil R., 182
Chittenden, Lucius E., 732
Chitwood, Oliver Perry, 654
Church, William Conant, 888
Clancy, Herbert J., 947
Clark, Allen C., 519, 752
Clark, Bennett Champ, 584

Cleaves, Freeman, 639
Cleland, Hugh, 332
Coffey, Joseph I., 68
Coit, Margaret L., 595
Coleman, Charles H.,899
Coleman, Elizabeth Tyler, 657
Colm, G., 44
Colman, Edna M. Hercher, 179, 180
Cometti, Elizabeth, 418
Commins, Saxe, 232
Conant, James B., 495
Condict, Lewis, 552
Confederate States of America. Congress, 649
Conger, Arthur L., 898
Connery, Thomas B., 942
Conway, Moncure Daniel, 238
Conwell, Russell H., 112
Cooke, Jacob E., 507
Cooley, Thomas M., 2
Coolidge, Louis A., 894
Coolidge, Thomas Jefferson, Jr., 407, 438
Corbin, John, 285
Corey, Herbert, 1267
Corwin, Edward S., 5, 9, 27, 42, 45, 1178
Cotter, Cornelius P., 66
Cousins, Margaret, 1395
Cowles, Anna Roosevelt, 1044
Coyle, David Cushman, 56
Craig, Hardin, 1204
Cramer, Jesse Grant, 895
Cramer, John Henry, 796
Cramer, Michael J., 884
Cranch, Mary Smith, 377
Crane, Katharine E., 189
Crawford, Valentine, 236
Crawford, William, 236
Creel, George, 1315
Crenshaw, Ollinger, 781
Cresson, William P., 536
Crocker, George N., 1350
Crook, William H., 177
Crownover, A. Blair, 1340
Cuba. Comisión ... de Teodoro Roosevelt, 1090
Cunliffe, Marcus, 336
Cunningham, William, 352
Current, Richard N., 783, 830, 832
Curry, Roy Watson, 1195
Curtis, George Ticknor, 691
Curtis, William E., 434
Cushing, Caleb, 634
Custis, George Washington Parke, 255

Cuthbert, Norma B., 803
Cutright, Paul Russell, 1087
Cutts, Lucia B., 517

D

Daniel, Marjorie L., 1165
Daniels, Jonathan, 146, 1186, 1384
Daniels, Josephus, 1172, 1177
Daniels, Walter Machray, 95
Daniels, Winthrop M., 1173
Dauer, Manning J., 370
Daugherty, Harry M., 1218
Daughters of the American Revolution, Indiana, 641
David, Paul T, 105, 1409, 1440
Davidson, John Wells, 1144
Davis, Harold E., 940
Davis, John W., 126
Davis, Kenneth S., 1404
Davis, Matthew L., 496
Davis, Oscar King, 1065
Davis, Richard Beale, 416
Dawes, Charles Gates, 994, 1241
Dawson, Moses, 633
Day, Donald, 1007, 1126, 1292
Dean, Elizabeth L., 520
Decatur, Stephan, 307
De Conde, Alexander, 1275
De Grazia, Alfred, 1410
De La Bedoyère, Michael, 313
Delaware. Public Archives Commission, 294
Dennett, Tyler, 767, 1066
Denslow, Ray V., 121
De Santis, Vincent P., 984
De Toledano, Ralph, 1430
DeWitt, David Miller, 738, 865, 866
Diamond, William, 1171
Dietz, August, 143
Dinneen, Joseph F., 1451
Dixon, Thomas, 1218
Dodd, William E., 1120, 1149
Dodge, Daniel Kilham, 749
Donald, David H., 797, 818, 834, 877
Donaldson, Thomas, 432
Donelson, Andrew J., 661
Donnelly, Thomas C., 1265, 1308
Donovan, Michael J., 1053
Donovan, Robert J., 145, 1413, 1441
Dorris, Jonathan Truman, 876
Dorsey, John M., 421
Dos Passos, John, 491
Dougherty, John Hampden, 74

150

Hicks, Frederick C., 1117
Hildreth, Richard, 634
Hill, Howard C., 1070
Hilliard, William, 418
Hillman, William, 1376
Hinsdale, Burke A., 935, 938, 940
Hinsdale, Mary L., 938
Hinshaw, David, 1273
Hirst, Francis W., 442
Historical Records Survey. New York
     (City), 138
Hobart, Jennie Tuttle, 1003
Hobbs, Edward H., 33, 44
Hoffmann, William S., 620
Hollister, Ovando J., 913
Honeywell, Roy J., 450
Hoover, Herbert, 1199
Hoover, Irwin Hood (Ike), 184
Hoover, Lou Henry, 1245
Horn, John S., 60
Horn, Stanley F., 615
Horner, Harlan Hoyt, 817
Horton, David S., 1379
House, Edward M., 1161
Houser, Martin L., 828
Houston, David F., 1162
Howard, Oliver Otis, 675
Howe, George Frederick, 949
Howells, William Dean, 715, 921
Howland, Harold J., 1061
Hoyt, Edwin Palmer, 106
Hubbard, Cortlandt Van D., 208
Hudson, J. Paul, 333
Hugh-Jones, Edward M., 1181
Hughes, Charles Evans, 126
Hughes, Rupert, 277
Hull, Cordell, 1322
Humbert, Willard H., 17
Hume, Edgar Erskine, 249
Hunt, Gaillard, 173, 269, 362, 433, 504,
     512
Hurd, Charles, 188
Hurwitz, Howard Lawrence, 1080
Hutchins, Cortelle, 317
Hutchins, Frank, 317
Hutchinson, William T., 505
Hyde, Arthur Mastick, 1271
Hyman, Harold M., 879
Hyman, Sidney, 34, 41

I

Iacuzzi, Alfred, 369
Ickes, Harold L., 1337
Irelan, John R., 112
Irvine, William, 237
Irving, Washington, 254
Irwin, William H. (Will), 1047, 1264
Ives, Mabel Lorenz, 298

J

Jackson, Robert H., 1312
Jaffa, Harry V., 835
Jaffray, Elizabeth, 181
James, Marquis, 613, 614, 1363
Jameson, John Franklin, 530
Janowitz, Morris, 1414
Jay, John, 507
Jefferson, Isaac, 487
Jefferson, Randolph, 414
Jeffries, Ona Griffin, 211
Jenkins, Charles Francis, 242, 405
Jensen, Amy La Follette, 215
Johnsen, Julia Emily, 90
Johnson, Cave, 660
Johnson, Donald Bruce, 1373
Johnson, Gerald W., 1175
Johnson, Walter, 61
Johnston, Frances B., 170
Jones, Cranston, 165
Jones, Edgar De Witt, 799
Jones, Harry Wilmer, 18
Joslin, Theodore G., 1249, 1269
Judah, Charles B., 96, 110

K

Kane, Joseph Nathan, 152
Kaplan, Milton, 141
Kearns, Michael, 1402
Keckley, Elizabeth Hobbs, 722
Keeler, Lucy Elliot, 925
Keen, William W., 963
Kelly, Frank K., 1207
Kerney, James, 1157
Kilpatrick, Carroll, 1303
Kimball, Fiske, 407, 462, 469
Kimball, Marie Goebel, 454, 457, 465, 476,
     485
King, Grace, 283
King, Horatio, 692
Kingdon, Frank, 1290
Kirk, Grayson, 1398

Kittler, Glenn D., 1418
Klapthor, Margaret Brown, 198, 492
Klein, Philip Shriver, 697, 701, 703
Knapp, Sally E., 1367
Knight, Franklin, 234
Knoles, George Harmon, 971
Knollenberg, Bernhard, 319
Knox, Dudley W., 299
Knox, Katherine McCook, 287
Koch, Adrienne, 343, 389, 466, 479, 486
Koenig, Louis William, 42, 62, 1313, 1378
Kohlsaat, Herman H., 120
Kraus, Sidney, 1448
Kreager, H. D., 44
Kuhns, William T., 993
Kurtz, Stephen G., 372

L

Lafayette, Marquis de, 250, 412
LaFeber, Walter, 974
Lambert, Oscar D., 653
Lambert, William Alexander, 436
Lamon, Ward Hill, 723, 741
Lang, Lincoln A., 1069
Langer, William L., 1197
Langford, Laura C. H., 168
Lansing, Robert, 1150, 1166
Larkin, John Day, 13
Laski, Harold J., 16, 27
Latham, Earl, 1200
Lathem, Edward Connery, 1239
Lawrence, David, 1158
Lazarsfeld, Paul F., 87, 97
Leahy, William D., 1328
Lear, Tobias, 307
Learned, Henry Barrett, 4
Leduc, Gilbert F., 321
Lee, Gordon C., 393
Leech, Margaret, 999
Leeming, Joseph, 199
Lehmann-Hartleben, Karl, 477
Leighton, Frances Spatz, 214
Leighton, Isabelle, 1307
Leonard, Daniel, 351
Leupp, Francis E., 1049
Levin, Peter R., 139
Lewis, Ethel, 186
Lewis, Lloyd, 757, 906
Lincoln, Robert W., 111
Lindley, Ernest K., 1306, 1309
Link, Arthur S., 1180, 1187, 1196, 1197,
    1203

Linthicum, Richard, 1121
Linville, C. Edwin, 46
Lipscomb, Andrew A., 382, 404
Lipsky, George A., 590
Little, Shelby Melton, 284
Lochner, Louis P., 1282
Lockridge, Richard, 1401
Lockridge, Ross F., 982
Lodge, Henry Cabot, 267, 1019, 1045
Logan, Rayford W., 487
Lomask, Milton, 880
Long, Everette B., 883
Long, John C., 140
Longaker, Richard P., 44, 71
Longworth, Alice Roosevelt, 1097
Looker, Earle, 1072
Lorant, Stefan, 92, 829, 1093, 1329
Loth, David G., 1170, 1383
Lott, Davis Newton, 158
Lowe, Gabriel L., 618
Lowe, Jacques, 1442
Luthin, Reinhard H., 683, 775, 777, 843
Lynch, Denis Tilden, 626, 967
Lynch, William O., 676
Lyons, Eugene, 1278

M

McAdoo, Eleanor R. Wilson, 1145, 1167
Macartney, Clarence E., 907
McCaleb, Walter Flavius, 1075
McCarthy, Charles H., 735
McClure, Alexander K., 733
McClure, Stanley W., 844
McClure, Wallace, 27
McCombs, William F., 1151
McConnell, Burt M., 149, 201, 206
McConnell, Jane Tompkins, 149, 201, 206
McCormac, Eugene Irving, 664
McCoy, Charles A., 671
Macdonald, Dwight, 1365
McElroy, Robert M., 965, 987
McGee, Dorothy Horton, 1279
McIlwaine, H. R., 411
McIntire, Ross T., 1315
MacKay, Kenneth Campbell, 1236
McKeogh, Michael J. (Mickey), 1401
McKinley, Silas Bent, 679, 1198
McKitrick, Eric L., 881
McKnight, David A., 74
McLaughlin, Andrew C., 570
MacLean, John Coyne, 38
McNaughton, Frank, 1382

154

McQuown, Ruth, 91
Magie, David, 1002
Malone, Dumas, 413, 451, 480
Manchester, William R., 1449
Manning, Warren H., 436
Marburg, Theodore, 1111
Marchman, Watt P., 930
Marcy, Carl Milton, 21
Markmann, Charles Lam, 1443
Marsh, Philip M., 526
Marshall, John, 252
Marshall, Thomas R., 1209
Martin, Asa Earl, 142
Martin, Edward T., 488
Martin, Laurence W., 1201
Martin, Ralph G., 1356, 1370
Marvick, Dwaine, 1414
Marx, Rudolph, 154
Mason, Edward Campbell, 3
Mattison, Ray H., 1089
May, Ernest R., 63
May, James T., 932
Mayo, Barbara (Lida), 460
Mayo, Bernard, 387, 414
Mayo, Katherine, 315
Mayo, Lawrence Shaw, 582
Mazo, Earl, 1431
Mearns, David C., 146, 716, 848
Merrill, Horace Samuel, 972
Meserve, Frederick Hill, 778
Meyer, Leland W., 629
Meyer, Richard, 109
Meyersohn, Maxwell, 1291
Michener, James A., 1444
Michigan. University. Survey Research
        Center, 1388, 1408
Middleton, Lamar, 220
Miers, Earl Schenck, 712, 846, 910
Milhollen, Hirst D., 141
Miller, David Hunter, 1152
Millis, Walter, 1385
Milton, George Fort, 20, 871
Minnigerode, Meade, 77, 498
Mitchell, Stewart, 377
Mitgang, Herbert, 827
Moley, Raymond, 1311
Monaghan, James (Jay), 782
Montgomery, Henry, 675
Moore, Charles, 246, 278
Moore, Edmund Arthur, 1276
Moore, Frank, 863
Moore, Guy W., 820
Moore, John Bassett, 689

Moore, Joseph Hampton, 1068
Moore, Powell, 666, 667
Moore, William G., 867
Moos, Malcolm C., 93, 107, 1409
Moran, Thomas F., 128
Mordell, Albert, 724
Morgan, George, 532
Morgan, H. Wayne, 991, 1001
Morgan, James, 150
Morgan, John Hill, 290
Morgan, Robert J., 655
Morganston, Charles E., 10
Morison, Elting E., 1005
Morison, Samuel Eliot, 300
Morley, Blaine, 109
Morris, Edwin B., 195
Morris, Joe Alex, 194
Morrow, Honore M. W., 857
Morse, John T., 361, 577
Morstein Marx, Fritz, 24
Mott, Frank L., 467
Motter, T. H. Vail, 1142
Mowry, George E., 1082
Murphy, James W., 1215
Muzzey, David Saville, 437
Myers, William Starr, 1178, 1251, 1270,
        1272

N

A Narrative of a Tour of Observation, 528
Nason, Elias, 912
Nelson, Anson, 672
Nelson, Fanny, 672
Nesbitt, Victoria Henrietta, 1323
Nettels, Curtis P., 327
Neustadt, Richard E., 35, 39, 44, 64
Nevada. Legislative Counsel Bureau, 101
Nevins, Allan. 540, 659, 708, 852, 904,
        953, 968, 1437
New York. Public Library, 273
Newton, Walter H., 1270
Nichols, Roy F., 688, 699
Nicolay, Helen, 743, 804
Nicolay, John G., 705, 730, 736
Nixon, Edgar B., 1304
Nixon, Richard M., 1432, 1448
Nock, Albert Jay, 443
Noggle, Burl, 1223
Nolan, James Bennett, 291
Norton, Anthony B., 635
Notter, Harley, 1168

O, P

O'Gara, Gordon Carpenter, 1081
Ogg, Frederic A., 608
Olcott, Charles S., 992
Orton, Vrest, 1240
Osborn, Lucretia Perry, 229
Overacker, Louise, 76, 84
Pach, Alfred, 132
Padover, Saul K., 233, 388, 392, 417, 461, 506, 1124
Page, Elwin L., 301
Paine, Thomas, 541
Palmer, John Macaulay, 125
Paltsits, Victor Hugo, 247
Parker, George F., 951, 960
Parker, Wyman W., 919, 931
Parks, Lillian Rogers, 214
Parton, James, 427, 497, 602
Partridge, Bellamy, 1078
Patterson, Caleb Perry, 23, 27, 489
Patton, John S., 435
Peckham, Howard H., 643
Peden, William, 343, 389, 396
Peek, George A., 344
Peel, Roy V., 1265, 1308
Peirce, Clyde R., 1094
Pendell, Thomas F., 171
Pepper, George Wharton, 11
Perkins, Dexter, 534, 1345
Perkins, Frances, 1316
Perkins, Hazlehurst Bolton, 458
Perling, Joseph J., 136
Peterson, Merril D., 494
Phifer, Gregg, 874
Philips, Edith, 444
Phillips, Isaac N., 739
Pickering, Timothy, 544
Pierson, Hamilton W., 425
Pius XII (Pope), 1302
Plischke, Elmer, 49
Pollard, James E., 137
Poore, Benjamin Perley, 864
Porter, Horace, 889
Potter, David M., 773, 800
Powell, Charles Percy, 846
Pratt, Harry E., 776, 779, 846
Pratt, Julius W., 535
Presidency in Transition, 27
Presidential Inability, 2
Presidential Office, 44
President's Tour; A Collection Of Addresses, 528

Preston, Howard W., 302
Prindiville, Kathleen, 202
Pringle, Henry F., 1076, 1116
Pritchett, C. H., 27
Prussing, Eugene E., 281
Pusey, Merlo J., 1415
Putnam, Carleton, 1091
Pyle, Howard, 264, 1132

Q

Quaife, Milo Milton, 658
Quarles, Benjamin, 853
Quincy, Josiah, 576
Quincy Historical Society, Quincy, Mass., 373
Quirk, Robert H., 1208

R

Rachal, William M. E., 505
Ragan, Allen E., 1115
Rahskopf, Horace G., 585
Randall, Henry S., 424
Randall, James G., 783, 791, 793, 808, 830
Randall, Ruth Painter, 860-862
Randolph, John, 239
Randolph, Mary, 185
Randolph, Sarah N., 426
Randolph, Thomas Jefferson, 380
Range, Willard, 1352
Ratner, Sidney, 902
Rauch, Basil, 1293, 1314, 1330
Ray, Perley Orman, 685
Rayback, Robert J., 684
Redfield, William C., 1159
Reid, John, 600
Reilly, Michael F., 1318
Reisner, Christian F., 1063
Remington, Frederic, 1014
Remini, Robert V., 628
Rice, Allen Thorndike, 727
Rice, Howard C., Jr., 379, 481
Rich, Bennett Milton, 19
Richter, Edward J., 73
Riddle, Donald W., 801, 831
Ridley, Maurice R., 784
Rigdon, William M., 216
Riis, Jacob A., 1050
Ritter, Halsted L., 292
Rives, William Cabell, 511
Robertson, Pearl Louise, 969

Robinson, Corinne Roosevelt, 1062
Robinson, Edgar Eugene, 86, 1319, 1341
Rock, Vincent P., 68
Rogers, Cameron, 1231
Rollins, Alfred Brooks, 1368
Roncière, Charles de la, 248
Rood, Henry, 177
Roos, Charles A., 159
Roosevelt, Eleanor R., 1361, 1362, 1368, 1371, 1374
Roosevelt, Elliott, 1288, 1317
Roosevelt, James, 1353
Roosevelt, Kermit, 1036, 1047
Roosevelt, Sara Delano, 1307
Roseboom, Eugene H., 100
Rosenau, James N., 1332
Rosenberger, Francis Coleman, 490
Rosenman, Samuel I., 1287, 1336
Roske, Ralph J., 875, 878
Ross, Ishbel, 915, 1243
Rossiter, Clinton L., 27, 29, 65, 507
Rovere, Richard H., 1387, 1416
Rowland, Eron O. Moore, 611
Rubin, Louis D., 920
Rush, Benjamin, 355, 367
Rutgers University. New Brunswick, N. J., 1427
Rysavy, Francois, 207

S

Sachse, Julius F., 243
Sage, Agnes C., 176
Sager, Benjamin F., 641
Sandburg, Carl, 753, 768, 778, 805, 821, 859
Sawvel, Franklin B., 403
Sawyer, Joseph Dillaway, 282
Schachner, Nathan, 493, 499
Scheiber, Harry N., 1206
Schlesinger, Arthur M., Jr., 1346, 1387
Schmidt, Karl M., 1392
Schnapper, Morris B., 1375
Schortemeier, Frederick E., 1213, 1214
Schouler, James, 430
Schroeder, John Frederick, 231
Schubert, Glendon A., 47
Schulz, George J., 75
Scoble, Harry M., 1419
Scott, George T., 934
Searcher, Victor, 845
Sears, Louis Martin, 128, 303, 337, 446, 1169

Segal, Charles M., 720
Seitz, Don C., 78, 1285
Selection of Eulogies (1826), 359
Seligman, Lester G., 40, 43, 44
Sellers, Charles Grier, 669, 670
Severance, Frank H., 680
Sewall, William Wingate (Bill), 1056
Seymour, Charles, 1153, 1193
Shalett, Sidney, 1353
Shannon, Jasper B., 91
Shapley, Harlow, 462
Shattuck, Frances M., 1421
Shaw, Albert, 758, 1054
Shaw, Archer H., 711
Shawen, Lena Belle, 1324
Shelley, Fred, 950
Shepard, Edward M., 625
Sherwin, Mark, 1443
Sherwood, Robert E., 1331
Shores, Venila Lovina, 924
Showalter, William Joseph, 304
Shrady, George F., 892
Sievers, Harry J., 985
Silva, Ruth C., 27, 30, 44, 1284
Sinclair, Sir John, 234
Singleton, Esther, 174
Sioussat, St. George L., 660, 661, 696, 867
Slemp, Campbell Bascom, 1225
Slocum, William J., 1318
Slosson, Preston W., 1217, 1233
Small, Norman J., 12
Smelser, Marshall, 330
Smith, A. Merriman, 190, 192, 1412, 1423
Smith, Abbot Emerson, 513
Smith, George Winston, 110
Smith, Harold Clifford, 310
Smith, Ira R., 194
Smith, John Malcolm, 66
Smith, Justin H., 675
Smith, Margaret Bayard, 173
Smith, Page, 374
Smith, Theodore Clarke, 944
Smith, Walter Bedell, 1417
Smith, Willard H., 914
Smithsonian Institution, 205
Smyth, William Henry, 918, 1096
Snyder, Marty, 1418
Somers, Herman Miles, 28
Sowerby, Emily Millicent, 419
Spanier, John W., 1391
Sparks, Jared, 225, 235
Spaulding, Ernest Wilder, 500

Villard, Harold G., 771
Villard, Henry, 771
Virginia (Colony) General Court, 400
Virginia born Presidents, 126
Volwiler, Albert T., 981

W

Wagenknecht, Edward C., 790, 1092
Waldo, Samuel Putnam, 528
Walker, Alexander, 601
Walker, Turnley, 1338
Wallace, Sarah A., 656
Walsh, Correa Moylan, 363
Walworth, Arthur Clarence, 1202
Wandell, Samuel H., 498
Ward, John William, 619
Warren, Harris G., 1280
Warren, James, 356
Warren, Louis A., 754, 836
Washburne, Elihu B., 885
Washington, Henry A., 382
Wasson, Woodrow W., 946
Waterhouse, Benjamin, 357, 453, 588
Waugh, Edgar Wiggins, 222
Webster, Homer J., 636
Webster, Sidney, 687
Weik, Jesse William, 728, 729, 748
Welles, Gideon, 724, 742
Weston, Florence, 616
Wharton, Anne Hollingsworth, 339
Wheare, Kenneth C., 806
Whicher, George F., 996
White, Leonard D., 25, 31, 36, 50
White, Theodore H., 1446
White, William Allen, 124, 1160, 1234
White House Historical Association, Wash-
      ington, D. C., 217
Whitehurst, Alto Lee, 627
Whiting, Edward Elwell, 1224
Whitney, Henry Clay, 770
Whitney, Janet Payne, 378
Whittemore, Frances Davis, 311
Whittier, John Greenleaf, 555
Whitton, Mary O., 193
Wieland, Christoph Martin, 573
Wilbur, Ray Lyman, 1271
Wiley, Farida A., 1008
Willets, Gilson, 175
Williams, Charles Richard, 916, 918, 922
Williams, Edwin, 111
Williams, Irving G., 221, 223
Williams, Jesse Lynch, 961

Williams, Thomas Harry, 713, 772, 815,
      834
Williams, Wayne C., 809
Willis, Edward Frederick, 1274
Wilmerding, Lucius, Jr., 102, 537
Wilson, Edith Bolling Galt, 1211
Wilson, Ellen Axson, 1145
Wilson, Fred Taylor, 130
Wilson, James Grant, 117, 885
Wilson, Rufus Rockwell, 764, 774, 785, 786
Wilson, Vincent, 166
Wilson, William L., 973
Wilson, Woodrow, 264
Wilstach, Paul, 288, 441
Wiltse, Charles M., 594
Winkler, E. W., 917
Winston, Robert W., 869
Wise, Henry A., 650
Wise, John S., 116
Wister, Owen, 271, 1074
Wolcott, Oliver, 253
Wold, Karl C., 154
Woldman, Albert A., 765, 816
Wolf, Simon, 119
Wolfe, Harold, 1277
Wolfe, Udolpho, 529
Wolff, Perry S., 218, 1453
Wood, Frederick S., 1071
Woods, John A., 1357
Woodward, Augustus B., 1
Woodward, William E., 279, 896
Woolery, William Kirk, 447
Woolfall, Lila G. A., 172
Wright, Benjamin Fletcher, 507
Wright, Esmond, 335

Y

Young, Arthur, 234
Young, John Russell, 887
Young, Klyde H., 220

Z

Zevin, Benjamin D., 1289
Zorn, Walter Lewis, 147
Zornow, William Frank, 823
Zwierlein, Frederick J., 1088

159

U. S. GOVERNMENT PRINTING OFFICE : 1963 O - 693-349